D0411985

Asking for Trouble

Also by Sheridan Morley

A Talent to Amuse: The First Biography of Noël Coward
A Bright Particular Star: The Life of Gertrude Lawrence
Review Copies: London Theatres 1970–1974
Marlene Dietrich
Oscar Wilde
Sybil Thorndike: A Life in the Theatre
Gladys Cooper
Tales From the Hollywood Raj: The British in California
Shooting Stars: London Theatres 1975–1983
Katharine Hepburn
The Other Side of the Moon: The First Biography of David Niven
Spread a Little Happiness: The First 100 Years of the British Musical
Elizabeth Taylor
Odd Man Out: The First Biography of James Mason
Our Theatres in the Eighties: London Theatres 1983–1989
Audrey Hepburn
Dirk Bogarde: Rank Outsider
Robert, My Father
Ginger Rogers: Shall We Dance?
Gene Kelly (with Ruth Leon)
Cameron Mackintosh: Hey Mr Producer! (with Ruth Leon)
Judy Garland: Beyond the Rainbow (with Ruth Leon)
Marilyn Monroe (with Ruth Leon)
A Century of Theatre (with Ruth Leon)
Spectator at the Theatre: London Theatres 1990–1999
John G: The Authorised Biography of John Gielgud

As editor:
The Noël Coward Diaries (with Graham Payn)
Noël Coward and His Friends (with Graham Payn and Cole Lesley)
Theatre 71, 72, 73, 74
The Theatre Addict's Archive
The Autobiographies of Noël Coward
Punch at the Theatre
The Stephen Sondheim Songbook
The Theatregoer's Quiz Book
Bull's Eyes
Out in the Midday Sun
The Methuen Book of Theatrical Short Stories
The Methuen Book of Film Stories
Raymond Mander and Joe Mitchenson's Theatrical Companion to Coward
(with Barry Day)

For the stage:
Noël and Gertie
Spread a Little Happiness
If Love Were All (with Leigh Lawson)
Law and Disorder

Sheridan Morley

Asking for Trouble

Hodder & Stoughton

First published in Great Britain in 2002 by Hodder and Stoughton
A division of Hodder Headline

1 3 5 7 9 10 8 6 4 2

Copyright © 2002 by Sheridan Morley

The right of Sheridan Morley to be identified as the Author of the Work has been
asserted by him in accordance with the Copyright, Designs and Patents Act 1988.

All rights reserved. No part of this publication may be reproduced, stored in a
retrieval system, or transmitted, in any form or by any means without the prior
written permission of the publisher, nor be otherwise circulated in any form of
binding or cover other than that in which it is published and without a similar
condition being imposed on the subsequent purchaser.

A CIP catalogue record for this title is available from the British Library

ISBN 0 340 82057 8

Typeset in Sabon by Palimpsest Book Production Limited,
Polmont, Stirlingshire
Printed and bound in Great Britain by
Mackays of Chatham plc, Chatham, Kent

Hodder and Stoughton
A division of Hodder Headline
338 Euston Road
London NW1 3BH

'I never tire of watching. I watch, therefore I am. I am what I watch, and what I watch entrances me . . . but I remain invisible to myself.'

Michael Holroyd, 1999

He, too, was brought up in the Thames Valley of the 1940s, and he, too, started out in the Maidenhead Public Library, reading biographies before he decided that he wanted to write them.

Hugh Kingsmill once demanded of a biographer some account of his or her life as a passport for travelling into the lives of others. This, then, is mine, and I can only hope that it is still valid, has all the right visas, and that the photographs have not become too laughable with age.

It is dedicated, with love, gratitude and amazement, to all those relatives and friends, sometimes enemies, too, who have been my travelling companions across sixty years, and with apologies to those whose details have, for whatever reason, fallen out of my scrapbooks, or vanished from the diaries that, until this moment, have existed only in my head.

Sheridan Morley, London, July 2002

Contents

List of Illustrations

Picture Acknowledgements

All photographs are from the author's family collection except the following: Marcus Adams/Camera Press, page 4; Corbis, page 5, above left; Hulton Archive, page 5, above right; *Illustrated London News*, page 6, above; Oscar Mellor, Oxford, page 9, below; Clive Barda/Arena Images, page 11; Catherine Ashmore, page 14, above; Alan Davidson, page 16.

Every reasonable effort has been made to contact the copyright holders, but if there are any errors or omissions, Hodder & Stoughton will be pleased to insert the appropriate acknowledgement in any subsequent printing of this publication.

I

A Weekend That Will Live in Infamy – Pearl Harbor and Me

How to begin? Alan Coren, for whom I was arts editor and drama critic at the old *Punch* for just over a decade – far and away the happiest office time of my entire forty-year-and-counting life in journalism – as usual had the best idea. Most memoirs start with birth, not (at least for the writer or, indeed, for his/her mother) the easiest or most tranquilly recalled moment. Why not, thought Coren, start about three months earlier? 'God it's dark in here, though there does seem to be some sort of an indoor pool. Am I the right way up? Is this the mother? Could she stop that bloody tapping? What if I'm a twin? Is there anybody else in here? That sounds like the father. What sort of house, I wonder? Desirable neighbourhood? Money for further education? Am I the first, last, or only one, or somewhere in the middle? Do they have television? On a good bus route? Holidays abroad? And what about the neighbours?'

You get the general idea, and I will, of course, leave it there in the vague hope that one day Coren will get round to doing it properly. That's what separates humorists from critics: they create, we react. There are, however, more of us. I can only think of four humorists in my lifetime who have made me laugh out loud: James Thurber, Alan Coren, Christopher Matthew and Craig Brown. Critics, on the other hand, make me laugh a lot, usually on the principle that either they have gone barking mad or I have. Sometimes it's a damned close-run thing to decide which.

How else to start an autobiography? Clearing the desk might be a help, not to mention the drawers. A postcard from John

Osborne: 'Watch out behind you, Fatso Morley, especially on dark nights, or the Playwrights' Mafia will get you'; I must have written something unusually unflattering about a play of his, but the trouble is that I can't remember now what or which. Still, the postcard might be worth a few quid at Sotheby's, if I can manage not to lose it. What else? An *Observer* 'Saying of the Week' from the late diarist Alan Clark, on being told ten or so years ago that Ruth Leon and I were about to get married: 'They deserve each other.' A telegram from Noël Coward: 'Darling Boy, I am absolutely mad about me. Love Noël.' That was after I had sent him the first published copy of his (and my) first biography, since he had given me all his letters and diaries, then agreed not to see a word of the book until it was in irrevocable print. Not a lot of people do that nowadays, though happily for me John Gielgud, rather more recently, was another, and I have just found an enchantingly engraved silver paper-knife, left to me in his will by way of approval.

John G didn't lived to see the book, which was roughly what he and I had agreed would be for the best, but I do still have the knife and a couple of his silver boxes to remind me that, in principle at least, he must have thought I was the right casting as chronicler of his long life. Or maybe he just thought I was going to do a knife job, which I wasn't.

We seem to be getting ahead of ourselves, and I can't find much else of interest on the desk. Photographs of my beloved Ruth, and my equally beloved two parents, sister, brother, three children and two grandchildren. I even have a rather lovely picture of my first wife, though I'm prepared to bet that she doesn't have a rather lovely one of me on her desk. More of all of that later – although I have just found a rather splendid press cutting sent by my son, who with my brother runs the best restaurant in downtown Tampa, Florida. 'We regret,' it reads, 'to announce the death of the man who built the first great five-screen multiplex movie house in the whole of Florida, at the age of 97. His funeral will be on Friday, at 2.30, 4.50, 7, 9 and 11 p.m.'

These memoirs are already getting out of hand: we need a little discipline, and perhaps a few facts. I was born on 5 December 1941, at a nursing-home called either Fivetrees or Twelvetrees (it was sixty years ago), overlooking the race-course at Ascot, which had always been my father Robert's spiritual home. When he was originally offered what became the Charles Laughton role in *The Hunchback of Notre Dame*, he declined it on the grounds that all Quasimodo did was grunt, and that, anyway, the filming would keep him away from the Ascot Gold Cup. Soon after that he transferred his allegiance to Windsor, a racecourse even closer to where my parents lived for half a century. When he died we put a plaque on one of the benches in the enclosure that reads, 'Robert Morley sat here, 1946–1992'.

Years later I once asked him if he ever regretted turning down the Hollywood fame of Charles Laughton: 'Not at all, darling. All that sitting around in overheated Californian swimming-pools, just waiting to be insulted by producers.' It wasn't a bad definition of Charles's life.

Two mornings after my birth something still more momentous occurred; the Imperial Japanese Navy bombed the hell out of the American fleet at Pearl Harbor and my uncle John, a glamorous but schizophrenic actor and painter who eventually took his own life, sent a politically incorrect telegram to my mother, his sister. It was duly censored by the Los Angeles post office, and only reached my mother some time in 1947. 'Congratulations,' it read, 'from me and the little yellow men who will soon be with us.' We often wondered, this being the kind of thing we did in my family in those far-off days, whether the telegram had been censored on the grounds of its appalling racism, or for exhibiting a lack of faith in the ability of Los Angeles to hold off the Empire of the Sun.

I was the eldest of three children, born at five-yearly intervals to Robert and the Joan Buckmaster he had married early in 1940, and to whom he remained devoted until his death on Derby Day 1992, one of the few he ever missed. I emphasise their mutual devotion and alliance across more than half a century, not only because it was (and is today even more so) theatrically unusual, but also because it was unusual in our family. Each of my mother's parents had been married three times, my brother Wilton and I have both been divorced, as have Ma's other closest surviving relatives in her own generation, her half-sister Sally and her step-sister Rosamund. Only my sister Annabel with her Australian husband Charlie and my two daughters Alexis and Juliet have held out in later generations against the family trend.

On my father's side, his only sibling Margaret was also divorced, and although his parents were too Victorian, or at least Edwardian, to contemplate such a scandal, theirs had never been what you could call a blissful alliance. In the midst and the aftermath of all this marital collapse, it was almost as though Robert and especially Joannie had decided to make their partnership work at all costs, having seen rather too much at close hand of the alternative.

My mother, almost ninety-two at the time of writing, still lives at Fairmans in Wargrave, which she and my father bought in 1940 when it was a two-up two-down gamekeeper's cottage in about three acres of woodland. My father paid the local farmer £500 for the lot, and always maintained, even into his eighties, that he should only have had to pay £450. Luckily the cottage came with a fair number of barns, all of which are now filled with the furniture, papers and other random leftovers of five generations of our family, ranging from my grandmother's school reports to my grandchildren's early attempts at Christmas cards. Given the aforementioned number of divorces and consequential moving of houses, all of us have left at Fairmans everything for which we couldn't find a new home, in the vague hope that it might some day come in useful for someone, even perhaps ourselves. If Ma ever dies, which happily she gives precious little sign of doing, we shall have to organise the garage sale of all time. Meanwhile, I think we still have all of her own mother's theatrical contracts, dating back to *circa* 1895, not to mention most of her furniture.

I was lucky enough to know both of Joannie's parents very well: Herbert Buckmaster (the founder in 1920 of Buck's Club and therefore also of Buck's Fizz, which maddeningly he never bothered to patent, thereby denying us the family fortune that has eluded us) and the actress Gladys Cooper, who lived long lives, well into my late twenties and their early eighties. On the Morley side, I never knew my father's father, who died soon after I was born. Of his widow I have only remote and shadowy childhood recollections of an old lady sitting up in bed doling chocolate biscuits rather cautiously out of a large silver box, looking remarkably like a man in drag playing the older Queen Victoria.

My father's immediate ancestors, at least on the female side, seem to have spent most of their lives in bed; in my grandmother's case, this was almost certainly to avoid too much contact with her husband the Major, a man of many careers, most of them disastrous. A compulsive gambler and – in a useful phrase of the period – ne'er-do-well, he lived a life of regular financial crisis, passing on to my father, his only son, a passion for roulette and the rare, admirable ability to live constantly on the financial edge without much loss of sleep or nerve. This talent was duly passed on to my brother Wilton and my son Hugo, but not, alas, to me or my sister Annabel: we have always lived lives of comparative financial caution. Even that, though, is relative: when I married for the second time, into the Leons, a family of Marylebone High Street fashion-shop owners who have never spent more than was in the till, I found to my astonishment that, by their standards, I was wildly spendthrift.

My lifelong financial rule has always been to owe the bank just fractionally less than the current market value of wherever I am living, but lately my in-laws have taken me sharply in hand. Now we seem to have no actual money but no debts, a state of affairs that, oddly enough, makes me faintly uneasy. Living in debt for half a century I found curiously restful, my theory being that Barclays Bank should be losing the sleep, not me. Now that, for the first time, there is a fractional surplus in non-VAT months, I lie awake worrying about whether the bankers are about to abscond with my takings.

My paternal grandfather the Major's principal ambition, he always said, was 'to lead a champagne life on a beer income', and by all accounts he was precisely the type of eccentric, larger-than-life figure that his son Robert took to playing in his late-life screen cameos. The Boer War had left the Major with little except a helmet that he later converted into a biscuit tin; he had, however, been slightly wounded in South Africa, maintaining ever afterwards that the bullet had entered too close to his heart to be safely removed surgically. Thereafter, in times of stress, he would clutch his stomach and cry, 'I feel it moving.' This was often enough to deter his creditors, at least temporarily. If it failed, he would take to his bed, threatening suicide with his old Boer revolver if his debts were not immediately taken care of by some unlucky relative. This could usually be achieved, because the Major's parents had thoughtfully entailed some of their assets for just such a purpose, hoping in vain to keep them out of their spendthrift son's hands. 'There never has been an entail through which a good lawyer cannot drive a coach and horses,' cried the Major, and many of Robert's earliest memories concerned his father's various searches for the right coachman.

Whenever his wife (known originally as Daisy but later as Poor Daisy and finally as Poor, Poor Daisy, as sympathy within her family grew for the difficulties she endured at the hands of the Major) complained about his wasteful ways, he would sigh and murmur self-sacrificingly, 'Only trying to make a few pennies for you and the children, dear,' before disappearing back into the welcoming gloom of the nearest *salon des jeux*. On those rare occasions when the roulette ball landed in the right socket, he would return to the steps of the casino and thrust thousand-franc notes at Robert and his sister Margaret, enjoining them to 'Take this before the rats get at it', the rats being whichever creditors, bank managers or taxmen were proving most troublesome at the time.

All my relatives, known and unknown, seemed to me larger than life, or did I just want them to be that way? As the son and grandson of actors I was, I suppose, a starstruck child but, curiously enough, of all the players in my family, father, grandmother, godfathers, uncles, the only one who corresponded to what we nowadays expect of actors, taking his career very seriously indeed, was and remains Robert Hardy, who married my aunt Sally.

He started out at Stratford after the war with John Gielgud, and has ever since led the life of a classical actor on stage and especially television, dedicated to his chosen profession. That could not be said of Robert or, indeed, his best friend and my godfather Peter Bull, for whom acting was often a branch of the travel business rather than a calling, a way of seeing the world and making friends, but not perhaps with absolute fidelity to the script in hand. Had you asked them the title of the movie they were making at any time, or even what it was about, they would often not have been able to tell you.

That generation of what were once called in agents' offices 'responsible gentlemen', available to play doctors, judges and kings, small but showy roles with a certain weight in more ways than one, has now vanished. If my grandchildren wish to know what Robert was like, I guess I would point them towards Peter Ustinov or John Mortimer, but when they go there will be nobody left like my father. He led his entire, and generally happy, life in the firm belief that just round the next corner, whatever continent we were on, would be the best casino, the best restaurant, the best hotel, the best pool and perhaps even the best audience ever. It never was, of course, but it kept us bumbling happily around the world for a good many decades.

I was also lucky enough, writing the Saturday Profile in *The Times* for about fifteen years from 1970, to interview the last of the Hollywood giants: Charles Chaplin and Cary Grant, Kirk Douglas and David Niven, Alfred Hitchcock and Joan Crawford, Audrey Hepburn and Billy Wilder, Lauren Bacall and Sophia Loren were all, in those days, available for lunch at the Connaught Hotel whenever they were in town flogging a memoir or a movie, or just themselves. They were all great storytellers, with wondrous recollections of the golden age of films and filming. In the 1980s, when the next generation of stars proved infinitely more difficult to reach personally, surrounded as they were by press agents and other acolytes unforgivably demanding copy-approval and details of the photograph and precisely when and on what page it would appear, I gave up newspaper interviewing. Not only do the younger stars appear to have no memories of anything but the film they are currently trying to hawk, they also have no gift for the elegant, wry, self-deprecating anecdotage at which their predecessors excelled. As a result, contemporary press coverage of stars is now reduced to interviews of those who have nothing much to say, written largely by those who cannot write, for those who cannot read. Once again, and it will, I fear, be a regular theme of this book, I was more than lucky to have been there when. And, as my wife Ruth often says, if only they had told us we were living through a golden journalistic and broadcasting age that was about to come to an end, we might have been a bit more bloody grateful or, at any rate, appreciative at the time.

2
The Original Man Who Came to Dinner

Where was I? Being born, I think. That seems to have happened uneventfully enough, unlike the subsequent birth of my sister Annabel five years later; she arrived so prematurely in 1946 that she had to be kept in Ma's airing cupboard for several weeks. Medical science in our corner of Berkshire was not greatly advanced. She thrived among the sheets and towels, however, and has remained about the healthiest of us ever since, even though her newborn legs were the length and width of my father's little fingers.

Five years later still, my mother had grown so expert at giving birth that our brother Wilton was born in her own bed, in the house just outside Wargrave where she still lives. An hour or two after the birth, Noël Coward rang in search of my grandmother Gladys. Ma regretted she was not around, but in response to Noël's ritual enquiry as to how she was, she replied that she was just fine, and had indeed given birth to her second son a little while ago. Noël was appalled. 'Disgusting,' he told her sharply. 'Just like all those African women who used to give birth behind trees whenever you weren't looking. I never thought it would come to Berkshire.'

Not much else ever did come to our corner of Berkshire, at least not in the 1940s; a cow was rumoured to have been killed by a German bomb in a field a couple of miles away from us, but all the war really meant was rationing and Robert having to bicycle two miles to the local station, uphill all the way back, to appear nightly in the title role of the long-running *The Man Who Came to Dinner* at the Savoy.

Robert had first been offered this when he was playing

Oscar Wilde on Broadway back in 1938, and had turned it down even though it was written by the two most triumphant comic dramatists in the whole pre-war history of the American theatre, Moss Hart and George S. Kaufman. Even so, in Pa's view the last act needed work; Kaufman and Hart disagreed, and the play duly opened to tumultuous success in New York and subsequently on tour and film, with Monty Woolley loosely disguised as the broadcaster and journalist Alexander Woollcott.

Though now almost unheard-of on this side of the Atlantic, and scarcely more familiar to Americans under eighty, Woollcott was a giant of his pre-war times; in Britain, one would have to imagine a curious amalgam of Malcolm Muggeridge, Melvyn Bragg and David Frost. Essentially, Woollcott was the man who invented books as a branch of showbusiness. Having started out in the 1920s as a waspish drama critic on the *New Yorker* and a member of the legendary Algonquin Round Table, he found his true form in the 1930s on a New York commercial radio show where, as the self-appointed 'Town Crier', he would recommend plays, books and movies to an adoring audience of hundreds of thousands of culture-hungry Midwestern matrons, to whom he would also deliver after-dinner speeches for considerable profit. Among much else, he invented what are now known as the celebrity lecture and the reading circle.

Privately, Woollcott was a closet gay of considerable arrogance and irritability, and the most impossibly demanding of weekend guests. After one such weekend, Kitty Carlisle, Moss Hart's actress wife, happened to remark how terrible it would be to have Aleck to stay for more than a couple of nights. From that slender beginning, Kaufman and Hart developed a riotous comedy starting with the notion that 'Sheridan Whiteside' breaks a leg while visiting an unsuspecting Midwestern family for dinner. During his enforced stay, he is joined by Harpo Marx, Gertrude Lawrence, Noël Coward, several penguins and a schoolboy choir. He also solves the mystery of the whereabouts of Lizzie Borden, and broadcasts his Christmas message to the nation from the fireside of a home he has now all but reduced to rubble.

Had the real Woollcott lived (he died in 1943), I would so love to have known him. In some almost mystical way I have always thought I might have inherited at least a few of his career tendencies; as it was, he agreed to be my godfather because I was born on the London first night of *The Man Who Came to Dinner* and had therefore been given his stage name – just as, almost exactly a quarter of a century later, my son Hugo was born on another of Robert's first nights, that of Peter Ustinov's *Halfway Up a Tree*, directed by John Gielgud, and acquired the Christian name of Pa's stage character, Sir Hugo FitzButtress. Two consecutive generations of us born on Robert's first nights and named after his characters seemed worthy of comment, though not to my grandmother Gladys: 'One names one's pets after characters in plays.' She sniffed. 'It's very common to name people after them.' Sadly she only ever got to play Lady Bracknell on a series of gramophone records; being born into the same generation as Edith Evans had its drawbacks, even for G.

As for Woollcott, on his last night on earth he went into a delicatessen on Broadway and from there sent me a large tin of unrationed American biscuits, much prized in wartime, before proceeding to his radio studio where he dropped dead on the air of a cerebral haemorrhage, having just announced that there was no such thing as a good German. Not a bad way to go, but he was only on the verge of his fifty-sixth birthday, and arguably the most famous pundit in all America.

A literary huckster way ahead of his time, had Aleck lived a little later or longer he would have been, like my father, one of the first great masters of the television chat-show, the author tours and the bookshop signings that we all now take for granted without ever knowing how they began, or even why. A prolific columnist, critic and women's-institute lecturer, he saw it as his mission to lead an often reluctant Middle American public down the highways and byways of theatre, music and publishing, drawing them in through his own personal network of gossip.

But because his entire career was in newspapers, magazines and radio stations, he has left nothing but a few anthologies of others' work behind him – that and the christening of Noël Coward as Destiny's Tot. Noël will figure prominently in these memoirs, but Aleck now disappears from them, leaving me only his stage name and the memory of an intriguingly powerful and pioneer arts broadcaster whom Robert Benchley nevertheless once mocked as 'Louisa M. Woollcott'. Like Coward, he was his own best invention and contribution to his own world, a man with a waspish sense of humour and considerable literary and journalistic courage. He once reviewed a book as 'Combining the homely charm of *Little Women* with the pulsing excitement of *The Hound of the Baskervilles*, the sturdy humour of *Huckleberry Finn* and the more engaging qualities of *David Copperfield*.' It was, of course, one of his own anthologies, and I like to think that if I have not inherited his brazen neck, then some of his passion for spreading the word about books, plays and films might subliminally have been handed down to me, the godson he never met.

The Second World War continued uneventfully in the Thames Valley lowlands of Crazies Hill. One day Cecil Beaton, an old friend of my mother, volunteered to take some baby pictures of me at a specially friendly rate. Pa duly met him at Wargrave station, carried all his equipment up the hill (Cecil was accustomed to native bearers even in wartime), and was later less than thrilled to discover that Cecil's specially friendly rate still ran to several hundred pounds.

Although soon after the war Pa acquired a wonderfully loyal dresser and driver in John Jonas, who stayed with him for nearly forty years to his death, at this time he was to be found, like John Mortimer and his blind barrister father, daily on the train to and from Henley-on-Thames. A passionate picker-up of stray passengers, Robert took the view that the public was never wrong, and relished brief encounters with strangers. Once, when I had grown up and joined ITN as a newscaster, he and I were as usual on the last train back to Henley one night. A woman was in the carriage, too, and as we reached Ealing Broadway she leant across to Pa. 'I do so admire you,' she said, 'and especially your work in the war.'

As I was aware that what Pa had done for much of the Second World War was tour army bases in Wales with *The Man Who Came to Dinner*, while inadvertently spreading chicken-pox to many of our brave lads on the brink of battle, I knew at once that she had confused him with Lord Brabazon, a lookalike figure who also lived near Henley, had been a flying ace and then run what was to become British Airways. 'Tell me,' she asked Pa, 'about the life of a pilot in wartime.'

'Well,' said Pa, 'it was surprisingly simple, really. One sort of got into the plane, drove along a bit, then up, along for a while and then one came down again.'

This ludicrous conversation continued all the way to Wargrave. As we left the train, I asked my father why he hadn't explained at the outset that he wasn't Lord Brabazon. 'Oh, but I was,' he replied. 'All the way from Paddington.'

Like the great hotel, casino or restaurant manager he so often resembled and had really wanted to be, my father maintained throughout his life a deep belief in the absolute, inalienable right of his customers to say and do whatever they pleased, once they had paid their money at his box office. The most faithful of his co-stars, and one of the few who could always put up with his frequent and lengthy on-stage improvisations, was the redoubtable actress Ambrosine Phillpotts. One night, coming offstage in the interval, she told my father that she had just seen the most disgraceful and disgusting thing ever: a couple of theatregoers copulating in the dress circle. 'Well, my darling,' replied Pa resignedly, 'if we can't entertain them, they must do it for themselves.'

On account of his flat feet, considerable bulk and general usefulness as an actor, Robert was classified for wartime call-up in the lowest possible group, the one that would only be mobilised if the Germans were spotted sailing up the nearby Henley regatta course. In order to maintain this status, he had to report every six months or so to a small office in Reading, where a weary civil servant would ritually ask him what he would like to do if, indeed, it ever came to pass that he had to be called up into uniform. 'I think,' said Pa unwisely, 'in that eventuality, I would quite like to sit in a small office in Reading asking other people what they would most like to do in uniform.' An apoplectic civil servant then tried to have him called up, until a physical check-up revealed the unlikelihood of that, even in our darkest days.

My parents had married on 23 February 1940 at Caxton Hall in Westminster – or, rather, in what was left of it after an air raid. My father's parents turned up, as did Ma's father Buck, though Gladys was now in California where she had opened a long film-studio contract. She was less than ecstatic about the marital news, writing to her daughter merely, 'Well, darling, if you like him, I suppose he can't be too bad.'

She already knew Pa slightly, as it had been her beloved only son John who, indirectly, had first brought my parents together. Just before the war, Pa had been on Broadway playing the title role in his first great success, *Oscar Wilde*. John was his Lord Alfred Douglas and, when the run ended, had decided to stay in America and fight there the war that seemed inevitable. Not knowing when he would see his sister again, he asked Pa to look her up at home and take her some useful American care packages. Had it not been for Johnny, it is doubtful that my parents would ever have met, let alone married. 'I told you just to look her up,' read his wedding telegram. 'Isn't this rather overdoing things?'

The service at Caxton Hall was short and only fairly sweet: Pa had not been too thrilled to see a newspaper placard reading GLADYS COOPER'S DAUGHTER MARRIES ACTOR, and because of the bomb damage there was only room in the registrar's office for the central players. Other relatives had to wait in a corridor outside. 'Is your father-in-law living?' asked the registrar, going down the usual checklist of questions.

'I'll just pop out and have a look,' said Robert.

Nevertheless, the marriage got off to a good start: Pa was filming *Major Barbara* with Rex Harrison and Wendy Hiller, and it took such an inordinately long time to make that he was able to get engaged, marry and buy Fairmans while all the time on a useful weekly salary from Gabriel Pascal, the mercurial Hungarian director. They were shooting mainly at Denham Studios, where Pa convinced Wendy Hiller that the wily foreigner had built himself a private waterproof shelter under the lake for his personal use in the event of an air raid. Relations between director and star were strained for several weeks. On another occasion, they were all staying at a country hotel for some location shots. There, too, on tour with an early play of Robert's (he wrote around fifteen in a long career) called *Short Story*, was the veteran actress Marie Tempest who, summoned downstairs in her hairnet in the middle of the night by a bomb falling nearby, spied Robert and Joannie in the hall and murmured, 'Oh, my darlings, *quelle vie de chien*', a phrase that lived on in our family for decades to come.

Apart from Woollcott, I was blessed at my christening with two other remarkable godfathers: Sewell Stokes, who with his brother Leslie had given Pa his first great hit by writing the first-ever play about Oscar Wilde, and Peter Bull with whom Pa had run, throughout the summers of the late 1930s, a seaside repertory company at Perranporth in Cornwall – it was reckoned to be the only one ever in regular receipt of food hampers from Fortnum and Mason. Among its regular players were Pamela Brown and the veteran director Frith Banbury who became one of our family's closest and longest-lasting friends.

As for Sewell, when he was barely into his twenties, he was rumoured to have been the last of many lovers of the great if eccentric dancer Isadora Duncan. He was with her in the South of France when she died, strangled by her scarf, which got caught in the wheel of a car; he had written her first biography (later filmed with Vanessa Redgrave, directed by Ken Russell), and much else, including novels, plays and journalism. He was gay, but so thoroughly closeted that neither my father nor I were ever allowed to visit his mansion flat just opposite the British Museum, or to meet any of his homosexual friends, assuming he had any in later life. His true passion was the cinema, and in particular the National Film Theatre of which he became an early supporter; he passed on his love of the silver screen to me, and far more usefully to another godson, Kevin Brownlow, who became the greatest of silent-movie historians in part thanks to Sewell's lifelong enthusiasm for them.

Sewell's war was spent at Bow Street Police Station as a special probation officer, experience he put to good use in several books demanding prison reform; he was thought to have a thing about young coppers in uniform. His time in court got off to a tricky start when the resident magistrate sent for him in chambers after his first day in official attendance. Imagining he had already committed some ghastly misdemeanour, Sewell was relieved to be asked if he had yet met his opposite number, a Miss Fortescue. Sewell said he had. 'I wonder,' said the magistrate, 'if when you get to know her a little better, you could do me a great personal service ... Could you ask her to shave?' Even if you were John Mortimer you couldn't have invented it, and Sewell spent most of the rest of the war trying without success to summon up the courage required.

By contrast, Peter Bull had a more spectacular war: he

was also gay, less closeted than Sewell, and in the 1950s
it was he who introduced me to such general London joys
as the pool underneath the RAC Club, and the number
nine bus to Chelsea. With Sewell I always felt I was learn-
ing something useful, if only about the silent films of Ivor
Novello; with Bully, as he was known, one always just had
a riotously good time. He and my father were devoted to
each other: they shared the same bulk, the same outgoing,
booming nature, and, above all, the same belief that films were
made so that the actors in them could have fun, preferably in
exotic, sun-drenched locations, and always at studio expense.
They would have made wonderful additions to the Three
Tenors, if either of them had been even faintly musical.

Peter's war had been conspicuously brave; he and his
beloved Alec Guinness (I have always believed, albeit on
slender evidence, that they were war time lovers) were both
commanders of flat-bottomed boats at the landings in Sicily
and Salerno, and Peter was duly awarded the DSC. On
returning to civilian life, he published a sequence of what
Kenneth Tynan called 'the funniest books ever written by an
actor', worked for many years with and without my father
in countless movies, ending up as the Russian ambassador in
Kubrick's *Dr Strangelove*. After a long London and Broadway
run in Harry Secombe's *Pickwick*, Bully developed considerable late-life stage fright, and took to running a zodiac
emporium in Notting Hill Gate, complete with cream teas
and a resident fortune-teller. He closed his life as a world
expert on teddy bears. Indeed, the bear carried throughout
Brideshead Revisited by Anthony Andrews, as Sebastian Flyte,
was on loan from the Bully Bear collection, as the title credits
acknowledged.

Peter's courage remained undiminished: when he got involved
in one of the first gay muggings in the King's Road, Chelsea,
he insisted early in the 1980s on writing a blow-by-blow
description of it for *Punch*, where I was then arts editor.

Nobody ever managed to construct a closet out of which Peter could not burst at full volume.

My favourite Bull story concerns the first night of *Waiting for Godot* at the Arts Theatre in 1956. A young Peter Hall had cast him as Pozzo in what became the greatest if most controversial critical hit of the season. But now Peter had a problem: for the first time his name was up in lights on Shaftesbury Avenue; his mother's faith in her youngest son – the others had all gone into far more Establishment lives – had at last been vindicated, and yet Lady Bull and Samuel Beckett were unlikely to be a marriage made in heaven. After considerable thought, Peter decided that, nevertheless, he had to invite her to the opening, with her faithful maid Jessie. The two eightysomething matrons, dressed as always in pitch-black bombazine, watched the play from the front row of the dress circle, then appeared in Peter's dressing-room. 'Well, Mother?' he asked nervously.

There was a critical pause.

'Jessie,' said his mother, 'takes the view that the railings of the dress circle in this theatre are most nicely polished.' The play ran for nearly two years, but Lady Bull never referred to it again. Neither did Jessie.

Some time later, when Peter celebrated his seventieth birthday, he was living in a flat in the King's Road, which he had acquired from Joyce Grenfell. Twenty years earlier, he and my father had been the only two actors who were not Humphrey Bogart or Katharine Hepburn in John Huston's *The African Queen*. Pa has about fifteen minutes at the start of the film as Kate's missionary brother, killed by marauding Germans in the First World War, while Peter has about twenty seconds at the end of the picture, as the German captain who tries to arrest Bogart and gets blown to smithereens for his trouble.

On the morning of Bully's seventieth birthday, we arranged things so that when he opened his bathroom curtains he would see above the cinema across the street, in blazing neon: PETER BULL IN *THE AFRICAN QUEEN* WITH HUMPHREY BOGART, KATHARINE HEPBURN AND ROBERT MORLEY.

3
Wargrave at War and Peace

'As you may have noticed,' wrote my grandfather Buck in all solemnity to me (I was just about to be three years old), 'there is a war on, and I shall not therefore be sending you a present until hostilities cease. If you take my advice, you will find an old tin and place a stone in it. I had many happy hours in my own childhood doing things with stones and tins.'

Somehow the joy of that escaped me. I was never, I think, a boy, or even a child, in the accepted sense of the word. I was born a very old adult, and I have never understood the theory that childhood is the happiest time of your life, not that I was ever an especially unhappy child, though certainly overweight and ungainly. When I try to bring it all back now in some sort of order or detail, I am surprised by how little I can remember. Partly, I think, this may be a Thames Valley problem: if you come from Wales or Yorkshire, your childhood memories come neatly prepackaged by the likes of Dylan Thomas or Alan Bennett. But nobody ever went down the mines in Maidenhead, nobody ever recorded an idyllic boyhood in Reading, and Slough only gets on to the literary map because John Betjeman was spectacularly rude about it in a wartime poem from which the locals have never entirely recovered.

True, Wargrave is briefly immortalised in *Three Men in a Boat* – the rather boring bit about the pub sign of the George and Dragon being painted in two different styles back to back – and *The Wind in the Willows*, and therefore *Toad of Toad Hall*, is almost certainly set around Cookham Dean, home of the author Kenneth Grahame, but that's about it until you cross the Henley border into Oxfordshire. There, of course, you run straight into John Mortimer country, and I only wish that I had known him and his blind barrister father when I was growing up and sharing the same branch line; Sir John has always perfectly understood the cultural non-relevance of Middle England's Thames-side communities, as well as their intricate but fundamentally unchanging politics. Indeed, rather than ramble on about them myself, I will refer you to his classic *Paradise Postponed* and its sequel *Titmuss Regained*.

Before it went missing from the *AA Book of the Road*, Wargrave was listed as having a population of 1500, early closing Wednesday, Henley 5 miles, London 32, Oxford 28, buses five past every hour, leaving for Marlow from just outside the Woodclyffe Hall – where, for half a century, Peggy Hannen and her gallant band of amateurs sparkled in Noël Coward – and for Reading from just outside Box Tree Cottage where the Youngs used to live. Not any more, however. Peter, their eldest son and my oldest friend, now presides benignly over a couple of large McDonald's franchises just outside Barcelona: 'Wargrave Man Triumphs In Cheeseburgers To Go'. His finest hour came a year or two ago when, at a college reunion in Oxford, the Warden announced that he could not possibly salute all of the reassembled graduates but that if any of them happened to be in Washington they could get a free tour of the White House from an ex-Rhodes scholar in their midst, President Clinton, and that if they found themselves in Barcelona, they would qualify for a free cheeseburger and jumbo fries to go, courtesy Mr Young (University College 1960–63).

But back to Wargrave: far and away the most exciting event of the day was watching the buses pass each other in the high street because it was, still is, curiously narrow; now it has yellow lines down it, and a traffic warden who is believed to come in from Henley on Tuesday and Friday mornings. The bank has gone, as have most of the shops since they built the large supermarket in Twyford. Apart from that, however, the village looks much as I remember seeing it from my pram in about 1942, although now it has on the outskirts entire estates of brand new, desirable and interchangeable 'Georgian' residences.

Talking of my pram, Robert was once wheeling me down the Strand when an elderly gentleman in a bowler hat with a cane patted me on the head. 'That,' confided my father proudly, 'was George Robey.' I was just over six months old, and have always felt slightly guilty that I didn't express more appreciation or even awareness at the time of the unquestionable honour. Later I always took care to acknowledge Bud Flanagan, a near neighbour, when I saw him in the local post office and village store combined, lest he, too, should feel unappreciated or ignored by a toddler. One can never be too careful with the egos of thespians.

The other possibility about Wargrave is, of course, that it and I have fallen apart over six decades but roughly in unison, so that we have failed to notice each other's disintegration. Of my sixty years, roughly half have been spent somewhere in the Thames Valley; during the other half, I have tried East Anglia, Oxford, Geneva, Honolulu, New York and London, but none of them is a patch on Wargrave.

I have always felt a little nervous elsewhere; 'elsewhere' is where the buses don't cross over at five past the hour, and you can't leave your bike up against the Youngs' fence while you go to the Odeon in Henley, which anyway is now a Regal in the middle of a vast car park. 'Elsewhere' is where they accept Barclaycards, and expect you to make something of your life; 'elsewhere' is the foreign country where they are always doing things differently.

In Wargrave we had a healthy sense of priorities: most things failed to arrive there until long after the war, including bananas and television. The greengrocer bought lots of the former and one of the latter, and the entire village stood munching happily in his shop to watch Princess Elizabeth being married, which was worth a whole morning off school. Or was that the Coronation?

The man who did all the local building, Clifford Maidment, also functioned as the undertaker; of his two roles, he always said he preferred the latter, as the customer complaints were vastly fewer, even if the coffins were apt to be a little out of true. He built an extension to my parents' cottage as soon as that became possible after the war, but all the ceilings slope sharply upwards. When asked by my father why this was so, Clifford said it was all to do with the joists, which kept my father happy for about forty years until Clifford, inspired perhaps by intimations of his own mortality, confessed that he'd measured it up all wrong.

Clifford outlived Robert by a year or two – and was thus in charge of his old friend's funeral – unlike Pa's other great friend in the high street, an electrician called Stanley Bennett who had never come to terms with electricity. He had a goldfish pond, and had trained the fish to come and kiss his fingers when called, an eccentric but unique talent that more than compensated for the frequent blackouts to which his wayward sense of wiring condemned us well into the 1960s.

Talking of Pa's funeral, it created a minor village problem in that although we wanted him buried at the local church, near which he had lived for fifty years, so far as we could recall he had only ever entered it once, to see his daughter safely married, and even then had had to hurry off directly after the service to play a matinée in London. In conversation with the vicar, however, it transpired that even had Pa been the most regular of village churchgoers, he couldn't have been buried in his local graveyard: it had been closed due to overcrowding in about 1740. The bodies since then had been shipped to a rather larger cemetery in Caversham. Just as I was reflecting that Pa had always hated Caversham, I noticed on the churchyard wall some newly inscribed names, people whom I knew from personal acquaintance to have lived in Wargrave rather later than 1740.

It turned out that you qualified for your name on the wall if you were cremated and sprinkled beneath it, so we settled for that, especially as the vicar added that he was starting a new wall of remembrance. 'My father,' I heard myself saying nervously, 'always felt quite strongly about top billing. I suppose we couldn't make sure that his name goes at the head of the new column?' Luckily that could also be arranged, and Clifford duly carved a plaque, on which Pa's name is slightly raised, not because Clifford had measured it wrong, as usual, but because he was tactfully leaving space for my mother. And still you wonder why I love Wargrave? Not only is my father buried there: so, too, are all the memories I have of childhood, which I seem to have spent, remarkably for the indolent, overweight child I was, almost entirely on a bicycle.

In 1790, the then Earl of Barrymore built Wargrave its very own theatre; like many subsequent producers, he soon went bankrupt and died. His grateful villagers popped him into the earth at dawn so that his many creditors couldn't claim the body and hold it against his debts. I have always hoped vaguely that they might be willing to do the same for me when the moment comes, even though I have shamefully failed thus far to build them a theatre.

What we Wargrave folk lack, of course, are the folk memories that others take for granted: although a non-mining village, we once had an underground passage where the treasures of the British Museum were stored in wartime, and for all I know they may still be down there, but the romantic gloom of the Rhondda somehow always stayed far to our west.

I searched for a local writer with whom to identify, and eventually came up with, and distantly befriended, Michael Holroyd. He is a Maidenhead man of roughly my vintage, but even he (in *Basil Street Blues*) can only recall that the town was 'without architectural merit' and that he lived with his grandparents, in conditions of Dickensian gloom and unhappiness, interrupted by brief attempts to run away to London and then, more surprisingly, to run home again.

I cannot pretend that my childhood was ever unhappy: my mother always kept dramas to a minimum, believing that they belonged with my father and her mother in theatres. The only real excitement was caused in wartime by her Pekinese, one of two sisters called Topsy and Mitzi, which took fright at a few fireworks one Guy Fawkes Night and hid under the bonnet of our Morris for several days until she emerged warm and curiously unharmed by the pistons.

From Joan's diary, 5 December 1945
Sherry's fourth birthday. Tea party with fireworks in garden. Height 3′7″, weight 4 stone 12 lbs. Counts to 100 accurately, knows some letters, can tell time and nearly dress himself. Likes being read to, playing snap and riding his tricycle. Think he may need to go on a diet.

Much as Wargrave was my home village, Henley-on-Thames was my home town. At first it was a toss-up between Henley and Reading for this honour; Reading took about fifteen minutes longer on the bus (I was never into physical exercise of any kind), and cost sixpence more, but it had five cinemas while Henley had only one, and as early as 1949 there was a place down by the station where they sold American-style hot dogs. But Henley was where my school was: Rupert House educated virtually every child in what was then still a small community, and was run by the formidable Miss Densham, who was the kind of character usually played by Joyce Grenfell in Ealing Comedies of the period. After her retirement the school changed hands frequently, on one occasion being bought by a man from somewhere in the Midlands. Amazingly, in those days, you were allowed to buy and run schools with no official qualifications or check-ups of any kind.

'And what,' asked my father, since I still had a brother and sister at the school when this changeover took place, 'made you want to buy Rupert House?'

'Well,' said the new self-appointed headmaster, thoughtfully, 'I've always had a bit of a thing about whipping very small boys in short trousers.'

My parents led a committee to get him out, and since then, I hasten to add, the school has been impeccably run. Henley was also where my grandmother lived, when she was not working in Hollywood movies: her garden at Barn Elms was one of the few on the regatta stretch, and though it was made of wood and prone to flooding in winter, in summer you could stand safely on her side of the hedge and shout cautiously rude things at the upper-class twits as they struggled upstream in preparation for the annual boat racing. An elderly coach on a bicycle also shouted at them, but through a megaphone.

Henley has always regarded the regatta much as Stratford-on-Avon regards Shakespeare: it brings money and undesirables into the town in roughly equal proportions. In my case the undesirables were hearty public-schoolmen with names like Roger and Reginald, who slung boats carelessly up on to their shoulders like sweaters, and stood around looking butch, thin and chinless, while ladies with lots of teeth and headscarves admired them.

I fear I was the wrong shape for the regatta, just as I have always been the wrong shape for everything else, except sitting around and talking a lot, preferably while eating and drinking.

Ever since I first fell off my bike into one of its locks, which happened to me often, right through school and Oxford, the Thames and I have lived side by side in mutual distrust. Once I expected it was all going to be Jerome K. Jerome, a river full of people in straw hats wittily getting wet, but somehow the fun of that always escaped me. Nowadays whenever I peer over one of its Berkshire or Chelsea bridges in summer, it always looks like a waterlogged M4.

Talking of that, when I was a child the M4 didn't exist. To get to London you had to drive all the way through Maidenhead, Slough and Chiswick, and it took exactly ninety minutes to reach Hyde Park Corner. Then they built the motorway, and for a while in the 1960s my mother could get to Harrods from her bedroom in under the hour. Then all the world, his wife and children came to live in the Thames Valley, and now on the M4 it takes exactly ninety minutes to get to Hyde Park Corner. That's what I have always loved best about Berkshire; you only have to wait forty years and you are back exactly where you started. Progress has never really been one of my objectives, which is why, I suppose, I have always been so happy living in England.

4
Relative Values

An autobiographer with a family of eccentric relatives is deeply blessed: my father lived for years off anecdotes about his uncles and aunts, but mine were less theatrical – except, of course, in the professional sense. I think perhaps there was enough real madness around internationally in the 1940s to have seen off those larger-than-life characters who populated Robert's childhood during the First World War.

I have always envied him neighbours like Mrs Boddam-Whettam, her name a schoolboy joke in itself, who gave afternoon teas in Folkestone for bridge players. Once she unwisely asked my father, then about seven, to deliver the invitations. Pa had a lifelong fear of the dogs that were then kept down long Folkestone driveways. To avoid them he went down to the beach, hurling the envelopes one by one into the waves as he muttered to himself, 'Alas, unable to attend. Alas, unable to attend.'

Then there was Mrs Agnes Pope, another Folkestone resident who had a thing about handkerchiefs, believing them to be the work of the devil. As the self-appointed life president of the Society for the Abolition of the Handkerchief, she forbade all visitors to use one. When she was very old and ill an uninformed guest blew his nose at her bedside: Mrs Pope took it to be the sound of the Last Trump and duly passed away, sniffing to the last.

Then, of course, there was Robert's father the Major who, determined that his son should be introduced to the seamier side of life, once took him to Limehouse as an example of the kind of place to be avoided, unlike casinos. Father and

28

son entered a small Chinese grocery, which the Major had decided was an ill-disguised opium den. It was July. 'Got any snow, Mother?' the Major asked, in what he took to be the colloquial language of Limehouse opium-traders *circa* 1915.

'Snow?' responded the old lady behind the counter. 'You'd need to come back in December for that.'

'A very secretive lot, these Chinese,' opined the Major, as they started the long journey back to South Kensington and a safe tea.

One afternoon in 1921, Robert's life was transformed; he was on a half-holiday from yet another miserable prep school, and he had wandered into the local Folkestone theatre to see Esmé Percy on tour in George Bernard Shaw's *The Doctor's Dilemma*. That afternoon, in a matter of three hours, Pa went from being a fat, unlikeable, bewildered teenager to a potential leading man. The speech that did it for him was that of the artist Dubedat as he lies dying: 'I know that in an accidental sort of way, struggling through the unreal part of life, I have not always been able to live up to my ideal. But in my own real world I have never done anything wrong, never denied my faith, never been untrue to myself. I've been threatened and blackmailed and insulted and starved. But I've played the game. I've fought the good fight. And now it's all over, there's an indescribable peace. I believe in Michelangelo, Velázquez and Rembrandt; in the might of design, the mystery of colour, the redemption of all things by Beauty everlasting, and in the message of Art that has made these hands blessed.'

I have often envied my father many things – his stardom, his invincible faith in himself, his conviction that whatever he did was undeniably right, at least at the time of doing it, and his ability to convince his nearest and dearest that what *he* wanted was what *they* wanted too. I envied him his lifelong curiosity about virtually everything, his unflagging optimism, his freedom from depression or fear or financial anxiety when broke, but most of all I think I envied him that Shaw thing: the moment when a voice in a seaside theatre at a dull, half-empty matinée of *The Doctor's Dilemma* suddenly showed him the rest of his life.

My life has never yet had a transforming moment like that, and I realise now that I have lived it perhaps too often through other people. As a biographer, as a critic, as a journalist, as a radio and television interviewer, I have spent the best part of half a century persuading others, sometimes strangers, to tell me their life stories – or, at any rate, those areas of them that they thought fit for public consumption.

But what about me? Do I have no inner life, or did I just find it too boring to spend time developing one? Too young to fight a war, too careful ever to get into deep trouble, my life has been lived almost always in the middle lane, travelling neither too slow nor too fast, and always fascinated by the cars on either side of mine. The rest of my time has been spent largely in the dark, at plays and films, again watching life go by at a distance: reality always seemed to happen to other people. Only relatively lately have I gone back to the acting and directing I gave up at college, as if aware, forty years on, that Kenneth Tynan was right that a critic is someone who knows the way but cannot drive the car. Suddenly, in my late fifties, I wanted to drive the car myself, then realised I had left it almost too late.

When I wrote my father's biography, soon after his death and really as a way of keeping him alive, one of its sternest critics was my second wife Ruth, who pointed out with alarming accuracy that I had described everything that my father had been and done, without ever dealing with the issue of what he had done to me. Everything I am, she believes – and, worse, everything I'm not – is to do with Robert, but because neither of us ever bothered to work out our relationship, the issue remains, and will now for ever remain, unresolved.

We do not like criticism, at least not on my side of the family: Pa did not speak to Godfrey Winn, a leading sob-sister journalist of the day, for nearly thirty years because Godfrey had unwisely remarked, when I was about five, that I was already decidedly overweight. True, of course, but neither Robert nor I took lightly to being criticised for our weight. The only trouble with the Winn boycott was that, after about twenty years, Pa began to forget whether it had been him, or possibly Cecil Beaton or Beverley Nichols, who had uttered the famous size-ist insult, and we had to cut all three at parties in a miasma of uncertain retroactive indignation.

But was I really paternally challenged, and if so was there anything I could have done about it? Eric Morecambe's son, Gary, once published a book called *Hard Act to Follow*, for which he interviewed a dozen or so of us actors' children. Nearly all talked of the agonies, the drink, the drugs, the insecurities, the multiple marriages and the sheer impossibility of living with a star. All I could recall were the holidays, the lunches and the sheer delight of a man who was only on earth to have a little fun and spread it around.

Sometimes, of course, it all went wrong. In my early forties I had a nervous breakdown, brought on by my decision to leave my wife and children for another life and another woman, as well as by the collapse of *Punch* where I had settled so happily. I still rattle with the pills it takes to keep depression at bay, but what I now remember best – I've worked hard to suppress the rest – was Pa's amazement that any child of his could so allow their private life to get in the way of a public career. Our family has always been good at parties; introspection we try to leave to others.

'We can be bought,' the great American actor Alfred Lunt once noted of himself and his long-time wife and partner Lynn Fontanne, 'but we can't be bored,' and that, in essence, was Pa's philosophy. In truth, I now think he was often bored by fatherhood. Not that he wasn't devoted to my sister, my brother and me, but somewhere in him there was a deep terror of the family he loved. Happy enough when leading us into restaurants or watching us splash about in his pool, he would suddenly remember that there was a world elsewhere, and that fatherhood was never as much fun as a night of roulette or a week on the Trans-Siberian Railway.

Robert never frightened me, or bored me, or tried to make me anything I hadn't already become by heredity, accident or desire, and in our own clenched, curious way we loved each other very much. We were like a couple of water-buffalo, splashing around in the shallows of his beloved Berkshire swimming-pool. Although fatherhood was one of Pa's longer-lasting roles, he had to act that too. I only hope he enjoyed the performance as much as I did; I was not only Pa's eldest child, I was also his travelling audience and it was a long, happy tour, with perhaps just a few bad houses along the way – and maybe something a bit wrong with the second act, but nothing that couldn't be fixed in rehearsal. Which, in a way, was where we always were, no matter the town or the country: we were in rehearsal for real life, which, luckily, only seldom got in our way.

The end of the Second World War seems to have passed largely unnoticed in our household: I recall no bunting or cheering, though I think we had a half-holiday from nursery school. Pa's long run in *The Man Who Came to Dinner* had been followed by an equally long one as the Prince Regent in *The First Gentleman*. On VE night, Churchill had come to see the play, and during a curtain speech Pa proudly announced that 'the first gentleman of Europe' was in the house. Winston did not go backstage afterwards: 'It is important to remember,' said Pa later, 'that Churchill was first and foremost a statesman, not a diplomat.' A few weeks later he lost the election and Pa, a lifelong Fabian Socialist after his first encounter with Bernard Shaw, was not entirely disappointed, especially as Labour-supporting audiences were still flocking to see him in a play that unashamedly celebrated one of Britain's most dissolute and luxury-loving monarchs, a bully, a wit and a drunk.

It was the critic and *Observer* editor Ivor Brown who at this time noted perspicaciously of Robert's now well-established West End stage stardom: 'Morley's peculiar talent lies in his ability to pass the first great test of a star, which is that he can play his hand in act one, and then replay it in acts two and three without ever losing our interest.'

It was effectively the hand that Pa was to play for the remaining fifty or so years of his life; unlike Alec Guinness or Peter Sellers, with whom he worked in several movies, Robert did not believe in disguise. Instead, he decided that a vast range of real-life historical characters had looked curiously like him, and played them accordingly. His art was in familiarity, and although he could be astonishingly good when he set his mind to it, he often avoided the greater theatrical challenges. He turned down Peter Hall's offer of a Stratford Falstaff 'because I shan't enjoy it, darling, and then nor will they'.

'They', of course, were his audience: wherever he was in the world, playing whatever theatre in whichever country, he would stand at the 'half', thirty minutes before the curtain went up, peering through it at the arriving customers, his customers. Depending on how many there were, what they were wearing, carrying, eating, talking about, he would do the show then and there, for them and for that night only. It was never the same twice and, of course, directors and playwrights (though Pa usually avoided their presence and influence whenever possible, preferring to speak his own lines and organise his own stage directions) found him difficult if not impossible to work with. When the young Peter Brook found himself directing my father and David Tomlinson in *The Little Hut*, he knew of their reputation for ad-libbing even as early as 1950, and told them that he must, if he was to work with them, have *carte blanche*. Pa replied that she was already getting a little deaf and very expensive.

Half a century or so later, I came back from New York where Twiggy had been magically starring in a version of my

Noël & Gertie, heavily adapted by her husband Leigh Lawson – with my blessing and encouragement – for her tap-dancing genius. Soon after I got home Alan Ayckbourn rang to ask for the rights in my show for his Scarborough theatre.

Hoping to re-establish my script as once it had been, I asked him nervously if he was planning any changes. Alan's reaction was unusually sharp. 'Changes?' he barked. 'You dare to ask if I am going to change your script? I'll tell you. We are in 1969. I am a young dramatist and your bloody father is doing one of my very first plays, *How the Other Half Loves*. The first day of rehearsal he comes over to me. "Mr Ayckbourn," he says, "my name is Robert Morley. I am now going to make you very, very rich and very, very unhappy."'

Both predictions came good: the play ran in the West End for two years, Alan's longest run to date, but well before the end of it Pa had done his usual 'editing' of the script. 'Do you wonder I have never again written a script for a solo star?' asked Alan. I need hardly add that he did my *Noël & Gertie* word for word, comma for comma, exactly as I had first written it. Actually he didn't: a guest director called Matthew Francis did, but I like to think Alan was somehow keeping a paternal eye on it for me.

Ayckbourn had only become a playwright because of another playwright: when, freshly trained as an actor and straight from drama school, he got his first job at a seaside rep, he was to be directed by Harold Pinter in one of his own plays. At lunch on the first day of rehearsal, it is said that Alan plucked up courage to ask Harold what his character was all about. 'Mind your own fucking business,' replied Pinter, and Alan retired from the stage soon afterwards, to become one of its most successful writers.

To my shame, despite reading French at Oxford, I have never ventured far enough into Proust to work out his thing about the madeleines, but I do rather fear for these memoirs: they are at best random, largely because the harder I try to stay within the chronology of my life, the greater the temptation to wander off down the highways and byways of random-memory association.

So, where were we? End of the war, still living in Berkshire, my sister Annabel just born, and I think I've already told you about her being kept alive in the airing cupboard. With the ending of hostilities, my parents decided that the little gamekeeper's cottage they had bought as newlyweds was hardly going to be large enough for a growing family, but as building restrictions were still tough, Robert bought himself a ready-made wooden hut, which still sits at the end of the garden. There he spent much of the rest of his life, smoking the cigars Ma had banned from the house, writing plays and journalism and sometimes just staring happily across the lawn.

Like most of us in his family, my father was good at doing very little; but there would be sudden bursts of authorial activity, and one of these was now starting to happen. Pa had been unusually thrilled by my birth; I don't think anything I ever did in later life impressed him quite as much, but the memory of the arrival of his firstborn, that moment when you first see a living thing that is partly your creation, never left him.

From Ma's diary, 5 December 1946
Sherry's fifth birthday. Party of 8 and fireworks. Knows 2 and 3 times table. Reads 3-letter words and can do simple mental arithmetic. Plays with soldiers and trains. Height 3 foot 10 inches; weight 4 stone 5 lbs.

I seem already to have been shrinking and putting on weight: was I also backward for my age? Probably, but local Thames Valley schools were not at the forefront of radical educational progress in 1946, though our local Wargrave establishment was soon able to boast the arrival of a young post-war refugee from Europe by the name of Tom Stoppard.

Meanwhile, backstage at *The First Gentleman*, Robert was running a regular bridge and poker school between and sometimes during performances, and one of its other members (alongside my godfathers Peter Bull and Sewell Stokes, now happily relieved of their widely differing war duties) was the writer Noël Langley, he of the *Land of Green Ginger* and the screenplay for *The Wizard of Oz*, whom Pa had first met in California when, just before the war, he was playing an Oscar-nominated Louis XVI in *Marie Antoinette* opposite Norma Shearer and John Barrymore. It was his first and arguably most distinguished movie.

One afternoon, these many years later, Robert began to tell Noël about the play that had been at the back of his mind. It was to be about the curious mix of delight and terror that you experience when you first see your own firstborn, and the belief that a child who grows up able to quote his own father is likely to be happier than one who cannot, or maybe chooses not to.

At first there wasn't a lot more that that to what was then called *My Son Edward*, and one of Pa's problems as a playwright was that he always needed someone to bounce his ideas off. Later, with the coming of radio and television comedy, such partnerships were common enough, from Frank Muir and Denis Norden all the way through to Ray Galton and Alan Simpson. In the immediately post-war London theatre they were, however, comparatively rare, despite the Broadway hits of Kaufman and Hart, and Pa was lucky eventually to find a series of co-authors, from Rosemary Anne Sisson to the late John Wells, who were able to spark him off. Or keep his nose to the typewriter when as usual he was wondering about lunch or a swim.

This first partnership did not run smoothly, and the omens for what became *Edward My Son* were not good: Robert was just coming off the back of two long wartime hits (*The First Gentleman*, like *The Man Who Came to Dinner*, had run almost three years in London and on the road, seen by more than 500,000 people), and there was some doubt in the business about whether he could complete the hat-trick with a play of his own devising, especially one that, like Topsy, grew and grew in the writing.

I guess nowadays, if anyone could ever afford to revive *Edward My Son* (a project I have long cherished as both a son and a director), you would assume it was about Robert Maxwell, and even I would have to admit that it has, to some extent, been overtaken by David Hare and Howard Brenton's brilliant *Pravda*. For *Edward My Son* is also about a newspaper tycoon who allows his passion for money and success to destroy his inner life. But the great trick of this play is that you never get to meet its title character: Edward, the son for whom Arnold Holt always says he is working, becomes a dissolute drunk who is killed in a flying accident during the Second World War, and the play is in reality the story of his father, a larger-than-life character loosely modelled on Lord Beaverbrook. But Holt was an original: a media mogul way ahead of his time, a man willing to sacrifice even his own wife and child to making his fortune by fair means or foul. If you know the story at all, it will be from late-night TV screenings of the film, which George Cukor made for MGM in 1948 with Spencer Tracy and Deborah Kerr in the roles created by Robert and Peggy Ashcroft.

During shooting, Tracy was staying at the Savoy Hotel and the stage version with Pa was still playing next door. He was told firmly that he was not to see the show, lest it should unduly influence his screen portrayal. On the night that shooting ended, just before he returned to Hollywood, the greatest film star of the day went to see the play, then knocked on Robert's dressing-room door. 'Mr Morley,' he announced sombrely, 'my name is Spencer Tracy and I have just made a monumental fuck-up of your script. I fear nobody explained to me that you played it for laughs.'

What Robert did, as usual, was play it for the audience, which he frequently addressed in monologues during the show: 'My name, ladies and gentlemen, is Holt, Lord Holt. You'll have seen my picture in the papers quite a lot these last few years. When you get home you can look me up in *Who's Who*, if you happen to have one. It won't tell you everything about me but there's quite a lot there now, nearly half a page. It will tell you where I was born and where I went to school, whom I married and what offices I've held under the Crown. It will tell you some of the committees I've served on in my time. I'm not asked to serve on many now. But it won't tell you that I happen to own this theatre – I thought that would surprise you. It won't tell you that I am proprietor of a great national newspaper, that I'm Hythe's Lager Beer and Hungerford's Stores and the Brewster Match Company, that I control Provender's, and through it six of the eight big biscuit firms in this country. I am telling you all this not because I want to boast, but because I want to establish my contact with you. Just because you read my papers or eat my biscuits or sit in my theatre, it doesn't mean that you have to like me – or I you, for that matter. But it does mean that our lives, like a lot of other people's lives, have already crossed to a certain extent. That is why I should value your opinion. What would you have done on that foggy February morning? Would you have gone on, or gone back? I wonder.

'The trouble is, of course, that none of you knew Edward, and now he's dead and it's too late. Mind you, you'll meet other people here tonight who are dead . . . But with Edward it's different because, you see, he was my son. My only son. He was twenty-three when he was killed, a pleasant-looking boy with charming manners and a lovely smile. That doesn't add up to very much, does it? But it's all I can tell you about him for now. Later on – well, you'll see for yourselves how it was.

'Supposing we make a start. It is November the eleventh

1919. A year ago today the Armistice was signed and my son was born.'

It must be almost fifty-five years since I first heard Robert open his best play with that monologue, and the fact that I can still quote much of it verbatim is because my mother, my sister and I (my brother had not yet been born) lived with *Edward My Son* for the next three years; Pa played it first at the Savoy, then at the Martin Beck on Broadway, and finally all over Australia and New Zealand. Towards the end of that tour, I was even allowed to go on at the very end for matinées only, appearing not as Edward but as his little son, born just after he was killed. I was paid two and sixpence per performance, and formed the impression, as I suspect did many Australian matinée-goers, that I would have to find some other profession once I had left school. Or even started to go to one.

5
Edward *Goes on the Road*

What made *Edward My Son* such magic was, of course, the relationship that Robert developed with what I always thought of as his audience. He would talk to them not only at the outset but during the show, taking them with him on its journey and finally ending it: 'Well, ladies and gentlemen, that's how it all happened, more or less . . . Look after yourselves. The way things are in this world, nobody else will.'

Both John Clements and Basil Sydney inherited the role of Holt in the West End when Robert took it to Broadway, and then there was Spencer Tracy on film, but none of them ever quite caught Pa's extraordinary affinity with his audience. Somehow they, too, became part of his family as, of course, did the cast.

Like many other great hits, however, *Edward My Son* had a distinctly uneasy start. Peggy Ashcroft, ill-at-ease in modern dress, found Robert's somewhat slap-happy rehearsal habits a far cry from those of Gielgud and Devine at her beloved Old Vic and, on the opening night of the tour, locked herself in the dressing room rather than face the play. Pa managed to get her out and on, by telling her, implausibly, that if she didn't play that night she would never work again as an actress. Peg took his word for it, and played Evelyn Holt for a year in the West End and another on Broadway before handing over the role, first to Adrianne Allen on Broadway and then to Sophie Stewart in Australia.

There was also, as James Cairncross, one of the original cast's few survivors, recalls, a long opening scene set in the hospital where Edward was born. This disappeared when, on its first night in Leeds, the play ran for three and a half hours.

It was just as well: according to Cairncross, 'It involved the somewhat embarrassing sight of Robert in a too-tight army uniform, ending the scene by kneeling in a spotlight to thank God for the birth of his son.'

During the run, James remembers Robert being good for several lunches and dinners; later Pa's beloved agent Rosalind Chatto took to cooking his companies full-scale meals in the dressing room between matinée and evening performances. Some months into the run, Cairncross was walking towards the stage door eating an ice cream when he was accosted by Pa: 'He told me he disliked seeing members of his company eating in the street, a message which would have made more sense had he not at the time been spitting out the pips from a vast bag of grapes.'

James also remembers, 'A fat little boy of six or seven, standing by the wings in the prompt corner,' and I guess that must have been me. Certainly it was how I spent the next three years of my life all around the world, and at least the prompt corner never changed: it was home to me, while New York, Sydney, Melbourne, Auckland and Wellington were the unreal backdrops, places I never got to know as we never stayed long enough in any of them. Backstage, paradoxically, was real and unchanging and where I knew everyone, no matter the country, town or even continent. Backstage was my Neverland, second star to the right and keep on till morning, the place where dreams are born and all that still-chilling legacy of *Peter Pan*. Even that was a family affair because my grandmother Gladys (whom I had still not met) had been one of the first great Peters, and her younger daughter Sally a goddaughter of J.M. Barrie. To this day I cannot take my grandsons to *Peter Pan* without being chilled by Barrie's passion for very small boys, his horror of growing up and his belief that 'to die will be an awfully big adventure'; but in writing the lives of Noël Coward and John Gielgud, both born within a year or two of *Peter*, and now my own, I cannot but be aware how Peter

Pan still lives, surviving quite literally on a wing and a prayer then suddenly discovering that the world has moved on and he is no longer its star. Peter Pan defines almost every showbiz life of the twentieth century: he is all of us, however hard we try to deny him. Just as Americans of my generation have always had Judy Garland going over the rainbow to Oz, so we always had Peter flying us to the Neverland.

School Report, Autumn Term 1947, Rupert House, Henley-on-Thames
A likeable little boy, eager to be friendly. Hopeless at art and handiwork: seems to have no co-ordination at all, but intelligent in curious ways and keen. Avoids sport whenever possible: inclined to be lazy. Imitates teachers well. Totally unable to catch or throw balls.

Robert played *Edward My Son* first at His Majesty's and then the Lyric, all through 1947 and well into the summer of 1948. For the first time he was making real money as star and co-author, and his agent had done a good deal with MGM for the film rights. But there was still Broadway to conquer: Pa had scored his first real success there back in 1938 as Oscar Wilde, and this was to be his only ever return. Peggy Ashcroft and Leueen McGrath stayed with the show, being replaced in London by Pauline Letts and a young Irene Worth. Ian Hunter, whom Pa had originally wanted to play the lead before deciding that only he could do it justice, was now the faithful doctor hiding his love for Lady Holt, and the plan was that we should all sail on the *Queen Elizabeth* to New York, cross America by train, spend the summer holidays getting to know my grandmother Gladys Cooper, then return to Broadway for a triumphal autumn opening.

I stymied that plan by inadvertently catching chicken-pox from a friend at my Henley nursery school. My sister, not yet two years old, was therefore flown ahead to California with her nanny before she could catch it, while my parents and I followed by ship several weeks later, once the spots had cleared up.

It occurs to me only now that my late-life passion for lecturing on cruise liners headed for faraway places with strange-sounding names was ignited that summer evening in 1947 when, at Southampton, we boarded the *Queen Elizabeth* for the six-day crossing to New York. I was not, as you may have gathered, a very bright child, and I think I never grasped the concept of a ship. At Southampton you walked up a gangplank into an amazing other place, where they had lights in windows of shipboard stores, and bananas, and things and people and clothes the like of which I had never seen in wartime Berkshire. I thought we had walked into a kind of mirror-kingdom, familiar to my generation from *Alice in Wonderland* and to my grandchildren, I guess, from *Harry Potter*.

It wasn't for a day or two that I noticed we were moving, and surrounded by sea. By that time I had ganged up with several other kids on the boat, and we derived considerable pleasure from irritating both Carol Reed and Graham Greene, who were on their way to launch *The Third Man* in America, but not thrilled to find their peaceful sea-break interrupted by screaming children.

For reasons that now escape me, neither of these great artists had bothered to acquire the correct immigration visas for landing in New York, and it was with an evil, childlike glee that we saw them transported to Ellis Island as undesirable aliens. It took some hours for their movie company in the US to get them safely immigrated, and I have always maintained that if they had been a little more gracious to us on the crossing, their misfortune would never have occurred.

We stayed only a couple of nights in New York before boarding the Super Chief, an amazing train that took five days to cross the United States. There were bunk beds, restaurants and bars on board, and an all-glass observation car at the back, from which we could view America – the Rockies, the Grand Canyon, the deserts and mountain ranges – in a breathtaking panorama. In Chicago, something still more exciting happened: because the rail gauge changed, you had to leave the train and the station, then cross Al Capone's city to a different terminal whence the journey to California continued.

Nowadays nobody does that five-day journey by train, and I regret that neither my children nor my grandchildren will see America as I first did, from ground level. At that time, just after the war, it was how everyone travelled: the major Hollywood studios all employed full-time aides to live in Chicago and facilitate their stars' changeover from one station to the other. George Kaufman even wrote a play about the train, *On the Twentieth Century*, which was later made into a movie with John Barrymore and Carole Lombard, then a Broadway and West End musical without them.

In those days, for a British actor or actress to take a Hollywood movie was a major, often life-changing decision. The journey to California lasted at least twelve days – seven on a boat and another five on the train – and was not to be taken lightly. Nobody went for just one movie – unless, of course, it was a disaster; you hoped that your first picture would miraculously expand into a seven-year contract, in which case you sent home for children, nannies, partners, and settled as surely as your parents and grandparents had in India or Australia.

In our Californian time, Deborah Kerr was one of the last of these imperial figures. Once her contract with MGM was safely established, she sent home for a Norland-trained English nanny and her two young children. It was around ninety degrees when they arrived, dressed as for an English winter school term, at Los Angeles station, and Deborah duly enquired of the uniformed nanny what she had thought of it all.

'Thought, madam? Of what?'

'Well, Nanny, the journey – the Rockies, Chicago, the Grand Canyon.'

'Ah, madam, you must mean America. We did not care for it.'

The rest of us did, though. For an English family, emerging from the Second World War – however disconnected Berkshire had been from hand-to-hand fighting – California was a paradise of sun, sand, safety and, above all, food such as we had never seen before: vast farmers' markets where fruit seemed piled up to the skies, and all of it ours for a few cents. You could also, for some obscure reason, buy tortoises cheaply, and one of my enduring memories of that magical Californian summer was Gladys and me trying to teach a recalcitrant shell to behave like a pet. That tortoise was one of the few animals that ever defeated my grandmother; ever since John Barrymore had given her a monkey back in the 1920s, as a token of love, irritation or who knows what, while he was playing his celebrated London *Hamlet*, Gladys had acquired a curious ability (much like Dr Dolittle) to talk to the animals. At various times she kept horses, dogs, peacocks, cats and other less domestic animals, and they became one of her many US projects, second only to growing oranges for her own brand of marmalade. Indeed, she finished her Hollywood life several years later as a guest star on the wildlife television series *Daktari*.

At this time Hollywood was haunted by the early murmurings of the House UnAmerican Affairs Committee, but Communism was never much of an issue among the old British Raj, whose major complaint was that, as John Gielgud later noted, most of their houses looked as though they had been rapidly constructed for an Ideal Home Exhibition and were about to be equally rapidly dismantled. Just as studio sets were by their nature impermanent, so too seemed most local dwellings – great façades, but few fireplaces.

It says much about my emotional insensitivity that I didn't

realise until many years later, when I came to write a book about her, that the glamorous granny I so loved in the Californian sunshine had been going through one of the worst times in her life. Barely two years earlier, the actor Philip Merivale, her third husband and the one she most loved, had died in Los Angeles of liver failure, which also killed his son Jack thirty years later.

Gladys and Phil had settled in California early in the 1940s; their marriage lasted nine years, and started badly with ugly divorces on both sides. Some curiously disastrous joint attempts at Shakespeare followed, first in the open air of Regent's Park and then on Broadway. It was only when Gladys picked up her first Hollywood movie from an old English admirer, Alfred Hitchcock – *Rebecca*, in which she was the sister to Maxim de Winter, played by Laurence Olivier, whose career she had started during her management of the Playhouse Theatre in London in the 1920s – that she and Phil discovered their place in the sun.

He went on to star with Rosalind Russell, whose impresario husband Freddie Brisson he christened 'The Lizard of Ros', in *Sister Carrie*, and then for Orson Welles in *The Stranger*, but his health was never good. As for Gladys, though she soon got a character-acting contract with MGM, it cannot have been easy to accept relegation to relatively minor roles while such local stars as Bette Davis made movies of plays like *The Letter*, which Somerset Maugham had written for G at the Playhouse.

Yet, as always, she survived, even winning the first of her three Oscar nominations for supporting Davis in *Now Voyager* while coping as best she could with a beloved, ailing husband, a severe shortage of cash and a career in apparently steep decline. Though she never talked of it, there is no doubt that the loss of her beloved Phil after less than a decade as his wife was the greatest sadness of her long life. She remained his widow for another quarter of a century, until her own death in England at eighty-two.

6

Tales from the Hollywood Raj

All the more reason, therefore, for us to be with her in that summer, if only to remind Gladys that she had another family at home in England. Her younger daughter Sally, and her wayward son John, who was already showing signs of mental instability, had been much with her in the aftermath of Phil's death, but now we, too, could be there at her little house in Pacific Palisades, with its pool and the orange trees, a life that had been unimaginable in rainsoaked, late-1940s England.

Then, as always, it was my father who wrote best about Gladys: while we lazed around her pool, much like the new tortoise, G headed off to work at MGM every morning, never quite sure which film she was making but certain it would only require a few days of her time to be Gregory Peck's old housekeeper, or somebody else's old English aunt, in yet another literary classic. Those were the days when, as often as not, a film would start with the opening of a leatherbound book, and Gladys's regular allies among the supporting cast were often billed shamelessly as 'Dame May Whitty' and 'Sir C. Aubrey Smith'. Elsewhere, Britain might be in full retreat from her Indian and African empires, but in Hollywood there was still much to be said for a title. This was, after all, the summer in which Evelyn Waugh wrote his classic parody of Hollywood and the American way of death in *The Loved One*.

When Gladys died some twenty years later, I published an obituary written by the son-in-law who had only really begun to know her that summer in the Palisades:

To start life, my father wrote, as a Genuine British Beauty on a

World War One postcard, and end it as a Dame of the British Empire, can't be altogether bad . . . The whole story of Gladys's success, from her first 1905 appearance in *Bluebell in Fairyland*, has an element of fairyland make-believe, although she would never discuss past triumphs or disasters, and if you ever asked her about her acting, all she would say was that (like Noël Coward) she had learnt everything from the old Edwardian actor-manager Charles Hawtrey, who seems to have been the first stage naturalist. She could be very sharp at times, was no good at feeling sorry for people, perhaps because she had never felt sorry for herself. If you were in trouble, you got out of it, with her help, of course, but in the end it was down to you. If you got ill, you got better. She was, in her way, something of an early health fiend. She never ate much, and worshipped only the sun . . . When we were with her that summer, she would come back from MGM every night, start cooking our dinner at dusk, and then, when everything was in hand, she would disappear and a moment or two later sweep back across the patio, wrapped in towelling, for her evening swim. Ten minutes after that, she would reappear in a sort of shift dress, gold bangles on her arms, her hair and makeup immaculate, to mix a final round of daiquiris before she took the lamb off the spit. How is it done? I used to ask myself. How can she be so elegant? If she was vain about anything, it was her cooking. Two things you were never allowed to criticise – her marmalade and her driving. Both, I always felt privately, left a good deal to be desired. But about everything else she was eminently reasonable. How good an actress she thought herself to be, how seriously she took her profession, I was never really sure. She acted like she did everything else, with utter naturalism.

But of one thing I was very certain: she was immensely proud of the affection and gratitude of her public. She answered every letter, she acknowledged every compliment, and no day back home in England was ever too wet or too cold for her to pause as she came out of the stage door, or later still the supermarket in Henley-on-Thames, to have a chat to a faithful patron who wished to compliment her on some play or film or television appearance, or just on still being Gladys Cooper.

We never really quarrelled, not even when she took me for a drive through Yosemite National Park and insisted on winding down all the windows to feed the bears lumps of sugar from her hand, while I crouched on the back seat, having first taken the precaution of locking the doors so that I would be unable to go to her rescue when, as I was convinced they would, the bears finally ate her. But they recognised a kindred spirit, and we drove on unmolested.

Once I tried to write her a play, secure in the knowledge that one morning she would come in from those impossible California flower-beds, put on her huge horn-rimmed glasses, and sit down on the porch overlooking the Pacific Palisades Golf Course to start reading whichever script was on top of the pile on the table. Something, perhaps the bark of a dog, or the scent of a flower, or the flight of a dragonfly, had suddenly reminded her that once again it was time to be off. Maybe to New York to see her son, or London to see her daughters, or Hawaii just to see Hawaii. On these occasions, she travelled on the first available flight, with the first available play. As a rule, the plane always proved the more reliable vehicle.

Years later, I realised that what to me and my baby sister Annabel was the most magical of post-war times did not seem that way to many of the surviving colony of English actors out in the midday sun. David Niven had just lost a beloved young wife, Primula Rollo, in a tragic fall down a flight of stone stairs when she, newly arrived from England with their two small sons Jamie and David Jr, had mistaken a cellar door for one opening in to a closet.

A few streets and months away in the Hollywood hills, Rex Harrison's extramarital affair with an American starlet, Carole Landis, had ended catastrophically when Landis killed herself in his apartment. Only the reappearance of his wife

Lilli Palmer, some brilliant if irregular body-shifting by his old friend Roland Culver, an astute publicity campaign and a Broadway hit with *Anne of the Thousand Days* combined to rescue Rex's career a decade before *My Fair Lady*. Somehow, to this very day, I can't hear even the echo of Rex definitively speak-singing 'I've Grown Accustomed To Her Face' without recalling the suicides of two women who loved him, Carole Landis and Rachel Roberts. Rachel, indeed, took the trouble to do away with herself, long after their divorce, in Los Angeles only a few hours before he was due to reopen there on a last tour of *My Fair Lady*. Sacred Rex may not have been; a monster he certainly was. At which point we may as well recall the night when, in pouring rain, he was leaving the stage door of Drury Lane after a performance of *My Fair Lady* only to find, on the pavement, an old female fan waiting in the hope of an autograph. Rex snarled that it was late and wet and he was going home; hurt, the old lady tapped him lightly on the elbow with her autograph book. At that moment, Stanley Holloway, the original stage and screen Doolittle, was coming out of the stage door behind him and caught the significance of the gesture. 'Rex,' he said, 'you have tonight made not only stage but world history. Just now, for the first time ever, the fan hit the shit.'

Years later, I asked another of Rex's five wives, Elizabeth Harris, who survived marriage to him (and another to Richard Harris), if she could define Harrison in a single sentence: 'Oh, yes,' she said. 'He was the kind of man who would always send the wine back in his own home.'

Yet I knew nothing of the troubles of Hollywood Brits until years later when I began to research for a book called *Tales from the Hollywood Raj*. Was I a peculiarly innocent seven-year-old? Or had Gladys just decided that the local difficulties of her old friends and colleagues from London were not to be allowed to disturb our summer in the sun?

I remember her announcing one day that Garbo was coming

to tea – 'She's a rather boring old Swede, darling, and very lonely, but luckily she loves doing the washing-up' – and on another occasion Marlene Dietrich came. I don't recall the latter offering help with the plates, although she too, as I discovered when I wrote a biography of her, had a similarly obsessive and curious passion for housework.

Then there was the Louis B. Mayer tea party, which I remember rather more clearly. Gladys had now been under contract to MGM for the best part of a decade ('I have every star in the heavens signed up to MGM,' Mayer once told my father proudly, 'except for that damned little mouse at Disney'), and LB, as he was rarely called to his face, had been irked to discover that every Sunday afternoon G laid on tea for the entire colony of old British character actors. This included everyone from Ronnie Colman and May Whitty through David Niven, Basil Rathbone and Nigel 'Willy' Bruce (Holmes and Watson, no less) to Deborah Kerr and Greer Garson. Gladys had started out with many of the senior ones in the London theatre of the 1920s and, like them, was determined to maintain as many traditions of the old country as possible. Hence the Sunday teas. Mayer's office let it be known that he, as their employer, would like to be asked so, graciously, Gladys agreed that he should come on the following Sunday.

She lived at 750 Napoli Drive, which was not by any means a mansion but a comfortable family home. At the bottom of the garden, there was a pool house where we all stayed and which later she made her home; she sold the 'big' house in about 1950 for several million dollars less than it must now be worth.

Mayer's limo, a Cadillac rather larger, it seemed to me, than G's entire garden, drew up and out clambered the tiny cigar-chewing Tsar of all the Rushes. It was widely noted at the time that if you had swung a scythe five feet above the California ground you would not have injured a single studio chief, so vertically challenged were they. But Mayer had only begun to approach Gladys across her lawn when I heard Niven, in an audibly appalled aside, say to Ronald Colman, 'Look out, old boy, there's an American on Gladys's grass.'

7
It's a Wonderful Town

But summers, even as magical as that, never last: all too soon we embarked on the Super Chief in the other direction, five days to get back to the chill of a New York winter. Robert opened *Edward My Son* at the Martin Beck to some of the best reviews of his life. There was an embargo on the Spencer Tracy movie, which meant it couldn't be screened until we were *en route* to Australia, and despite the play's English setting, American audiences – more accustomed than we were to the rise and fall of millionaires and the private price to be paid for public success – took it to their hearts.

Years later I asked Robert what it was about *Edward*, a thoroughly effective but somehow workmanlike melodrama, that made it his greatest hit. 'Difficult to answer, darling boy,' said Pa, 'unless you remember a very minor American dramatist called Clyde Fitch. He once said that when you write plays, just very, very occasionally you weave in a golden thread. We had woven in the golden thread.'

And golden it was: we lived in an apartment on Park Avenue that had a living and dining room so large that when my parents gave me, at Christmas, a Lionel electric train set, complete with an engine that puffed real smoke, it could run all the way through one room, out of sight across the passage, then round the other and back.

Although that December I was just seven, I had never been to school in America. My parents decided then, however, that the time had come for a little light education, and I was duly sent to the Town School, a chic Manhattan day school where I made my first real friend, one whom I have kept for more than fifty years.

He, too, was an actor's child, and he, too, had a father then appearing on Broadway: Bert Lahr, the great Cowardly Lion of *The Wizard of Oz*, was in the last of his legendary stage revues with Ethel Merman, and Johnnie and I became firm friends. What happened to us later has always struck me as decidedly eerie: we lost touch in 1949, met again in 1960 at the beginning of our first Oxford undergraduate term, then lost touch until 1969, when his first book (a wondrous tribute to his father entitled *Notes on a Cowardly Lion*) and my first, the life of Noël Coward, were published on both sides of the Atlantic in the same season.

Once again we lost touch, and the next time I saw him we had both just divorced our first wives, Johnnie in far more tragic circumstances than I. We met again soon after he had married Connie Booth and I Ruth Leon, and for ten years while he was (and remains) drama critic of the *New Yorker*, I held a similar job on that magazine's nearest British equivalent, the *Spectator*. Once I was able to give him an award for writing the theatre book of the year, and I have always told him that if for any reason he feels he is, God forbid, about to die, he is to telephone me at once. That way I get a few hours at least in which to put my affairs in order.

Though Johnnie Lahr is, historically, my oldest friend, we have never been close, which allows me to say that he is far and away the best theatre writer I know. His *New Yorker* profiles have only ever been equalled by Kenneth Tynan, another golden boy of our business, but less disciplined and meticulous. Johnnie is technically something more than a critic: his deal with the *New Yorker*, envied by the rest of us mere mortal hacks, allows him to roam the world and to live with productions, actors, writers, directors, for as long as it takes to research a 20,000-word essay that becomes a review not just of their current show but of their lives, their body of work, their entire claim to public attention.

Johnnie understands, from all those years of staring at his

dad in dressing-room mirrors, the essence of showbusiness, what Tynan once called 'high-definition performance'. Unlike most critics, who are either overnight reporters or would-be professors of drama, Lahr has Leichner greasepaint running through his veins. This does not make him always a showbiz fan and, indeed, some of his most savage and bitter-sweet writing has always been about his own family – especially his mother, who could somehow never apply heat to food, and the father who never really knew him. But if you want to know about late-twentieth-century theatre, about the business of showbusiness, about those faces in the dressing-room mirrors, Lahr remains the best guide, by blood, instinct and genius. I am proud to have known him as long as I have, and I have always secretly hoped that whatever I have written would reach and please him. What I envy him most is not his talent – it would be futile – but that, thanks to a remarkable marketing operation, there are little plastic models of his dad and all the other stars on the yellow brick road to Oz in every New York souvenir-shop window. On his way to yet another Broadway opening, Johnnie can thus wave at his father forty or more years after his death. I have posters of Robert all over the house, but somehow I think I'd rather be talking to a little plastic model. Curiously, English actors don't often seem to qualify for those, although my son once gave me for Christmas an almost lifelike Patrick Stewart from *Star Trek*, which stands about six inches off the bookcase, while an old college friend called Oliver Ford-Davies has finished up in his sixties as a statue from the new *Star Wars*. Not even Gielgud became one of those, although Alec Guinness did.

Is that really all I can recall of New York that first winter? Not quite. I made two other friends, and they, too, were already steeped in theatre. Anna and Daniel Massey were almost exactly my age, the children of Adrianne Allen, the actress who had taken over as Lady Holt in *Edward* from Peggy Ashcroft. Adrianne was a formidable star of the H. M.

Tennent management who had also been Sybil (as in, 'Don't quibble, Sybil'), in the original London production of Noël Coward's *Private Lives*. Around 1930 she had married the actor Raymond Massey and had her two children; a decade or so later, she picked up the phone to hear the cultured tones of an American in London, Bill Whitney, suggesting a meeting. Adrianne went to his office and Bill told her two things: that his wife was having an affair with her husband, and that he was one of the best divorce lawyers in the business.

Bill organised both divorces, then married Adrianne and adopted her children: the four of them were now living a highly social life near us on Park Avenue, which often had room for me although, as I was painfully aware, I was never the elegant little guest that Adrianne somehow always expected. My recollection is that I was forever falling over her exquisite arrangements of small tables with elegant flowers in tall cut-glass vases.

But one of the curious things about childhood friendships, I now know with some regret, is that you have to work at them in later life. Anna and I still see each other frequently in the corridors of Broadcasting House, where we make much of our radio living. After a difficult first marriage to the bisexual, disturbed, infinitely neurotic *Sherlock Holmes* star Jeremy Brett, which produced an award-winning novelist in their only son David Huggins, she has found happiness with a distinguished Russian scientist for whom she learnt his language: initially he spoke almost no English. We still hug each other, but with seemingly little recollection of those months in New York fifty years ago. As for her brother Dan – whom I came to admire as much as any actor of his generation, save perhaps Corin Redgrave – we met up often in the months just before he died far too young. There, too, I have a sense of a friendship never fully realised.

As for Adrianne, our lives continued to overlap in foreign countries: she remained a West End actress, frequently replacing Celia Johnson or Wendy Hiller, until 1959, when her old friends John Gielgud and Binkie Beaumont, the H. M. Tennent manager, cast her in Peter Shaffer's first play, *Five Finger Exercise*, with another Tennent veteran, Roland Culver, and three starry newcomers: Juliet Mills, Michael Bryant and Brian Bedford. However, when it was time to take what had been one of Adrianne's greatest personal successes to Broadway in 1960, the local management insisted on an American name for the posters, and replaced her with the long-time expatriate Jessica Tandy. Neither Gielgud nor Beaumont had the courage to tell Adrianne, and she found out when she overheard backstage gossip in the last week of the London run. By that time – she was known as 'plannie Annie' – she had already started to pack. In one of the most defiantly furious gestures ever made by an actress, she instead collected her belongings on the play's last West End night, removed her name from the theatrical *Who's Who* and herself from England, to settle with Bill in a Swiss village near Noël Coward. He had not been involved in this disaster and was about the only theatrical figure she ever spoke to again. She never again returned to England, even for a weekend.

Her sense of exile and betrayal was worthy of King Lear himself: later she quarrelled bitterly with both her children, and went to her grave thirty years later nursing a marathon sense of grievance – out of all proportion to what had happened, you might have thought, until you recalled that her whole life had been about the London theatre and showbiz friends, and they had destroyed it. She remained fond of me, however, and our paths continued to cross while I was teaching in Switzerland, later at the University of Geneva, and eventually writing the first biography of Noël Coward.

There was one other New York encounter that I still recall with some awe: for reasons that now escape me, my mother, father and I were once invited to the apartment of Leonard

Bernstein, who had only recently made his name as the boy-wonder conductor of the New York Philharmonic. As usual Pa was working, so Ma and I arrived first and the conversation turned, unsurprisingly, to music. The curious thing about Pa, I told Mr Bernstein, was that, like many of our family, he was tone-deaf – which became all too apparent some years later when he starred in a Drury Lane musical called *Fanny*. Mr Bernstein was not amused: 'That,' he told me indignantly, 'is the most disgraceful thing for a boy to say about his own father. No man is without music.'

At that chilly moment, my father walked into the room. 'Just for Mr Bernstein's benefit,' I asked him, 'would you sing "God Save the King"?' My father did so.

After a moment Bernstein turned to me in considerable shock: 'I am most terribly sorry for what I said to you just now. I never would have believed it possible, but this man is indeed entirely without music.'

Forty years later, when I was conducting one of the last interviews Bernstein ever gave, I reminded him of our first encounter. His face showed considerable retrospective pain.

What else about New York in 1948–9? There were snow-drifts in Central Park taller than me, and on Christmas Day, although Pa's theatre was closed for the holiday, the musicals played on. He took us all, including the Masseys, to see Ray Bolger in *Where's Charley?*, the Frank Loesser musical of *Charley's Aunt* (the composer's first wife was known even then as 'the evil of two Loessers'). Bolger sang 'Once In Love With Amy' and 'Make A Miracle' and wished us all the compliments of the season, which was when I knew suddenly, beyond all reasonable doubt, that I wanted to spend the rest of my life in a theatre, a decision I reached at an even earlier age than my father.

That winter, I also saw Ezio Pinza and Mary Martin in the original *South Pacific*, bitterly envied the two children who got to sing 'Dites-moi pourquoi la vie est belle', and failed to understand why the boy's role could not have been played by a podgy, tone-deaf English child with spots and a slight stammer. Modesty, self-awareness and sheer practicality have never been regarded as assets in my family, let alone virtues, any more than have thrift or common sense or the ability to stick to a diet or, indeed, to for-God's-sake-just-shut-up.

As winter turned into the spring of 1949, my love-hate relationship with New York was consummated. In later years, I married one American wife and another who, though born in London, has spent most of her working life there. In addition I have three American-passport-carrying children, have worked for thirty years or more for two American publications, the *International Herald Tribune* and *Playbill,* and have proudly co-hosted Don Smith's *Cabaret Conventions* at Town Hall for more than a decade. So why am I not a New Yorker? Why, however happy I have been there, am I always relieved to see Heathrow in the rain on my return? Partly, perhaps, because I have always lacked the work ethic that drives New Yorkers ever onward and upward: the desire for self-improvement is not in my character, and I shall regard it as something of a miracle if, when I die, I am still in roughly the same place as I was when I was born. This is very unAmerican, I need hardly add.

My other problem is that if I am working there, either reviewing Broadway or bookselling, and if I have somewhere to go every hour of the day and night, all goes fine. But the moment work stops, for the night or the weekend or whatever, I never know what to do with myself. New Yorkers are not good at doing nothing, which I have developed into an art form.

And yet, as I write this in the aftermath of the events of 11 September 2001, I am somehow aware that Americans now behave with precisely the 'grace under pressure' that we had told ourselves was a uniquely European virtue, and is no longer anything of the kind. When the unthinkable became the unbearable as it did on 11 September 2001, neither Ruth nor I could wait to get back to New York: we had work to do there, but for once it wasn't that which drove us back. It was the desire to see New York survive, and even draw a kind of triumph from disaster. We were too young for the Blitz, familiar only with a post-war England forever divided against herself, and to be in New York, working with Americans if only in such a marginal endeavour as cabaret, was to understand what it must be like to take pride and patriotism seriously and to heart. Suddenly the flags made sense, and if I have ever been ashamed of my own country it was in our inability to understand how, in their reaction to the devastation of the Twin Towers, Americans were defining what mattered most to them. I was, suddenly and stupidly, more proud to be in New York in those days than I have ever felt about being at home in London.

8
Bush Babies

But back to 1948. In those days even hit shows closed in June: air-conditioning had not yet been installed in theatres and the heat became unbearable. We returned to my grandmother in California, because we knew now that our next destination was Australia. After London and New York, *Edward* went on to Sydney, Melbourne, then all over New Zealand, or at least those parts of it where sheep did not outnumber the audiences, and where the local cities did not appear to have closed for the 1940s.

In less than thirty words, I see that I have already killed any chance of this book being widely distributed in New Zealand, so I should explain perhaps that it was then, as I'm sure now, an altogether enchanting if quiet country. After Broadway and Hollywood, though, it seemed so laid-back as to be comatose.

Gladys joined us on the first leg of the new adventure. This entailed going to Los Angeles airport one evening, being strapped into bunk beds on an old wartime Pan Am seaplane, sleeping through the night and waking eight hours later to find ourselves literally on the beach at Waikiki. If, in barely a year away from Berkshire, I had already fallen in love with New York and California – or, more precisely, Broadway and Hollywood – I now became obsessed by Hawaii. This group of islands somewhere on the way to Japan from Los Angeles, where rain falls on only five days a year – they call it liquid sunshine – was now to become the only home outside the Thames Valley that I have ever really coveted or missed.

I went back to Hawaii as a postgraduate student to work in

the university drama department for a year in 1963–4. I met my first wife there, and we took the children back for at least one long vacation. When I remarried in 1990, Ruth and I had our honeymoon there; she had fallen in love with the islands while on a film jury there with her first husband. Since then we have been back for vacation after vacation, and wonder quite seriously if we might ever manage to retire there.

And all of that because, one summer morning, a Pan Am clipper landed us off Waikiki beach. Then there were perhaps less than half a dozen hotels on the sands, which now support around fifty. Moreover there was a shipping strike, which meant that we had the sea and the beach more or less to ourselves: a family photo shows my parents, sister, grandmother and me running out of the surf looking as happy as I can remember any of us.

Pa and I spent several weeks frolicking like overweight dolphins in the surf and sometimes, to the hilarity of the few Hawaiians hanging around the beach, we even went out on a catamaran. Once we came ashore to find my sister in floods of tears. We had not been in serious danger of drowning, we reassured her. No, no, she explained, she was crying tears of humiliation because the locals were making fun of our chubby ungainliness.

I think it was at that moment that I first became aware of one of the sharpest divisions in our family, the one that separated those of us (Gladys, Robert, me especially) who would settle gladly for any public attention, even mockery, from those who lacked our abiding, lifelong fear of anonymity.

As soon as the shipping strike ended, we said farewell to G and set sail from Honolulu to Sydney aboard a ship called the *Aorangi*, about which all I recall is the captain telling us rather sadly that he never liked to look over the side, since it depressed him to see how slowly we were sailing.

When we arrived down under, it was my family's turn to fall in love. In the fullness of time my brother, Wilton, as yet unborn, would settle for a time into Sydney theatrical management; our sister would marry an Australian actor-director, Charles Little, and spend twenty years in Sydney bringing up two Australian children, while my parents, until the end of Robert's life, went there virtually every January. Robert paid their way first with the proceeds of a series of his West End hits, and later his role as Mr Heinz in a long-running campaign of soup commercials. Indeed there were times in the 1980s when my parents had as many children and grandchildren in Australia as in England, and I feared they might settle there too.

We lived for the next year in an affluent suburb called Double Bay – or, by envious non-residents, Double Pay – overlooking Sydney Harbour. In 1949 Sydney had the Harbour Bridge but, of course, no opera house, and I can think of no city in the world that has changed more radically in my lifetime. Then it was effectively a small English market town, somehow bizarrely airlifted to sunshine on the other side of the known world. The influence of the Pacific Rim, the accessible proximity to the Far East, open-air bars and five-star cuisine were all still twenty years away.

The deal for the down-under tour of *Edward My Son* had been done with the venerable firm of J.C. Williamson, which monopolised Australian theatre from the 1890s until well into the 1960s, and specialised in bringing out hits from London. Recently the Oliviers had been sent out from the Old Vic as a kind of thespian reward to Australia for her help in the Second World War, although their 'royal progress' ended catastrophically: Vivien Leigh went into the first of her manic nervous breakdowns and fell head over heels in love with the young local talent, Peter Finch.

The Morley tour was less dramatic, although Robert fought a pitched battle with the Williamson management. The company was controlled by the five Tait brothers, who were locally and irreverently known as Hesitate, Agitate, Cogitate, Militate and Meditate. The brothers regarded London actors as little better than disruptive and ungrateful hired hands; backstage conditions in Sydney, and on the road, were kept Spartan at best. They wrote weekly reports to each other on their imports. 'Morley is nothing but Trouble,' read one.

It was alarmingly similar to the report I received from Cranbrook, a distinguished local school that had agreed to take me for a term or two while *Edward* played the old Theatre Royal in Sydney. The truth was that my education had still not really started: a couple of Berkshire terms, another couple with Johnnie Lahr in New York, and one in Pacific Palisades while we were summering with Gladys in California hardly added up to a stable scholastic routine, and it was with mild shock that my Cranbrook masters discovered that at the age of eight I could barely read or write. Luckily the school had other interests: my Australian scrapbook still proudly contains a boxing diploma (presumably heavyweight all-comers under ten), and a certificate to the effect that I had successfully swum Sydney Harbour, although we cheated by crossing at one of its narrowest inlets.

Robert continued to court unpopularity with the Williamsons by querying their showbusiness practices, which were admittedly eccentric by London standards. For example, to save costs they would open the box-office only an hour or so before the show. If you wished to book a ticket during the day, you did so from hard-to-find counters in downtown department stores. They also declined to pay for coffee or tea during rehearsals, which Pa immediately countermanded. 'Thank God,' read another sour report from Tait to Tait, 'he is only doing *Edward, My Son* and not *Annie Get Your Gun.*'

At this time, Robert began to perfect the rebellious but responsible gentleman personality that was to serve him so well in later years on the lecture circuit. Always an astute self-publicist, he had noticed that visiting British actors only ever gave the local Sydney press a bland, patronising quote of the type traditionally associated with newly arrived ambassadors, which consequently rated little space. He chose another tack; he criticised Sydney, 'a honky-tonk town with nothing but a Harbour to recommend it'; Melbourne, 'a city of Hogarthian squalor'; and the ludicrous licensing laws, which closed all bars at 6 p.m. having opened them only an hour earlier – the regulars poured down so much alcohol so fast that they spent the rest of the evening throwing up in the gutters.

Robert's criticisms of the Oz status quo, at a time when other British actors behaved like visiting royalty condescending to the underprivileged natives, always guaranteed him a sizeable audience whenever he gave a press conference. Indeed, on one occasion in Melbourne it was reported that 'three women fainted in the mob, and others suffered minor injuries'. If it wasn't quite the Beatles, at least it was a start; and at that time, little else was going on in Australia.

But we remained, I suspect, a curiously innocent family: the locals reported that early in 1950 my father and I travelled solemnly up-country to prospect for gold, and I even recall keeping, with my sister, a grain or two in the 'Aspiring Tin', until it got lost on the long journey home. The Klondike it wasn't.

I also recall, though by this time we had travelled on to New Zealand, watching water bubble up through the ground at Hot Sulphur Springs, which smelt as nasty as their name warned, and took hours to reach by unpaved roads. In those far-off days, this hot bubbling water was the only thing, apart from sheep, that they showed you in New Zealand, and there was a limit to its fascination. It was far more exciting to fly in a tiny plane from North to South Island. Below us, as we peered out cautiously, some sort of regatta had been struck by high winds, which overturned several boats whose valiant crews now sat in their own sails awaiting rescue. Around them we noticed, with considerable horror, several sharks circling. Should we attempt an air-sea rescue? No problem, said our pilot cheerfully: in this country, sharks were not allowed to attack if you were sitting in the sails of your own boat. We never liked to ask who had told the sharks.

Others touring from Britain at this time included Anthony Quayle and Diana Wynyard from Stratford (the first Shakespeare I ever saw, and still among the best), and Arthur Askey in *See How They Run,* the old Aldwych farce with the funniest single line I could remember hearing in a theatre, 'Constable, arrest several of these vicars.' Oh, well, I guess you had to be there, and luckily I was.

I was also lucky with the backstage crew on *Edward*: the Scots actress Sophie Stewart and her husband Ellis Irving had taken over as Evelyn and the doctor, and were kind enough to adopt me on those few occasions when my long-suffering parents needed a break. There was also Pa's business manager, the American Mort Gottlieb, who had started out as Gertrude Lawrence's publicist and was to finish up one of the richest and most successful of all Broadway producers, thanks to his 1960s discovery of the late Tony Shaffer and *Sleuth*.

Robert never kept a diary, but by piecing together his travel writing it is possible to form some impression of what he first made of the Antipodes:

Nobody really prepared me for Australia, and what was worse nobody had prepared Australia for me . . . We arrived on a boat via Fiji, where they had only recently stopped eating people and were not unnaturally obsessed by my plumpness: 'What a meal he would have made for Grandfather,' one seemed to hear them say . . . Then we stopped briefly at the Great Barrier Reef, which was wildly uncomfortable and a very good preparation therefore for Australian hotels, which were still of Victorian discomfort . . . The countryside was endlessly flat . . . We used to drive for miles, convinced there would eventually be something to look at, which there never was, and the High Commissioner told us that his life had been much more exciting in Cardiff. But I think I managed to be of some interest, especially in New Zealand where the only rival entertainment seemed to be sheep-dog trials. I once saw forty thousand people in Auckland utterly enthralled by the spectacle of three dogs and a man penning six sheep. It was the ultimate economy in public entertainment, and curiously impressive.

But best of all, there was a young stage assistant on *Edward*, still in his early twenties, called Michael Blakemore. The son of a Bondi doctor, a surf baby, he became, first at the National Theatre and subsequently all over the world, one of the greatest stage directors of my lifetime, also one of the most modest and consequently still curiously low-profile in his seventies, even though in 2000 he made Broadway theatre history by winning, on the same Tony night, awards for his productions of a straight play, Michael Frayn's *Copenhagen*, and a musical, *Kiss Me Kate*.

But as usual we are getting ahead of ourselves: in 1950, Blakemore was just starting out in the theatre and eager to be an actor. A dozen or so years older than me, he was kind enough to teach me how to read and write properly while writing in his still unpublished memoirs what I think remains the best account of my father backstage:

Like all actors at that time, Robert believed in the full slap: sticks of Leichner blended together until the face came up a burnished tangerine, followed by rouge on the cheeks, blue on the eyelids, and the whole lot swamped with powder, which would then be reduced by scrubbing the face with a very soft brush. A cloud of talcum would sink to the floor like stage smoke. The effect was as startling as a totem pole, but highly effective from the front, where you could see those penetrating blue eyes from the very back of the theatre . . .

During these preparations, anyone who came into his dressing room, and most did, was expected to be amusing. Robert had no time for shyness, which he considered a product of laziness or pride. If you didn't put up a fight on behalf of your own personality, he tormented you until you did; or worse, he just dropped you to the side like a dull magazine.

The most alarming thing about him was his low boredom threshold, and few things were as discouraging as seeing those eyes glaze over in the middle of your sentence and that lively mind go wandering elsewhere . . . but this was only one aspect of an abundant and recklessly generous personality, whom it amused to enlarge the pleasure in life of those who collected around him.

He was then in his early forties, at the height of his fame as a performer and playwright, a prodigious earner and blessed in his private life. Resolve and talent accounted for part of this, but, as he often insisted, so did luck. Like a big winner at the race track, he wanted to spread some of that good fortune around, and did so by the handful . . . Throughout the Australian tour, Morley was an indefatigable performer, and whatever the house and his own frame of mind, I never saw him give a slack or inconsistent showing. This professionalism was at odds with a provocative flippancy about the theatre in general. Morley liked to give the impression that there were other and always more important things to do beyond the stage door. In Sydney, for example, he changed the day of the mid-week matinée so that he could enjoy the races. While approving of comedy, because it gave him and his audiences a good time, he pretended to balk at dramatic scenes. 'Couldn't we get Freddie Valk in to do this bit?' he would ask in rehearsal, referring to the distinguished German-born actor who had just had a big success in London as Othello.

Yet, in one of the Lux Radio Theatre broadcasts, which Robert would often do on Sunday nights in Australia to boost his income there, I once saw him give a performance as Crocker-Harris in Rattigan's *The Browning Version*, which it would be hard to improve on. Because he was an actor through sheer force of personality, with only one voice and one shape at his disposal, his moments of emotional exposure had a kind of autobiographical authority about them. Areas of pain and longing, left behind somewhere in his youth, were unexpectedly then on show and the result could be extraordinarily touching.

Rereading that now, ten years after my father's death in 1992, I realise with shock that I am already twenty years older than Robert was at the time Blakemore wrote of their first encounter, but so many aspects of the character he glimpsed in those Australian dressing-room mirrors remained true of my father throughout his life. He was insanely generous, remarkably so, in that although he spent years in casinos and on racetracks he was seldom lucky there. He gave the impression of considerable wealth while hardly having enough ready cash to cover that week's expenses, let alone the tax bill. He bored more easily than anyone else I have ever known, and would sometimes leave the country for a weekend in Le Touquet rather than carry on a conversation he already knew too well.

Where he was lucky, I think, was in the timing of his life: it would be hard to make a living today as Robert did, and his belief in the theatre of pure entertainment – that audiences wanted only to be taken out of themselves and that actors were better off when unencumbered by playwrights or directors – has fallen out of fashion even among the regulars at the Garrick Club bar.

Yet the ever-astute Blakemore had noticed something else: that Pa was acting even when offstage, often giving a more convincing performance as himself in real life than ever he did as a character onstage, and that he was a better actor than he pretended or perhaps allowed himself to be.

He was brought up in the theatre of 'Anyone for tennis?' and his early ambition was to be the next Basil Loder, a long-forgotten Shaftesbury Avenue supporting player. Loder's speciality was to wander onstage in tennis whites at the end of act one to take the hero off to the court when an exit was needed, reappearing once more in the last act for another exquisitely understated little scene.

The problems with that scenario were that Robert was always too big and ungainly to be the 'best friend', and that he was capable of breaking your heart onstage. Curiously, it was again in Australia, but some thirty years after that first *Edward* tour, that I saw my father give the best performance of his life; he was making his farewell appearance there, and I had encouraged him to take the plunge in a play by Alan Bennett called *The Old Country*, about Guy Burgess and Donald Maclean in Soviet exile (not to be confused with the later, better play Alan wrote about Guy Burgess and Coral Browne in Moscow, *An Englishman Abroad*).

Alec Guinness had played Burgess in London, not very well, in my view, but for Sydney audiences Pa gave an unforgettably haunting performance, precisely capturing the 'areas of pain and longing' that Blakemore highlighted. At least, he did for those who bothered to come: Sydney audiences had long since decided they only wanted Pa to make them laugh. I got off the plane from London and went straight into one of the emptiest matinées I have ever seen. Stunned by Robert's performance, and wishing it could have been seen by my London colleagues who could never be persuaded of his greatness as an actor, I went backstage feeling guilty that I had persuaded him to take out so evidently unsuitable a play.

'My darling boy,' was all an unperturbed Robert had to say to me, 'you can have no concept of the enormity of the outback of Australia until you have seen our dress circle at matinées,' and, indeed, you could have shot kangaroos across the aisles. He returned to Sydney only to shoot Heinz commercials, a job he preferred to acting since both the hours and the money were better, and never again had to deal with recalcitrant critics or audiences.

But to return to Blakemore's analysis, Robert did not always balk at the dramatic: before the war he had starred in *Pygmalion* at the Old Vic and the film of *Major Barbara*, and I don't believe anyone seeing him now in late-night cable television reruns of *Oscar Wilde* would doubt that he could be a more serious and dedicated actor than his image would normally allow.

He came, though, of the most remarkable generation of classical actors that the world had ever seen: by the time he started in the early 1930s, so too had Olivier, Gielgud, Richardson, Redgrave and Guinness, and that was just the men. The classical market was somewhat overcrowded, so my father came at the stage and screen public from a different corner of the field.

Did he ever regret the lack of a more serious career? Only, I think, occasionally: there's a moment in the courtroom scene from *Oscar Wilde* when Robert in the title role and Ralph Richardson (to whose wife, Meriel Forbes, Pa had once been engaged) as the prosecuting counsel, Carson, go eyeball to eyeball in close-up contest. It is an even match, and you suddenly start to wonder just how different my father's career might have been if he had taken up the more challenging role-call of Ralph. But the truth is that Pa would not have enjoyed a classical career, and if he didn't enjoy it, neither would the audience. Theatrical careers have been built on worse philosophies than that.

This did not indicate undue modesty on Robert's part: he was well aware that he belonged to an already dying tradition, that of the gentlemen players, and that his stage work as both actor and dramatist, sometimes even director, put him in a class above, say, James Robertson Justice, who was often up for the same sort of movie casting.

Robert was also what was known then as 'a useful actor', which essentially meant available, not too expensive, and perfectly willing (nay, eager) to rewrite any scene in which he appeared during the shooting, thereby giving it immediacy, a little added humour and depth of character. 'Mr Morley,' wrote Dilys Powell, the greatest and longest-surviving of all film critics, 'joyously lifts up whatever dire film he happens to be appearing in, before neatly putting it back on the floor where he found it as he leaves the screen.'

If he had been born just a few years earlier, he would have fitted perfectly into the team that Ben Travers gathered for his Aldwych farces: Tom Walls, Robertson Hare, Alfred Drayton, names forgotten now but once the essence of semi-impromptu stage comedy. As it was, Pa had to gather his own team around him; it was led throughout the 1950s by Wilfrid Hyde-White, David Tomlinson, Ambrosine Phillpotts and later William Franklyn, all adept stage comics with brilliant timing and the much-needed ability to follow Robert as he went off nightly at some bizarre tangent only loosely connected to the play at hand.

The *Edward* bandwagon rolled happily around Australia and into New Zealand for the rest of the 1949–50 season, with Robert still good for a few scandalised local head-lines – 'Ridiculous to call a city Sydney,' he once told an astounded local reporter. 'You might as well call it Bert.' He also decorated Mort Gottlieb and Michael Blakemore for their conspicuous gallantry in fending off the Tait management as they travelled from town to scheduled town. Before we left for the creation of similar backstage unrest in New Zealand, John Tait despatched an irate memo to his long-suffering partners and staff:

Morley is a very difficult man who finds fault with almost everything in our organisation and country. He can even be rude to the man in the street. He is an outstanding actor, and his is an outstanding play, but Morley has been so antagonistic to the stage manager that he has begged to be relieved from the New Zealand part of the tour; we are therefore replacing him with his assistant, who can cope with temperamental artists and seems not to get on Morley's nerves.

Before setting sail for Australia, Robert had been told that many British artists either died there (literally or metaphorically) or returned home in tears. 'I determined there and then,' he later told me proudly, 'that by the time I left, it was the Williamson management who would be in tears.' After nearly two years of us they undoubtedly were.

One of the essential problems with Robert was that what you saw was not what you got; his screen and sometimes stage image of a dyed-in-the-wool Conservative country squire was about as misleading as you could get. The grandchild of Jewish immigrants, who had left Wellington at sixteen proudly aware of having learnt almost nothing, he lived comfortably in the Thames Valley, but in a house that had cost him only five hundred pounds in 1940. And although only sporadically politically aware, he developed in his seventies as deep and radical a loathing of Margaret Thatcher as I have encountered anywhere. Those who still wonder why he never got a knighthood (and better yet those millions convinced that he did) need only recall the vitriol he showered on Mrs Thatcher with every public utterance, and that before her lengthy reign he had declined the honour from Harold Wilson for two eminently good reasons. One was that my mother felt that if she was called Lady Morley her Henley shopkeepers might be embarrassed, and the other was that Pa had noted that some of the group of honorees he was being invited to join, that of Marcia Falkender's notorious Lavender List, looked distinctly dodgy. One or two, indeed, ended up in prison, and Pa went blissfully unknighted to his grave. He regretted only that when invited to Buckingham Palace garden parties (he attended them all his life, but largely for the Fuller's chocolate cake, which in his expert view was among the best in the world) he always ended up having to make polite conversation with the late Duke of Gloucester, who was not noted for his showbiz interests.

I wish now that, like my contemporaries Clive James and Barry Humphries who must have been ten-year-olds in Sydney at roughly the time I was, I had been able then to detect the greater lunacies of Australian suburban and educational life. All I can recall was the miraculous absence of rain, cold and fog, the envy people seemed to feel when we told them we were only out there for a year or so, and splashing about every day in Sydney Harbour with my father.

New Zealand seemed closed for all of the six months we stayed there, and by the time we reached Wellington, or was it Christchurch?, it felt as though we had reached the end of the world. Logically the next stop on the tour would have had to be the Antarctic, and as the audiences had fallen away quite drastically after Pa announced that whitebait, the local pride and joy, was one of the nastiest fish imaginable, we took the hint and began to pack our tents for home.

'I would like,' my father told an unimpressed local travel agent, 'a large suite capable of accommodating about eight people on your next boat home to England.'

'That, Mr Morley,' said the agent, 'will be one leaving in about two years' time. I might however manage you a small double cabin to Bombay in a few weeks.'

By now, although Mort was headed straight back to Broadway, the Morley party had grown considerably: my parents, my sister and me, our faithful nanny Nancy Stubbs, the H.M. Tennent manager and later restaurateur Daphne Rye, and, of course, Michael Blakemore, intent on a new career as a London actor. His father had been opposed to this, insisting that his son join him in medical practice until Robert, always up for a good row especially if it was somebody else's family business, stormed into his surgery one morning and announced that Michael would indeed be leaving with him for a new life upon the wicked stage in England. So keen was Dr Blakemore to get Pa out of his consulting room that he agreed at once and without demur. 'I shall be keeping my eye on your boy,' was Robert's parting shot, 'but almost certainly my blind one.'

The sigh of relief from Dr Blakemore as Pa quit his surgery

for ever and went down to the docks to catch the boat was probably heard and echoed all over Australia and parts of New Zealand. I don't think we ever troubled the peace in Tasmania.

9
Going Nuclear

The ship that had agreed to transport us home was the *Stratheden*, and we went aboard with me still bickering with my sister as to who should get to keep the Aspiring Tin in which we had preserved our few grains of gold. It was all we had to show for eighteen months in Australia, unless you count my boxing and swimming certificates, as I certainly do.

The *Stratheden* was not exactly state-of-the-art, and its captain was planning to take about eight weeks to deposit us back in Southampton by way of the Suez Canal. Half-way there, Robert decided that he had seen more than enough of life at sea, and he and my mother left us at Bombay to fly home by way of their first-ever foreign holiday in Rome.

In later years, Rome became almost a second home to us: during the 1950s, Hollywood studios discovered that epic historical or biblical movies could be made much more cheaply there than in California, and if they couldn't get Charles Laughton for the mad emperor or whoever, they would offer it to Pa then move on to Peter Ustinov. Such was the casting order of the day.

But on this first occasion, my parents went to Rome purely on holiday. In their hotel they found Graham Greene, newly converted to Catholicism and indeed so devout that when he finally met the Pope, His Holiness said, after half an hour's one-to-one conversation, 'Ah, Mr Greene, I so understand everything you say ... You see, I too am Catholic.' Ma and Pa also got an invitation to meet His Holiness, along with the veteran character actor Felix Aylmer, who was also staying in their hotel. In the bar one night, Pa asked Aylmer what he did on those rare occasions when presented with a script that needed no last-minute doctoring. 'Usually then,' confided Aylmer, pulling thoughtfully on his pipe, 'I find it sufficient just to act it.' It was a lesson my father rarely took to heart. Aylmer conducted my parents to what was billed as a 'private audience' with the Pope, Pius XII, who was already widely regarded to have been too compliant with the Germans during the Occupation. The private audience was held in a large room, and His Holiness paused graciously for a little chat with Robert: 'He asked me, in immaculate English, where I came from and I replied, "Australia." Then, for some reason terrified that His Holiness might actually take me for an Australian, I hurried on to explain that I was in actual fact an actor from England, but had recently been touring Australia with my play *Edward My Son*. I don't think it is possible to confuse a pope, but I fear on this occasion I may have bored one. He moved on just a little too swiftly for my liking.'

Back in the hotel bar Graham Greene, livid not to have been included in Aylmer's party, was awaiting a full report on the papal proceedings, and this was too good an opportunity for Pa to miss: 'Darling Graham, we were so sorry not to see you there. His Holiness displayed a remarkable interest in the British film industry, asking in fluent English after both Anna Neagle and Jessie Matthews, and took a particularly close interest in my career. After a very good papal lunch, it occurred to me that perhaps we were outstaying our welcome, so I plucked up my courage and said that I felt we had already taken up too much of His Holiness's valuable time, and that we should now be taking our leave. His Holiness would have none of it: "I was in fact very much hoping that you'd be able to stay for tea," he said, "because my wife will be joining us, and she was so much looking forward to meeting you."'

Greene never spoke to any of my family again.

Back home from their Vatican rag, Robert and Joannie were reunited with us children and we duly returned to

Fairmans in Berkshire, which, under my aunt Margaret's guidance, had been enlarged during our two-year absence. Margaret, herself newly divorced, had been living there with her two daughters – Felicity, later tragically killed in a riding accident, and Catherine who, married for many years now to David Barham, leads the Kent division of our extended and extensive family.

Living just down the road from Fairmans, though not for much longer, was the actor, screenwriter, composer and matinée idol Ivor Novello. He had started out with my grandmother Gladys, making a silent movie of *Bonnie Prince Charlie* in 1922. Throughout the rest of his life, which ended all too early in 1951 following a prison sentence for illicit wartime use of black-market petrol – handed down by a famously homophobic magistrate who really wanted to penalise him for being gay – Ivor had been elegantly pursued by Gladys, who took the view that homosexuality could be cured by the love of a good woman. The actress Judy Campbell, with whom she was soon to star in *Relative Values*, took the same view with Noël Coward; she had once been encouraged when, during a wartime tour of *Blithe Spirit*, which he wrote for her, on stage one night in Aberdeen he put his hand some way down between her breasts. 'I am so terribly sorry,' he murmured to her after the show, just when Judy was thinking she had achieved an amazing breakthrough, 'but, you see, there's no heating backstage, or in the hotel, and I fear my hands were frozen solid. I was only trying to warm them up.'

Anyway, to get back to Ivor and Gladys in 1950: thanks to a long succession of hit musicals at Drury Lane, with titles like *Careless Rapture, Glamorous Night, Crest of the Wave* and *King's Rhapsody*, and a long silent-screen career as the 'Welsh Valentino', then a bizarre period as a Hollywood scriptwriter, during which time he coined the phrase 'Me Tarzan, you Jane', Ivor was as famous as Noël, and had once been rather more so. On the last night of *Cavalcade* after a two-year run at

Drury Lane with a cast of two hundred, Noël had rushed up to the box-office demanding a ticket. 'We are totally full,' said the dragon lady behind the counter.

'But I wrote this show,' expostulated Noël. 'I composed it, directed it, worked on the sets and costumes, the orchestrations . . .'

'Proper little Ivor Novello, aren't you?' said the box-office lady, and slammed down her window for the night.

Gladys sometimes took me for tea with Ivor at Redroofs, the Hollywood-style house he had built just outside Maidenhead. There I came across Garbo again, and her passion for washing-up, as well as Marlene Dietrich, Noël Coward, and other celebrities, many of whom I had then to look up in the Maidenhead public library. Stars from the fabled Hollywood Hills, in London to make a movie or promote one, would motor down to Ivor's for a glimpse of the Thames Valley, and a reminder of the luxury they had temporarily abandoned at home.

There was a huge living room with a piano, where Ivor would sing his latest score, rather unfortunately entitled *Gay's the Word*; there were also several good-looking young men around to entertain the old bats from the West End and Hollywood, and presumably for other purposes, though these were not divulged to a chubby child of ten.

But there were now more pressing personal problems to attend to, and some essential homecoming dilemmas to face. My father had to find work as soon as possible: he had begun what became a lengthy battle with the Inland Revenue, which claimed that as he had never intended to live abroad, his American and Australian income was subject to British tax. Pa retorted that he *had* intended to live abroad, possibly with his mother-in-law in Hollywood, and only changed his mind when he saw at close quarters what abroad was really like, and how far away it was from Windsor Races. Unfortunately this became known to the Revenue as the 'Morley Loophole', whereby any British actor with a brief stage or screen job abroad could claim to have emigrated in order to save on taxation. The Revenue was not inclined to forgive Robert; several years later they got him into the high court, only to hear the judge pronounce that Robert was an actor of probity and distinction, an artist who little deserved to be hassled by a bunch of pen-pushing accountants. As a result, my family's accounts have been closely investigated by the Revenue ever since. They managed eventually to close the Morley Loophole, albeit only after several million pounds had gone abroad.

The employment problem was rapidly and happily solved by the arrival in Pa's mail of a play called *The Little Hut*, a Parisian boulevard hit by André Roussin, which had been translated loosely from the French by Nancy Mitford, then our most distinguished Society resident of Paris. Over the next decade or two, Robert performed no less than three long-running Shaftesbury Avenue comedies all derived from Roussin, who had, as far as Pa was concerned, two great advantages: he spoke not a word of English and, because he was agoraphobic, seldom left his Parisian apartment, least of all to travel abroad. This meant that his plays were not so much translated as rewritten for British audiences without a word of complaint from their author. All have proved unrevivable anywhere in the world outside Paris since my father's death, not least because in English they were vehicles reconstructed for Robert alone.

The Little Hut opened at the Edinburgh Festival of 1950 and kept Robert gainfully employed on the road and in the West End until well into 1952, solving his immediate cash and taxation problems, in so far as they were ever solved, which was not very far. At the end of his life, after fifty plays and a hundred movies, he left just about enough to cover his funeral expenses: 'The trick, darling boy, is to live well, and ultimately to defeat the Revenue by death. There's not a lot the buggers can do to you after that.'

The last of our homecoming problems was not so easily

resolved: my sister was now nearly five, and therefore eligible for Rupert House in Henley to which I also returned for a term or two. Now that I was ten, though, some other school clearly had to be found for me, and my parents and I spent a good deal of the autumn of 1950 touring various establishments, auditioning headmasters and checking out dormitory and canteen facilities.

Eventually Pa decided – I suspect to the relief of several headmasters – that no public or prep school we visited was the kind of place he would send his worst enemy, let alone his beloved and thus far only son. Finally, he inserted an advertisement in the Personal Column of *The Times*: 'Father with horrible memories of his own schooldays at Wellington is searching for a school for his son where the food matters as much as the education, and the standards are those of a good three-star seaside hotel.' It achieved a kind of instant fame: the *New Statesman* even used it in a competition, soliciting replies from the fictional likes of Wackford Squeers and Dr Arnold. Amazingly, a number of schools responded to the ad, male pupils presumably being in short supply at the time.

As we auditioned the applicants, Pa having neatly reversed the position of school and parent, I like to think we pioneered a change in scholastic recruitment in Britain. Until then, parents just sent children to school, as often as not the ones their parents and grandparents had attended; Pa enquired about the beds, the food, the swimming-pools, the half-holidays, the sexual habits of the staff. Nowadays, admittedly half a century later, when you read glossy school brochures, apparently written by the same people who pen them for hotels and foreign tours, I believe it is my father you have to thank. Unwilling as they were, Pa dragged British schools into the era of the consumer society and parent and pupil power.

The lucky headmaster who won me in this bizarre parental lottery was a man who resembled my father in almost every way, more closely indeed than anyone else I have ever met. Harry Tuyn was a chubby, joyously extrovert Quaker Dutchman, who should really have become an actor and was one in every way that mattered. After an early life in Dutch Indonesia, where he had become a master chef, a calling he pursued all through his teaching life, he had been a distinguished Oxford undergraduate, then made a brave stand as a pacifist in the Second World War, which he therefore spent chopping logs in Wales.

After the war, he and his ever-loving, loyal and patient wife Elaine had taken a long lease on a large, rather chilly country house called Sizewell Hall, which stood just above the beach a mile or two north of Aldeburgh on the Suffolk coast, and turned it into a radically progressive co-educational prep school. Confusingly, it was situated only a mile or two away from a still more radical educational establishment, A. S. Neill's Summerhill in Leiston. But where, according to scandalised local press reports, some of Neill's pupils went in for drugs and free love, we were comparatively conservative in those areas, not least because the average age of the pupils when I joined was ten going on eleven. In other, quieter ways, Sizewell was deeply revolutionary. Harry believed in tutorials rather than classes, and although the skills of the staff were inclined to be a little patchy, he himself taught with messianic fervour; like a great evangelist, which he was for Shakespeare and the romantic French poets, Harry was mesmeric, larger-than-life, and so reminiscent of my father that I seldom felt homesick. The school motto might have been, 'If you don't succeed the first time, give up', and Harry's genius lay in finding out what his pupils could do best then encouraging them to go further with it, rather than depressing them by keeping their noses to the grindstones of what they either couldn't or wouldn't do.

In short, he treated us at ten as if we were already eighteen, giving us a wide choice of what to study, and an even wider one of what to do when we didn't. He himself cooked, swam and played volleyball when not in the classroom and most of us followed suit, not out of fear or the desire for conformity but because he was such fun to be with. Harry, like Robert, was a perpetual one-man show designed for the amusement and edification of others, and all he asked of us was that we were a good and attentive audience.

And if you are thinking that Sizewell sounds more familiar than you might expect of a school that never attracted more than about forty pupils and closed in about 1956, you would be right: several years after Harry left it, defeated by increasingly orthodox, conservative parents and the economics of private education, it became home to the builders of a nuclear power station, which occasionally hits the headlines and stands a mile or so out at sea, towering ominously over the beaches of Thorpeness and Aldeburgh. Just as Robert was always transfixed by any down-the-page newspaper story involving the beloved Folkestone of his childhood, so I am regularly brought up short by 'Sizewell Shock' headlines, assuming egocentrically that somehow they must refer to me.

The great thing about Sizewell as a school was that it attracted all kinds of eccentrics, not only on the teaching staff but among the pupils, who tended either to have been expelled from more routine establishments or to have failed to get into them, or else to have fathers like mine with a deep-seated loathing of traditional British education. When Pa was invited, as often actors are, to give prizes on speech days, he would always reply, 'Only if I may burn your school down,' and there were those who thought he was joking. He never was. On the other hand, he loved Sizewell almost as much as I did, I think because he at once recognised his *alter ego* in Harry, and realised that I would come to little harm in his company. Indeed, it was Harry who taught me what little I know academically; he taught me to hear the music in Shakespeare, and to admire inordinately the French language, especially in verse. Above all he taught me how to be happy in my own – admittedly too voluminous – skin, how to settle for and make the best of what I was, rather than wasting my time striving unsuccessfully to be different or better.

As was to be expected, Sizewell did not appeal to those in search of a traditional education: certain subjects, like geography and maths, Harry hardly bothered to teach at all, on the grounds that they were boring, and he did not see his school as a preparation for any other – it was more of a total once-in-a-lifetime experience. In that respect going to Sizewell was not unlike going abroad: like Australia, it was a self-contained country with its own rules and traditions, and the only problems arose when you had to re-enter the real world.

Luckily for me, that did not happen for almost another decade. I was ten when I first got to Harry, and the rest of the 1951 intake included an enchanting little girl from what we could still call Persia. Her father ran a number of successful Tehran restaurants for the Shah, and had decided that one of his beloved daughters at least should have the benefits of a British education. What made him choose Sizewell I have never known, but my earliest memory of the school in a traditionally frozen Suffolk winter is of this kitten-like child who spoke no English and ached to be loved, perhaps even understood, in a very foreign climate.

I have loved her ever since. She married the school doctor's son, who had also been one of Harry's pupils, and after forty years of running some of the greatest restaurants in the world, has ended up with him in charge of the best private dining club in Bakersfield, California. Haleh and Richard Burlingham are one of the many reasons why I am so grateful to Sizewell.

Even we three children, however, noticed that Sizewell was not growing in numbers. Although Harry ran a thriving summer school for foreign students, which effectively paid for everything else, the ranks of the regulars seemed to shrink almost from the time I arrived there, as parent after parent took their children away in search of some more conventional academic establishment. By the late 1950s, Haleh, Richard and I were almost the only pupils Harry had left on a year-round basis, and he was able at last to re-create the college conditions he had always loved. Hour after hour, day after day, he would take us through English and French literature; we got so good that, at about fourteen, we had no trouble in getting the O levels that were supposed to come a year or two later.

The only problem was that we didn't know or do anything else. Indeed we had become so much a part of Harry's family that when he had to quit Sizewell, and started up a more profitable English girls' finishing school in Chateau d'Oex, close to Gstaad in Switzerland, we followed him there to complete our education.

But then Richard and I faced a considerable problem: Haleh was already set on a culinary life, and had won herself a place on a Cordon Bleu course in London; she had studied Harry in the Sizewell kitchen as well as in the classroom. Equally inspired by Harry, Richard and I were determined to get into Oxford; the problem was that we lacked the requisite Latin, maths, and virtually everything except English and French.

I am ashamed to realise I don't recall how Richard solved the problem; I only know that he did, and spent a successful three years playing croquet at Pembroke College. However he managed it, though, I know I took a different route. My grandmother had had an understudy, Una Venning, whose husband, Gordon Hamilton-Gay, was an old friend of the then Warden of Merton College; both were tiny men who in the twenties had triumphantly coxed Merton crews to boat-race victories. Even in those days friendship – and mine with Gordon and Una was somewhat distant – was not enough to get you into Oxford, but it did get me a meeting with a craggy, pensive don called Robert Levens, whose wife Daphne ran the local Oxford Amateur Players, and who was himself the admissions tutor at Merton, as well as a distinguished classical scholar.

Levens told the eager sixteen-year-old me, over some very good teacakes, that I had come to the right college, given that not only was he theatrically connected but so were two of the other resident dons, Nevill Coghill and Hugo Dyson. However, he said sadly, a couple of O levels in English and French, even though achieved unusually young, were so far below measurable entrance requirements that I had better stop wasting his and my time.

When I was half-way out of his door, I knew suddenly that I wanted to go up to Oxford more than I had ever wanted anything in my life. I didn't know why, and I'm not sure I ever found out: I just knew I wanted to be there. 'What, sir,' I asked him, 'would you do if you were me?'

Levens thought for a minute. 'I think,' he said, 'I would choose to read a subject in which the college has no real interest or resident tutor. In your case French would do nicely. I would get some kind of diploma in French from some continental establishment, which will impress them here. Then I would try to get at least an O level in maths and Latin, because having only one foreign language you will need to study Latin in your first year. Do all that, and we'll see what we can do for you, though understand I am not holding out much hope.'

I have never been one to take up a challenge, believing all my life that if something can't be achieved pleasantly from an armchair, preferably in the sunshine, it is almost certainly not worth achieving at all. But Oxford was worth the effort, and somehow I knew it, just from wandering around the city peering through the archways of its colleges. Then it also had two thriving theatres, five cinemas, including two arthouses, and was conveniently on both bus and train routes to Wargrave for weekends at home, laundry and supplies.

I spent the next eighteen months doing precisely what Levens had suggested.

Before we leave the 1950s it occurs to me that we should do a spot-check on the rest of my family. My mother had given my sister and me a brother in August 1951: Wilton and I were ten years apart, in some respects a distance I have never bridged to our entire satisfaction, but he was an infinitely amiable sibling and remains so to this day. In a way, though fifteen years apart, my brother and my son strike me now as more alike than I am like either of them; at fifty, my brother has just remarried and had his first child, Roberto because of our father and Roberto's Spanish-American mother Olga. Paternal and domestic life may change him, but he and my son Hugo take after Robert's father, the gambling Major, I believe, while I belong, albeit not physically, to my mother's side of the family. We are instinctively cautious and home-loving where they tend to be travellers. They have always, like Gladys, longed for a place in the sun, and now they have found one in Florida. They also have the courage to live by and for the day, while I plan, usually unsuccessfully, how to get through the next decade. They are not irresponsible but – at any rate until my brother had his recent conversion to family life – they have avoided domestic responsibilities in a way I admire and even envy. I seem always to have had people to pay for, although both my wives and all three of my children would doubtless tell you, and probably rightly, that I am the one in their debt.

IO
Robert, My Father

If my 1950s were largely taken over by Harry and Sizewell, I was not entirely unable to realise that, at my other home in Wargrave, Robert was having the best decade of his life thus far. On his return from Australia, although technically without any work after more than two years abroad, he found that he had not been forgotten: indeed, something about his overseas success, about his refusal to settle (as so many of his character-actor contemporaries now had) for a place in the Hollywood sun, endeared him to directors of British movies and plays as never before.

The 1950s were when my father consolidated his position as a star, which he remained until the day he died. For the next forty years, he was mercifully spared the drastic highs and lows that marked so many others in theatre and cinema. He was simply an actor who went on acting, largely thanks to the efforts of his ever-loving, loyal and devoted agent, Ros Chatto. On those few occasions when he was out of work, we all knew where to find him: in the saddling enclosure at Windsor Races, or the casino that had recently opened on the Edgware Road. If he ever had a dark night of the soul, if he was ever unfaithful to my darling mother, whom he so loved and relied on for a sense of reality, we sure as hell never found out about it. In those days you didn't ask and you weren't told, and that was how we liked it. There was a lot to be said for the 1950s, especially by the Thames in Berkshire: it was already a lost world, but we lived in it, much like Badger, Ratty and Mole, taking care not to get too caught up in real life or go too deep into the dark, dark wood.

Binkie Beaumont at H. M. Tennent had intelligently persuaded

Nancy Mitford to translate *The Little Hut*; she was our most distinguished *grande dame* in Paris and took to this, her only theatrical venture, like an elegant duck to new water. As she wrote to her mother early in 1950:

It's a terribly funny play about husband, lover and wife on a desert island – lover gets very low all alone in the little hut, while husband and wife sleep in the big one, insists on them taking turns. Husband not altogether delighted, but sees the logic that they have shared her for six years and might as well go on doing so. Then a handsome young Negro appears, ties up husband and lover by a trick, and indicates that he will only let them go if the wife will go into the hut with him, which she is only too pleased to do as he is very good-looking.

Disgusting, I hear you say . . . and yet it is terribly funny, though I don't have much hope of it in London, as the Lord Chamberlain will never pass it. Here in Paris it has been a wild success for over three years, and I've skated over the worst indecencies, in fact the reason I was asked to do it is that I am supposed to be good at making outrageous situations seem all right.

Rather surprisingly, the Lord Chamberlain passed it with a couple of minor cuts, and Robert was already in a strong enough position to control the casting: for the wife he chose an old New York friend, the American actress Joan Tetzel, who had been married to the dramatist George S. Kaufman, and for the lover he went to David Tomlinson, who became a lifelong friend and ally. There was also a monkey up a tree, and inside that costume at various times in the two-year run could be found the actor Geoffrey Toone, the choreographer Billy Chappell and the future movie star Roger Moore. This was also where Ros Chatto graduated from assistant stage manager to cooking the gourmet meals that would be served to the entire company between matinée and evening performances. 'In my experience,' Pa told the Inland Revenue, when they queried the expense, 'a cast always performs better on a full stomach.' I suspect that that particular insight doesn't turn up in any Stanislavski or Peter Brook manual of stagecraft.

On the surface, Robert and David could hardly have been more different: Tomlinson had been a heroic fighter pilot in the Second World War, and was now established on stage and screen as a light comedian of considerable eccentric, offhand talent. His private life, which he seldom discussed, was the stuff of novels: as a young trainee pilot in wartime Canada, he had been given a seventy-two-hour leave to go to New York, had fallen head over heels in love with a young American beauty of intense, neurotic vitality he met in a bar, and married her over a long weekend of passion. Returning to his air base in Britain, he had answered the phone a few weeks later to be told by her parents that his beloved young wife had jumped to her death off a skyscraper. 'If only we'd had the chance to meet you,' said her parents, 'we would have been able to tell you that she had a long history of suicide attempts.'

And that was not all: soon after the war, David got his first overseas acting job in the film *Where No Vultures Fly*. Travelling out to Heathrow on the top deck of a bus, suitcase in hand, he happened to glance out into an upstairs window in the Chiswick High Road where, to his amazement, he saw his father sitting up in a double bed, enjoying tea and toast with a strange lady. Unable to delay his departure, David duly went to Africa, made the movie, and returned to London some weeks later. There, he phoned his hugely respectable solicitor father and suggested a meeting at the club where Tomlinson senior always lived from Monday to Friday. The two men were never close, but David told his father all the stories of his first film location before, over coffee, he mentioned with some embarrassment what he had seen through the Chiswick High Road window.

'Ah, yes,' said his father, 'that would have been me and my wife having breakfast in bed.'

David decided, not unnaturally, that his ageing parent was

starting to lose it. 'No, Father,' he said patiently. 'Mother is your wife. Has been for many years. Since before I was born, in fact.'

'Her too,' said the older Tomlinson, and explained that he had maintained two wives, two families, two entire households for many years; weekends in the country with David and his brethren, weekdays in Chiswick High Road. Nowadays I guess the coming of the mobile phone would make such sustained bigamy impractical, but sixty or so years ago, David's father had persuaded his first wife that he could be contacted only via the porter at his club, since no other telephones were available to him, and thus he maintained a happy double life for more than twenty years. I have always thought it says a great deal for his 'extended family' that when the old boy's marital sins finally came to light all of his children happily acknowledged each other as brothers and sisters and have remained, like their children, on excellent terms ever since.

Like Wilfrid Hyde-White, who was to co-star with Pa in his next long-running West End hit *Hippo Dancing*, also by André Roussin, David was a perfect foil to Robert, Laurel to his Hardy. All three men were actors of immaculate, understated but instinctive comic timing of a kind that has virtually disappeared now from the stage. They shared a deep distrust of directors and playwrights other than themselves, and an absolute belief in the theatre as a temple of escapism and post-prandial entertainment.

All three were gamblers, either in casinos or on racetracks or, in Tomlinson's case, with his own life as a pilot, and they shared an instinctive, intuitive understanding of their audiences and the changing nature of the stage moment. No two performances they gave, even in the same play at the same theatre in the same week, were ever much the same; they were master jugglers, first-class improvisers, and all could take the temperature of an audience within seconds of reaching the stage. In modern television terms, they offered 'an audience with'; the play and its original production always came second to the mood of the customers in front that night. In that sense they had more in common with great soufflé chefs than with modern actors.

But to watch them in action, as I did from the wings for the best part of a decade, was an education for any incipient drama critic: they taught the volatile craft of the live performer, on the wing and on the hoof, staying always just that split second ahead of their audiences and sometimes, indeed, of their play. They were all acrobats on the high wire of stage comedy; looking back, I am amazed at how seldom any of them had a fall. Even then, to watch their recovery was an education in itself. Look, no strings.

The Little Hut opened triumphantly in Edinburgh in August 1950; the morning after the first night, Pa was awoken by a phone call from a delighted Nancy Mitford, saying she had so enjoyed her first experience of playwriting that she would like to give my parents a celebratory dinner in the hotel the very next evening. Lovely, said Pa, shall we say about 11 p.m.? No, no, said Nancy, she always dined around eight thirty. Pa regretted that in this case she would have to do so alone because, he added, 'I shall at that time be performing your play again.' There was a stunned silence from Nancy, accustomed only to gala nights at Versailles. Then, 'You mean,' she asked incredulously, 'you do it twice?'

In fact, they did *The Little Hut* several hundred times, first on the road and then at the Lyric on Shaftesbury Avenue. Relations with Peter Brook had been somewhat strained from the first day of rehearsal, and he had been reduced once to tears, but fifty years later, almost the last thing my father did on television was an interview about him for a documentary celebrating the man who had become the great guru of world theatre. After everyone from Peter Hall to John Gielgud had paid their respects to Brook, the camera cut to Pa, sitting as always by his pool at Fairmans on one of the last sunny afternoons of his life. 'Peter Brook?' he says thoughtfully to the camera, racking his brain for the recollection. 'Peter Brook? Oh, yes. Jolly useful little chap. He always took my coat at the start of rehearsals, and always gave it back at the end.' Sometimes with Robert the most joyous sound was that of entire backstage worlds colliding around his considerable presence.

I I
The Outcast *and the* Queen

No sooner had Pa settled into the long *Little Hut* run at the Lyric than his screen career came back into focus for the first time since the war. Although he had originally made his name and won his only Oscar nomination for *Marie Antoinette* in 1938, his films since then had been eccentric and essentially undistinguished, with the one great exception of *Major Barbara*: his Undershaft, the armaments millionaire who, like the devil, gets all the best tunes, remains in my wholly biased critical view definitive and unchallenged to this day, outstanding even in a cast that also features Wendy Hiller, Rex Harrison and Sybil Thorndike.

He had also played, somewhat implausibly, the 'Lily of Laguna' composer Leslie Stuart in *You Will Remember*, a 1940 biopic of remarkably low budget, and had been one of *The Ghosts of Berkeley Square* in a haunted-house period piece derived somewhat loosely from an S. J. Simon–Caryl Brahms comic novel. Apart from that, and a few minor roles in rather better pictures such as *The Foreman Went to France*, *The Young Mr Pitt* and *The Small Back Room*, Robert's film life seemed to have flickered to a standstill when, early in 1951, the director Carol Reed offered him his first really good screen role since the war.

This was to be in *The Outcast of the Islands*, a Joseph Conrad adventure of the South Seas for which Reed had already assembled an amazing cast led by Trevor Howard, whom he had effectively discovered for *The Third Man*, Ralph Richardson, Wendy Hiller, Wilfrid Hyde-White and a new discovery called Kerima, who rapidly gave up acting

94

and married the James Bond director Guy Green. 'The great thing about Kerima,' explained Reed, of her casting, 'is that if you wet her hair and shoot her through a Venetian blind, you can cut her into any part of the picture you like.' Which, indeed, was what he did. Reed proved to be one of the few directors Pa ever liked ('Where Hathaway shouts, Huston mocks, Asquith cajoles and Pascal screams, Carol charms'), especially when he agreed that the four-year-old child needed in the picture for several key plot scenes could be played by Pa's own daughter Annabel.

All went well with the filming of *Outcast*, even though Pa, Ralph and Wendy were all, as was customary in those days, hurrying back from Shepperton every night to play in their various West End stage hits. This was to be a pattern in Pa's life over the next ten years. Nearly all of his films were studio-based, at either Shepperton or Pinewood, and where the roles were especially demanding or time-consuming he slept at the studios, leaving them only to travel to the theatre and back every night, and, of course, to go home for the occasional weekend when not required on set.

In the time it took to get *Outcast* edited, the ailing King George VI and Queen Elizabeth had chosen the film as one of their first Royal Command Performances. The night before the Leicester Square gala, Robert's agent Robin Fox (who headed the agency which Ros had joined) asked the producer Alexander Korda for an urgent meeting. Korda was essentially the only Hollywood-type mogul that the British film industry ever enjoyed. Like so many of the middle Europeans who had effectively invented and were still running the studio system in California, Alex was tiny, Hungarian, cigar-chewing and immensely theatrical. He was also hugely talented: among the stars he had spotted and made, sometimes in more senses than one, were Charles Laughton, Merle Oberon and Vivien Leigh, not to mention Sabu the Elephant Boy. Forty years later, it was with considerable delight that I found myself being published in America by his nephew Michael who, as the head of Simon & Schuster, has inherited many of the old man's best impresario qualities and also wrote, in *Charmed Lives*, the best ever book about him and his awesome power over the great years of British movies, just before and after the Second World War.

'I do just want to congratulate you, Sir Alex,' said Robin, silkily, 'on the tremendous honour our King and Queen have done you in selecting *Outcast* for their Royal Command, and on the tremendous good that that will doubtless do the film at the box-office.' Korda basked in the praise, unaware of what was coming next. 'There is, however,' continued Robin smoothly, 'just one little problem. One of the players in the film has, I fear, never signed a contract, and without her signature you will not be able to show your film, even to royalty.'

Korda went ashen. 'What you mean? Morley, Hiller, Richardson, Howard, I have all their contracts.'

'My client is Miss Annabel Morley,' said Robin. 'I think you will find that she is in several key plot scenes, which your editors will be unable to cut.'

'She child of four,' said Korda, not unreasonably. 'We give her bicycle.'

'My client instructs me to say,' continued Robin, 'that, in the light of the Royal Command, a bicycle will not be sufficient. Shall we say a thousand pounds?' And this was in the currency of 1951. Korda capitulated on one condition: he was a man who knew a great deal about moving pictures, and still more about pictures that did not move. 'There is,' he told Robin, 'a little art gallery on the corner of the Burlington Arcade with, in the window, a small Pissarro landscape for a thousand pounds. You will take my cheque and buy it for the child.' Robin did as he was told. A quarter of a century later, my sister sold the painting and bought a small house in Shepherd's Bush with the proceeds. Those were the days when we really did have a British film industry, and its name was Alexander Korda. But the days were shortlived. Ten years later, when my brother

Wilton landed the role of Oscar Wilde's son in the film Pa was making of Wilde's life, he got a bicycle for his efforts. By then, it was all that the industry could afford.

After *Outcast*, Robin and Robert decided that the new medium of television had to be tackled, and the result was the first of three major failures for Pa on the small screen: although towards the end of his life he made a whole new career as a talk-show guest, starred in countless American and Australian commercials and even in a pioneering how-to-cook programme called *Celebrity Chefs*, made by an American cable station, his attempts to write and play in new material for the small screen were seldom less than catastrophic, because his genius was for a live audience. Also, he was, apart from me, the most uncoordinated man I have ever known, and therefore forever falling over cameras, cables and standard lamps in the unwonted intimacy of a small television studio.

The first series Pa wrote and played in, for what was then the only television channel in British broadcasting, was called *Parent Craft*. It was an early attempt at a sitcom about family strife, and it is impossible now to gauge how well it worked since at that time there was no system of audience measurement, and precious little television reviewing – Fleet Street regarded the new medium as one that, if they kept very quiet about it, might go away of its own accord. Nor, of course, were any recordings made. All that exists now in the files is a memo from the then head of BBC children's broadcasting, a formidable woman called Freda Lingstrom: 'Working with Mr Morley is not an experience I would care to repeat.'

Pa decided that, on balance, he too didn't care to repeat the TV experiment: minimal money and no detectable audience in exchange for a lot of writing and acting did not seem to him a reasonable deal. He went back happily to *The Little Hut*, and a more distinguished offer to appear in what might now be considered the greatest movie he ever made.

The African Queen was based on the First World War

adventure novel of the same title by C. S. Forester. It told of a ramshackle boat, the *Queen* of the title, being sailed down a dangerous African river by an odd couple consisting of the buccaneering Charlie Allnutt, its owner, and Rose Sayer, the clenched schoolmarm spinster he rescues from marauding Germans. The only other role in the entire movie, give or take several dozen leeches and my godfather Peter Bull, who turns up for about thirty seconds at the end, was that of the missionary brother whose murder by the Germans, at the start of the picture, forces Rose into the arms of Charlie. It was this for which John Huston, the director, chose Robert. Huston had always liked large, over-the-top character men, and had been largely responsible for the Hollywood careers of Sydney Greenstreet and Peter Lorre in such movies as *The Maltese Falcon*; he was also, of course, an actor's son, in that his father was the Walter Huston who first told us, in Kurt Weill's classic song, that it was a long, long way from May to September.

Huston had already cast his old ally Humphrey Bogart as Charlie, with Katharine Hepburn as Rose, and the film had largely been completed on location in the Congo before the unit returned to Shepperton and engaged Robert to shoot, out of sequence, the opening scenes. It had not been an entirely happy location: several of the crew had caught either malaria or dysentery, Bogart had initially wanted his wife Lauren Bacall for Rose, and Hepburn, of course, had wanted her long-time lover Spencer Tracy for Charlie.

But Huston thrived on such dissent, and several books of memoirs as well as one entire though oddly little-known movie, Clint Eastwood's *White Hunter, Black Heart*, have already been based on the African adventure, during which Bogart found Hepburn unsufferably pretentious. She had trouble with her role until Huston gave her the key one day on location: 'Play her,' he said simply, 'like Eleanor Roosevelt.' She was a character Kate knew well and had emulated in her own courageous private life.

Now, back at Shepperton, there was another problem: Robert, who usually seemed not to have a nervous bone in his body, found himself overwhelmed by suddenly having to join three of the greatest figures in all the Hollywood firmament on a picture they were almost due to finish. An anxious first day ensued, at the end of which Pa went back to his *Little Hut* well aware that he had managed his opening scene very badly indeed, so badly that he even vaguely thought he might be about to get fired, which had not happened to him, and never did again, since an early tour of *Treasure Island* in about 1934.

After the show that night, to cheer himself up, he went on to a party given by some visiting Americans at the Savoy. To his horror, as he entered the room he saw Kate being interviewed by one of the leading showbusiness reporters of the day, David Lewin. 'And what,' Lewin was asking her, 'is it like now you are back in England and are being joined by Robert Morley?'

Hepburn clocked the question, and Robert's entry: 'Mr Morley,' she drawled, in that unmistakable, inimitable East Coast voice, 'joins us tomorrow.' It was all Pa needed to hear, and he finished the movie in ten days with scarcely another retake.

I have always loved Hepburn for that, though I fear she has not always loved me: I once wrote a book about her, a hanging offence in her eyes, but was eventually forgiven even for that. Years later still, I had the joy of spending a day or two with her in a wondrous townhouse in New York's Turtle Bay that had been in her family for generations.

At that time, elderly fans frequently confused her with another Hollywood legend, Joan Crawford. This annoyed Kate intensely as, rightly, she had always regarded herself as Broadway royalty, not to be confused with Californian rubbish like Crawford. I was with Hepburn on the day that Crawford's death was bill-postered all over New York. It was a snowy morning, and we were walking up Park Avenue when an old lady slithered across the ice towards us, proffering an autograph book. 'Sign, please,' she told Hepburn. 'I know you. You're Joan Crawford.'

'Not any more,' said Kate, indicating one of the placards in a nearby store.

Living next door to her was a young pianist whose music Kate would welcome by thumping irately on their shared wall. Many years later, when I was writing a book about him, I discovered that the pianist had been Stephen Sondheim. And a few years on from that, when I was writing a book about Dirk Bogarde, he thumped the floor of his Chelsea flat with a large stick when those living just below him played the piano somewhat loudly. Eventually I found out that they were the classically famous Lebecque Sisters – but we have drifted rather too far away from *The African Queen* and 1952.

John Huston recognised in Robert, as he had a decade earlier in Sydney Greenstreet, the kind of larger-than-life, comic villain figure that he most loved, and their alliance led to two other pictures, *Beat the Devil* two years later and then the one we'd all rather forget, *Sinful Davey* made in 1969, by which time Huston was losing his magical talent and, indeed, his interest in making great movies. Robert recalled that they once bought a horse together: 'John was a strange and rather magical man, who always told everyone they were going to be "just fine" whatever the perilous indignity to which he was about to subject them on location, where he regarded all film-making as a challenge, with himself as the challenger . . . We bought the horse at Newmarket after it had won a selling plate. "He'll be just fine," said John reassuringly, and as he said so the horse fell dead at his feet. Another time John was walking down Fifth Avenue and suddenly noticed a corpse on the sidewalk; the rest of his party climbed over it and hurried on but John knelt to feel the lifeless pulse, and reassure the surprised ambulance men that "He'll be fine, just fine."'

As I have doubtless told you too often, my father had remarkably little time for directors. In the words of his old friend Ralph Richardson, 'I give them ten minutes on the first day to see if they know any more than I do, and after that I just go my own way.'

In a long life on stage and screen, Pa must have worked for hundreds of directors, but only two made a favourable impression. One was Tyrone Guthrie, with whom he had started at the Old Vic in the 1930s and whose habit it was to close every rehearsal with the words 'Astonish me in the morning.' When Tony died, on horseback surveying his own considerable estate in Northern Ireland, his farm manager brought the news to his devoted wife: 'Lady Guthrie,' he said sadly, 'the great oak has fallen.' I always thought, secretly, that was how Pa would have liked to have his own death reported – wouldn't we all?

The other director he came to love was John Huston who, though seldom interested in stage actors and certainly not in the theatre-building that obsessed Guthrie and his only true heir John Neville, had many characteristics in common with Guthrie. Both believed in a kind of reality that was often impossible for stage actors to achieve: Guthrie had 'discovered' both Michael Redgrave and Margaret Rutherford when they had already spent several years as teachers, and Huston had taken Sydney Greenstreet out of an academic life to make him into a film star. In that sense both cherished the amateur, and both believed in the sheer fun of entertainment rather than its technical aspects; actors like my father suited them best, because they never took the business too seriously, and were ever eager to wander off down whatever highway or byway caught the attention of their directors. The fact that it required a vast professionalism to deliver such an apparently amateur style was one of the central contradictions of my father's working life, and why I persist in believing that he never really got his critical due, perhaps not even from me.

But what about me?

School Report, Sizewell Hall Suffolk, Spring Term 1953
When Sheridan first joined us two years ago he seemed to have
considerable difficulty settling in. He also seemed to be the oldest
10-year-old we had ever met, and in a way he has had to learn how
to be a child all over again. He is intelligent, pleasant to get on with
and unusually courteous, but he closes his mind to subjects that
are of no interest, and I have seldom seen him move on the sports
field. His intelligence is above average and he is a keen eater, but
I suspect he would have trouble fitting into a more 'orthodox'
school than ours. Socially he lumbers around Sizewell perfectly
happily, and when teased on account of his weight he tends to
deflect hostility by telling jokes or lengthy anecdotes about his
early life in Australia and America, although I am told that his
tongue can curl in bitter acridity from time to time. We like having
him around, and he seems happy to be here.

12
Truman Capote and the Raven

Of all the movie locations on which I was lucky enough to spend my school holidays from Sizewell during the 1950s, the one that lives most vividly in my memory is *Beat the Devil*, filmed in Ravello during the spring of 1953. By the time Pa was reunited with Huston, a couple of years after *The African Queen*, he had managed to get out of the clutches of the Inland Revenue by staying in constant work, not only concluding *The Little Hut*'s long stage run but also working by day in several other movies, not least *The Story of Gilbert and Sullivan* (as Gilbert), *Melba* (as Oscar Hammerstein), *The Final Test* (as an eccentric poet) and *Curtain Up*, a splendid forerunner of Michael Frayn's backstage farce *Noises Off*, in which Robert was cast, as so often, opposite Margaret Rutherford, his exact equivalent in drag, I always thought, playing here precisely the kind of domineering stage director he had learned to avoid in real life. The reunion with Huston came about suddenly, however, and through tragedy.

Humphrey Bogart and Huston, both aware that in Hollywood the McCarthy Committee on UnAmerican Affairs was making life uncomfortable for anyone with views even faintly to the left of Ronald Reagan and Melvyn Douglas (not to mention Ginger Rogers' mother, one of the most formidable witch-hunters of them all), had decided to set up their own production company in Europe. This, rather than the new threat of television, was what marked the beginning of the end of the studio stranglehold on Hollywood talent, since many actors, directors and even writers now also chose to take their talents elsewhere in a dodgy political climate.

Talking about this years later to the actor Jose Ferrer, I asked how he had survived the blacklist, given that he had spent much of the early 1950s touring America as Iago to the Othello of Paul Robeson, himself an avowed and proud member of the Communist Party. 'I dreaded the blacklist more than anything,' said Joe, 'not least because I already had several ex-wives including Uta Hagen and Rosie Clooney, who were not cheap. So I got this wonderful lawyer, and when they call me to the tribunal he stands up and says, "Gentlemen, before we come to my client Mr Ferrer, there is something you have to know. He is a notable actor, but a man of tremendous political and social naïvety, and for all the two years that he toured in *Othello*, he had absolutely no idea that Mr Robeson was a Communist. Indeed, he had no idea he was black."'

Thus did Joe survive, since even Senator McCarthy decided he was unable to try a man who thought that, like Al Jolson, Paul Robeson went home every night and took it all off in the bath. Others were not so lucky, though, and Huston and Bogart saw no reason to chance their arm by staying in a hostile climate. Once they had established their new picture company in Rome, which proved a home-away-from-home for Hollywood exiles of whatever kind, they chose as their first project *Beat the Devil*, a curious comic novel by Claud Cockburn. It had escaped much critical attention when first published a year or so earlier in Britain, but what Huston saw here was the possibility of a complex, in-joke parody of his beloved *Maltese Falcon*, one in which Bogart, Peter Lorre and Sydney Greenstreet would play minor variations on their original roles, while the new cast would include Jennifer Jones and, in her first English-language picture, Gina Lollobrigida, carving up the old Mary Astor part between them. The tragedy to which I referred earlier was the sudden death of Sydney Greenstreet just as the film was about to go into production. Casting around in some desperation, Huston recalled Robert's performance for him in *The African Queen*, and that here might be another chubby villain capable of some fine, sinister moments. Thus it was that, in April 1953, my mother, my sister and I found ourselves staying in an elegant palazzo – it is now the home of Gore Vidal – on the main and only square of Ravello, an enchanting hillside town high above Amalfi in the Italian hills south of Naples and facing out to Capri.

It was an idyllic location curiously fraught with problems, the first of which was the young American scriptwriter Truman Capote who, flush with his first novel's success, had been drafted in to make sense of Cockburn's baroque, confused tale of a gang of latterday pirates trying to fix a uranium deal in East Africa. For reasons that now escape me, Truman had left his pet raven in a hotel suite in Rome, but could only function if he rang the hotel from Ravello each morning, on a somewhat primitive telephone line, for the raven to speak or at least squawk to him. If it felt hoarse, or simply disinclined to converse, Truman couldn't write and the film fell yet another day behind schedule.

And that was the least of the problems. Indeed, I am almost unable to believe my own memories of life in Ravello – especially the long, languid evenings when we ate in the square and a deaf-mute dwarf ran around the tables begging for coins in sign language; one night Truman said, 'Ooh, I do wish he'd shut up,' and surprisingly he did – except that, happily, it has all been preserved on film, and by that I don't just mean the movie. About thirty years later, Ruth and I happened to be doing a Stephen Sondheim programme at the National Film Theatre with the great songwriter himself when, at the reception afterwards, she heard him talk about a spring in Ravello. We rapidly discovered that the twenty-one-year-old Steve had been a friend of Huston's son, and had got a job as a runner on *Beat the Devil*. Moreover, by way of camera practice, he had shot several hundred feet of home movies on the location, which he had then consigned to a box in his attic. The next time we were with him in New York, we persuaded him to dig out the footage, now distinctly foggy with age. Ruth ran it through a wetgate, transferred it to video, and we gave Steve for his sixtieth birthday, and Robert for his eightieth, the Sondheim film of the filming of *Beat the Devil*.

Nor were we the only visitors to that location; a few miles down the coast, Ingrid Bergman was filming with Roberto Rossellini, for whom she had just left Hollywood, home and husband in the greatest movie scandal of its day, which effectively ruined her American career for more than a decade; Jennifer Jones's husband, the *Gone With the Wind* producer David O. Selznick, who had also been involved in a scandalous divorce from his first wife Irene Mayer Selznick, was also hanging around keeping an eye on his wife's interests and especially her choice of wardrobe, in which he seemed to take an almost transvestite interest.

So, in that one small Italian hillside village, for a few short weeks in 1953, were gathered several of the leading players of the old Hollywood; it was like meeting the Hapsburgs in some sunny but exiled retreat shortly after the First World War, and I wish I could say now that I had realised at thirteen that I was in at the end of perhaps the greatest era in movie history. Already, in both the finished film and Steve's background shots, Bogart looks old and ill far beyond his years, coughing with the cancer that was to kill him, still in his fifties, less than three years later. Lorre too was soon to die, the Selznick marriage was rocky, and God knows how many wives Huston had worked his way through. Somehow *Beat the Devil*, intended as a jokey black comedy, comes to seem more and more like a requiem mass for Hollywood.

The other problem with the finished film is that it is almost entirely incomprehensible. In his eagerness to make an almost shot-for-shot parody of *The Maltese Falcon*, Huston had forgotten that the earlier picture had been released more than a decade earlier and, in those pre-video, pre-DVD, pre-National Film Theatre days, nobody had seen it since. It was only some years later, when *Beat the Devil* began to turn up in Huston or Bogart retrospectives back to back with *The Maltese Falcon*, that critics and audiences alike could begin to work out what the hell it was all about.

'There are,' as Robert once noted, 'really only three questions to ask about a film contract: how much, where, and when do we start?' In this case, thanks to Robin Fox – who was, with Ros, now running not only Robert's affairs but those of virtually every leading actor and director in the business, to say nothing of the Grade Organisation and the Royal Court, while finding time to maintain a loving family, sleep with most of his female clients and still give Robert the impression that he alone really mattered – the money was around eighty thousand dollars, which more than justified the time it took to bring *Beat the Devil* home.

It was a vastly complex movie, not only because of Capote's near-unfathomable script and all that was going on behind the cameras, but also because Huston and Bogart seemed only to have a tenuous grasp of independent production skills. Both men had grown and prospered within a Hollywood studio system where armies of accountants and other support staff dealt with the technicalities: now, on their own in Europe and freelance for the first time, they were like schoolboys who had taken over an establishment whose rules they only vaguely understood.

This problem was brought home to Pa, himself not the most technically adept of men, during a lengthy sequence shot aboard a yacht: leaving Amalfi harbour, cast and crew sailed out to sea for several days while the sequence was completed, whereupon Bogart asked the real-life captain how long it would take them to get back to shore. 'Well,' said the captain thoughtfully, 'about the same three days that it has taken us to sail to here.' Bogart was amazed: in the world of movies, if you wanted the next shot to be home, it was home.

But for an incurably starstruck teenager like me, *Beat the*

Devil was a joy: not only were there all these larger-than-life Hollywood legends around, there was also a supporting cast of vintage English character actors like Bernard Lee, not yet the M of Bondage, Edward Underdown, an elegant, languid gentleman jockey who also did a little light acting when his horses weren't performing, and the truly sinister Ivor Barnard, who carried a walking stick that unscrewed to reveal a lethal sword. I was intrigued to learn from him that he always carried it, and that Huston had merely incorporated it, like so much else that happened in Ravello, into the storyline.

I realise now, of course, that Ravello was where I learnt my lifelong craft of interviewing actors. They all had a story to tell, and in those days their stories were always more interesting than the one they were filming. Only Bogart seemed grouchy and uncommunicative, not least because on the journey from Rome, his chauffeur had driven him straight into a brick wall, thereby breaking several teeth: he was now eagerly awaiting the arrival of a new bridge from his dentist in Hollywood.

There was also the atmosphere of people suddenly released from the school rules of Hollywood and having a ball. One night the legendary cameraman Ossie Morris and his assistant Jack Clayton returned to their hotel to find Huston's bedroom ablaze. Staggering to bed in a more than usually drunken stupor, the great director had kicked over an oil heater, which had ignited his bed. 'Ah,' he said, as they dragged him to safety in the nick of time, 'sure 'tis a wonderful thing, the smell of burning pine.'

When Truman Capote eventually arrived on the location from Rome to deliver the long-awaited rest of the script, he was immediately dubbed 'Caposy' by the homophobic Bogart. Truman challenged him to a series of arm-wrestling contests, all of which, to general amazement, Truman won. On another occasion, a vintage and very expensive Rolls-Royce had to be pushed over a cliff with Bogart apparently at the wheel. The plan was that a small Italian mechanic would be secreted on the floor of the car to jam on the brakes in the nick of time. As the car was about to leave the road, Bogart glanced down and saw that the mechanic had wisely failed to put in an appearance. He leapt out with seconds to spare, screaming, as the car went over the cliff into the sea several hundred feet below, 'I could have been killed!'

'Yes,' said Huston, thoughtfully, 'but you weren't, were you, kid? So now you're fine, just fine.'

As the shooting came to an end and we all returned reluctantly to real life, Pa noted, 'I became a firm fan of Truman Capote, reading everything he ever wrote. Except of course the script for *Beat the Devil*.' Once we were safely back in England, Pa sent a wire to the film's nominal co-producer John Woolf of Romulus Pictures: 'We have now all returned to our capital, but I doubt that yours will ever be returned to you.'

And so, alas, it proved: to this day, some fifty years later, *Beat the Devil* has never shown a profit anywhere in the world. All the same, it was a lovely picture, especially if you were there at the time. One more Ravello story, and this, I promise, is the last. We were billeted for a while in the palatial home of the production manager, Prince Alessandro Tasca. His last guest before us had been a sister who much irritated him, not least because she was forever telling him how wise she had been to move to New York and an apartment full of labour-saving devices, instead of remaining in an old-fashioned Italian hill village.

Finally Sandro could take no more: 'Ah, but here, my dear sister,' he told her one night, 'we have the most amazing modern gadget of all, far ahead of anything the Americans could invent. I only have to press this button here, and iced champagne with glasses becomes immediately available.' He pressed it, whereupon his butler appeared with Dom Perignon and two glasses on a tray.

13
A Woman Without Veils

Life at Sizewell and Fairmans was something of an anti-climax after those heady days on location in Ravello, but I seem to have settled back into the school routine:

Headmaster's Report, Sizewell, Summer Term 1954
Sheridan seems happy enough here and has taken to working independently, which augurs well for his future. The morbid spectre that seems to haunt you day and night as parents, of the rather plump and timid deer ruthlessly pursued by his mates, should now give way to that of a young and bold Caesar, who bestrides our narrow school world like a confident Colossus. He will be more than ready for Common Entrance, and probably is so already, but why push a boy who is already running? He might well stumble. His conversation and sense of humour are at times alarmingly adult, and I have to remind myself sometimes not to ask him to come along after school hours for a drink and a cigarette.

Sometimes I think Harry was wasted as a headmaster: he should have been a novelist. On the other hand, we, his pupils, were happily never wasted: by the time I was thirteen he had me directing, albeit not very well, the school play. Only when I came back to the life of a stage director with the Redgraves some forty-five years later did I realise, admittedly a little late, that he had been right from the beginning, and that directing was really what I had wanted to do with my life all along – I had been sidetracked happily into journalism and broadcasting for half a century or so.

Robert's career was still in full flood: *Hippo Dancing* gave him another two-year West End hit, in another Parisian boulevard comedy by the reclusive André Roussin, but this time Pa wrote the adaptation himself, thereby guaranteeing himself a double percentage of the considerable profits, as well as finding his only other truly brilliant stage partner in Wilfrid Hyde-White, who shared his passion for the horses to such an extent that they insisted, when on the road, on not playing matinées if there was an important race meeting in the vicinity.

Like David Tomlinson, Willy also became a firm family friend and a rich source of anecdote. In David's case, the stories usually centred on his prowess as a pilot, in which he took considerable pride. Indeed, when he died some years after my father, having retired far too early on the proceeds of his role in *Mary Poppins* and driven his long-suffering family to distraction with his late-life boredom, he insisted on a massive memorial slab to be installed in his garden, which reads: HERE LIES DAVID TOMLINSON: ACTOR, PILOT, IRRESISTIBLE TO WOMEN.

You were never to question his brilliance in the air – or not, at least, until one celebrated weekend when he agreed to fly Pa to Le Touquet for a little brisk gambling between the Saturday and the Monday performances of *The Little Hut*. They took off on the Sunday morning, in David's two-seater plane and considerable fog. After they had been flying for about an hour, Pa enquired nervously if David had the faintest idea where they were: 'I am a trained pilot and war hero,' replied David. 'I have instruments. I am in touch with the ground. I have radar. We are even now just circling Paris.'

At that moment the fog cleared and, looking down, Pa saw Lancing College. 'I had no idea they'd moved that to France,' he said. David refused to speak to him for the rest of the weekend.

Wilfrid Hyde-White was less touchy, but no less fun: like Pa, he had regular cash crises and, also like Pa, he nearly always had bad luck on his beloved turf. After several uneasy bankruptcy hearings, however, he finished up happily enough in a late-life Hollywood career, most notably, of course, as the definitive Colonel Pickering in the movie of *My Fair Lady*. Intriguingly, if you watch that film now on television or video/DVD, what you notice is how, in all their shared scenes, Rex Harrison takes his lead and his timing from Willy, who was the great master of the art of light comedy and recognised as such.

Towards the end of his long life, Willy finished up, thanks to American Equity's generous pension fund, in a luxurious old actors' home in Palm Springs, California. 'Why,' I asked him once, 'are you, the most English of men, living out your retirement abroad?'

Willy thought for a moment. 'Two reasons, old fellow. Couldn't bear me last wife, couldn't bear the Inland Revenue.' And then he paused for the perfectly timed moment: 'I fear,' he added, 'I have just made a very caddish remark about the Inland Revenue.'

Oh, God, I miss them all so much: the gentlemen actors, and the semi-alcoholic journalists, and all those who believed that the great thing was to have fun, whatever the expense. There are, indeed, a few of us left, but the problem is that the world into which we were born has gone ambitious, and serious, and earnest, and dedicated, and nervous. It is no longer considered enough to be able to write on your tombstone, 'All in all, he had quite a lot of fun, and didn't do anyone any lasting harm, or at least not intentionally.'

What did you do in the Great Peace, Daddy? Well, my darlings, I tried not to annoy people too much, and only to work at things and in places with people I would have chosen anyway, even if there hadn't been any money in it.

Hippo continued dancing along Shaftesbury Avenue throughout 1953, and in the daytime Pa went from film to film, almost as if they were going out of fashion. Few of those pictures were notable, but he established a useful line in dotty monarchs for MGM, who by then had moved their overseas centre of operations from Rome to London, and were constantly making expensive costume epics in Britain. *Quentin Durward* found him bullying Kay Kendall, and in *Beau Brummell* he was opposite Elizabeth Taylor, with whom, years later, he was to make George Cukor's last disaster, an amazing musical attempt at Soviet-American co-production called *The Blue Bird*. On the first day of shooting in what was then still Leningrad, Cukor assembled his all-star cast – among them not only Taylor and Pa, but Ava Gardner and Jane Fonda – and told them how lucky they all were to be filming, historically, in the same studio where, in 1917, the great Eisenstein had made *Battleship Potemkin*. 'Yes,' added their Russian producer, 'and with the very same equipment.' After that things were never quite the same on *The Blue Bird*.

In *Beau Brummell*, Pa had been cast as the mad King George III, some thirty years before Alan Bennett rewrote the monarch for the late great Nigel Hawthorne, and Ustinov was playing his equally unattractive son, who became George IV. Once again, the film was chosen for a Royal Command, this one among the first to be attended by our new Queen Elizabeth and Prince Philip. After ninety minutes of watching Pa and Ustinov literally at each other's throats, chewing up the scenery as her mad ancestors, Her Majesty let it be known that if, in future, the selection of Royal Command films was to be equally regally tactless, neither she nor her husband would be attending them. Even the *Royal Variety Show*, Her Majesty noted privately, had to be less painful entertainment.

Meanwhile, my life continued happily enough at Sizewell, though it was clear even to me that the school was somehow shrinking, as parent after parent withdrew their children to more orthodox establishments. This however suited me admirably, as it meant that I got more of Harry's exclusive attention, and his teaching was now in full private-tutorial mode, with Haleh, Richard and I and only one or two others forming his entire daily classes in Shakespeare and the romantic French poets and, luckily for us, little else.

It was as a result of this almost one-to-one attention that I first managed to get my name in the national press, something that has remained of ludicrous importance to me ever since and led, not unnaturally, to my long career in journalism, not to mention my lifelong quest (usually unsuccessful) for the photo-byline. When I reached my sixtieth birthday, *The Times* was kind enough to print a colour photograph of me, an honour I never warranted in the time I worked there as a deputy editor, while that of my co-celebrant (albeit deceased) Walt Disney was merely in black and white. 'Hardly surprising,' muttered my younger daughter Juliet, who has inherited her great-grandmother Gladys's role as the cynic in the family. 'When Disney was alive, they probably hadn't even invented colour photography.'

My first bid for fame resulted, however, in a *Daily Mail* diary paragraph in 1955 announcing that, at thirteen, I had passed my O level in English some two years ahead of the normal academic timetable, thanks, of course – although this was not acknowledged by the Nigel Dempster of the period – to Harry's intensive Sizewell immersion coaching. My grandfather Buck, always keen to establish that any success in our family came from his rather than Robert's side, and a compulsive writer of letters-to-the-editor on a vast range of barmy topics (he had recently suggested to the *Daily Telegraph* that, in the light of Sir John Gielgud's tragic arrest for homosexual soliciting, all gay actors should henceforth be banned from the British theatre), was immediately in print with the news that as I was, thanks to him, distantly related to Professor Alfred North Whitehead, my schoolboy genius was hardly to be wondered at. *I* have wondered, rather shamefully, ever since who Professor Alfred North Whitehead was. I think he was either mathematical or scientific, so an alien being despite the blood connection.

My grandmother Gladys had also come back into our lives and had bought Barn Elms, the nearby house on the regatta stretch of the Thames at Henley where she was to spend much of the rest of her life. After Phil's death her career had gone into a sharp decline, but in 1951 Noël Coward had written expressly for her the stately-home comedy *Relative Values*, which ran for nearly two years at the Savoy, and thereby brought both him and her back from exile into the hearts of British theatregoers.

It wasn't until a year or two before her death at eighty-two that I began to realise how little I knew about her. I knew, of course, that she was an actress who had started out as a Gaiety Girl, and ended up a Dame of the British Empire. Unlike contemporaries such as Edith Evans and Sybil Thorndike, who had stayed resolutely attached to the Old Vic and the London theatre and therefore received their honours in their fifties, Gladys was punished for her years in the Hollywood sun by being made to wait well into her late seventies for the call to the Palace. When it came, she wasn't remotely as impressed as we were. I knew, too, that she had been the great pin-up poster girl of the First World War, and I'd met Chelsea Pensioners in their eighties who'd carried her picture on a postcard through the trenches. I knew that a whole window of Selfridge's had once been devoted to her own brand of cold cream, and that she had only narrowly missed, through fog, being the first woman to loop the loop. I also knew that Somerset Maugham – who wrote several plays for her when she was the first woman to run a West End theatre (the Playhouse) in the 1920s – had once called her 'a woman without veils'. The Playhouse still nestles just under Hungerford Railway Bridge on the Thames Embankment. 'What did you do about the noise of the trains?' one of her greatest late-life friends, Dirk Bogarde, once asked. 'Trains, dear?' replied G. 'We had them stopped, naturally.'

When I was making a radio obituary soon after she died, I asked Dirk what he had really thought of G: 'All the charm,' he said, 'of an electric carving knife.' On the same programme, Olivier called her 'one of the great long-distance hurdlers of twentieth-century theatre and cinema', and David Niven, her frequent co-star in a long-running 1960s American television crime-caper series called *The Rogues*, and in the film of Terence Rattigan's *Separate Tables*, concluded, 'Acting was something Gladys did for a living, not something she ever really thought about.'

Like L.P. Hartley's Go-Between, Gladys always believed that the past was where they did things differently, but unlike him she never saw the point in applying for a re-entry visa. Indeed, I think I managed to annoy her inadvertently, or perhaps especially, by becoming a theatre historian. When I told her, proudly, that I had been chosen by her lifelong friend Noël Coward as his authorised biographer, she looked at me in some amazement. 'Why would anyone,' she asked, 'want to read about Noël?' I suppose what separated us was that I did. When I tried to write her life, which I only achieved some time after she died, she was equally amazed. 'Tell me,' I would say, during the long summer afternoons on her Henley lawn or by her Californian pool, 'about your friendship with John Barrymore,' suspecting that they might have had an affair back in the 1920s, when he first brought his radical *Hamlet* to London. 'Jack Barrymore, dear?' she would reply. 'He's dead.'

And that, maddeningly, was always the end of that.

Gladys never understood about nostalgia, any more than she ever understood about fear, exhaustion, illness or old age, and she was never one to believe in the existence of something she couldn't understand. I can think of nobody further removed on the scale of human entertainment from Gladys than Samuel Beckett, of whom I suspect she had never heard. But he once said something that I have always thought held true for her, and perhaps for all of us in her immediate family: 'Fail. Fail again. Fail better.' G's whole career, indeed her whole life, was a triumph against the odds: as an actress she was never especially talented, or disciplined, yet she could break your heart. It was something to do with sheer survival in a rapidly changing world.

Though never very poor (her father had been the first journalist to edit a successful food-and-wine magazine back in the 1890s) yet, like all of us, for ever in debt to the Inland Revenue or its ugly American sister the IRS, there were short periods in Gladys's life when she enjoyed the comparative financial security of an earning husband or an MGM featured-player contract. Yet well into her eighties, she was still providing for a younger sister deaf from birth, and the son whose working life as an actor was ended prematurely by a severe mental illness that G could never even acknowledge.

Her two daughters, my mother Joan and her half-sister Sally, were frequently roped in – as were her two actor sons-in-law, my father and Robert Hardy, and her step-children Jack and Ros Merivale – to help her sort out the innumerable pets, cars, houses and relatives she had a habit of gathering on one side of the Atlantic then abruptly abandoning when, for some reason either personal or professional, she needed to be on the other.

In the manner of many born in her late-Victorian generation, Gladys kept herself to herself, much as her two daughters do to this day. She was not inclined to delve too deeply into her innermost soul, at least not in public, and neither did she encourage others to try to find out what, if anything, lay at the heart of her existence. To her generation, psychiatry and self-analysis were new-fangled and unnecessary; and that, too, I now find enviable – indeed, even admirable.

Her love for babies and small children was boundless: she lived just long enough to know Hugo, my son, Alexis, my elder daughter, and Emma and Justine, her two granddaughters from Robert and Sally Hardy. Watching them all playing on the Henley towpath in the last summer of G's life, separated by nothing but eighty years or so, I finally realised that they knew something that the rest of us, born between them, had somehow missed. I have never found out what it was.

Despite that, I never found it easy to think of her as my grandmother, certainly not the kind of grandmother who, like Robert's mother, might need trays of tea carried up to her bedside. If there were any trays to be carried around her house, it was invariably Gladys who carried them.

'Getting On' was G's lifelong philosophy. I don't think it mattered to her where you got on to, or in what precise direction, just so long as there was discernible forward movement. Like Noël Coward and Somerset Maugham, both of whom wrote plays for her, and like her daughter Sally and her granddaughter Justine – the travel writer Justine Hardy – she was a compulsive traveller across eight defiant decades; but unlike them she had little interest in discussing where she had been in a long and often courageous life. What always concerned Gladys was where she was going next. Don't stop, don't look back.

Gladys took the view that her life was for her to lead and others to follow if they so chose, and it was a belief that carried her undaunted and undefeated through more than three-quarters of a century. By her bedside when she died were the usual dog-leads, photographs of the grandchildren, and notes about gravel for the drive and food for the ducks on the winter towpath beneath her window, but nothing by way of a diary.

Perhaps we need now to look again at the cast-list for these memoirs. Some of the people who either made me, or just helped me not to fall flat on my face too often, you will already have met, if only briefly: Gladys, of course, and my parents, my brother and sister, my aunt Sally, Haleh and Richard, Harry Tuyn and his loving, long-suffering wife Elaine. Others – my wives Margaret and Ruth, Margaret's mother and Ruth's parents, my own children and grandchildren, Peter Young and

My parents outside Caxton Hall on
their wedding day, 23 February 1940

My mother and her mother,
Gladys Cooper, at the height of G's
'postcard beauty' fame in 1912

My grandparents on both sides of the family: the Major and his 'Poor Daisy'

Buck of the Club and the Fizz; and Gladys Cooper

My strikingly handsome, talented and doomed Uncle John, and my Aunt Sal,
photographed in the 1940s. Together and apart, they were the most
glamorous of all my relatives

Robert and me, at home
sometime in 1942: like
father, like son?

Robert as Alexander Woollcott in *The Man Who Came to Dinner*, the play which gave me my name and him a three-year wartime hit

My three godfathers: the real 'Man Who Came to Dinner', here playing himself on Broadway; Peter Bull; and Sewell Stokes, who taught me about life and London well before I came of age

1940s life at Fairmans: my mother, her mother and me

My mother, me, my sister Annabel and Topsy the Peke

An already chubby and deeply unenthusiastic sportsman in California, 1947

With Joan, Robert and Gladys, emerging from the surf in Hawaii, 1948

Home again: the family (thus far) back at Fairmans after the world tour

Christopher Matthew who became my best friends at school and college, the people I went to work with at ITN, *The Times*, BBC2 and *Punch* – you will soon get to meet, as well as the agent Barry Burnett, who showed me how it was possible to start a whole new life as a director and actor in your late fifties, and the American impresario Don Smith who gave me a whole new life in New York cabaret, as well as actors, from Vanessa and Corin Redgrave through Kika Markham to Patricia Hodge and the late, lamented Simon Cadell, all of whom either brought my scripts to life or let me direct them in those of others. I also owe a vast and unrepayable debt to three theatre managers, Sally Hughes at the Mill at Sonning, Dan Crawford at the King's Head, and Penny Horner at Jermyn Street, and to the greatest British choreographer of her generation, Gillian Lynne, who never taught me to dance but was generous enough to produce three very different productions of mine in three consecutive years.

In unique ways, all of these people, with what seems to me unfathomable courage and generosity, allowed a journalist with little previous experience – and moreover a drama critic who had, doubtless, at some time insulted them all in print – to start directing his own and other people's scripts on their premises or within their budgets.

I slide these credits in here because I know, from long experience of watching people in bookshops, that nobody ever reads them in a preface, and also because, already a little late, I realise that I have never found an adequate way of thanking them. There are others who, even as I write, I realise I have never acknowledged: for instance, I have shared countless radio panels, *Punch* lunches and literary gatherings with Clement Freud over the last thirty years, and even made one entire theatre series for Melvyn Bragg at London Weekend Television with Freud's enchanting daughter Emma. Only now do I realise that I owe to him my passion for cabaret, which has led me over the last fifteen years to countless seasons at the genial if eccentric Peter Boizot's Pizza on the Park and elsewhere, usually under the management of either Barry Mishon or, in America, the aforementioned Don Smith, or else on the road for Clive Conway all over the world in shows devised by Ruth, or me, or our friend the constant pianist and singer Michael Law, who is in his own considerable right the founder, conductor, lead singer and, with his partner Alan Bennett, the manager of the Savoy Hotel's Piccadilly Dance Orchestra.

All of that has thoroughly Freudian beginnings: early in the 1950s Freud persuaded the management of the Royal Court, even before they lucked into John Osborne and Jimmy Porter, that their rooftop space (the one that subsequently became the Theatre Upstairs) could be used as a late-night cabaret restaurant. By about 1954, a still ungainly teenager desperate to belong to the nightlife of the West End as glimpsed through my father's stage doors, I was fortunate enough to be taken – by my godfather Peter Bull, the ultimate Man About Chelsea – to this magical space up about four flights of stairs where things only started to look lively around midnight, and where entire cabarets and hot meals would be offered until two or three in the morning.

Shamefully I cannot remember who I first saw at Freud's club, or even what it was called, but in the late 1950s I know that the stars included a young Cleo Laine, then also doubling as an actress on the main stage downstairs, as well as the undergraduates Jonathan Miller and Dudley Moore. Although Peter Cook's later Soho cabaret club is always credited with giving birth to *That Was The Week That Was* and the satire boom, in fact it was all started some years earlier than the establishment of The Establishment, when Clement Freud first opened his restaurant at Court. By such happy accidents is showbiz history made, and I am always amazed that my historian colleagues, focusing endlessly on the revolution that overtook the Royal Court downstairs in 1956 with the coming of *Look Back in Anger*, never look also at what was happening in the same theatre at the same time upstairs. There, an altogether different musical and satirical kind of theatre history was being made. It was effectively the rebirth of post-war intimate cabaret, and perhaps the nearest we ever got on this side of the Channel to the Berlin of Lenya or the Paris of Piaf.

Returning to my lifelong inability to hear the beat or put one foot musically in front of another, when I was about five my ever-hopeful mother sent me to the dancing academy of the legendary Madame Vacani, who had only recently taught Princess Margaret and a pre-Hollywood Elizabeth Taylor to waltz elegantly around the floor; she then still maintained a dancing academy reassuringly close to Harrods in the heart of Knightsbridge. I had been there for less than a couple of hours when I was sent for by Madame Vacani herself: 'Mr Morley,' she addressed me regretfully, 'I have been running this academy of dancing for the best part of forty years, and in all that time I have maintained one absolutely golden rule, which is never, never to admit defeat, no matter how hopeless the student. However, this morning . . .'

14
Tales from Venice and the Vienna Woods

For reasons that I have never identified, the male members of my family have, for several generations, taken especial pride in saying the wrong thing in public. My grandfather would sit in the hallway of his own Buck's Club, lashing out with his walking-stick and his tongue at members to whose views he had taken exception. Robert developed this to a fine art during his last years, when he would accept speaking engagements at usually Conservative ladies' luncheon clubs up and down Britain. On these occasions, after a flattering introduction from the club secretary, he would rise to his feet, an apparently conservative old buffer, and deliver a blistering attack on Margaret Thatcher and all her political ways. Robert went to his grave in the belief, probably accurate, that she had single-handedly destroyed everything he held most dear in Britain. What I remember best of these occasions is the amazement of the old ladies. They could hardly have been more surprised if Mrs Thatcher herself had turned out to be a man in drag.

Back to Wargrave in the mid-1950s: in the few terms I had spent at Rupert House in Henley, immediately before and after our world tour, I had made some firm friends around the area, including one family of three enchanting sisters, Judy, Anna and Corinne, the daughters of Kay and Michael North, a man after my father's heart. He was a bear-like, lovable BBC radio light-entertainment producer whose early death of a heart-attack brought me up against the reality that no one lived for ever, as my family seemed to do, and that death could happen to the least deserving candidate. Then there was Sue Jackson, who always seemed – with some reason –

to prefer the company of her horses to us pimply youths, who pursued her and them hopelessly on bicycles around a village where, at least in my memory, there were always more bikes and horses than cars or people. Henley had other, more distantly glamorous figures, like Karen Pilzer, who still lives there, having succeeded her father as the best dentist in the town.

But my best and closest friend was always Peter Young, who lived in the middle of Wargrave with his redoubtable mother and grandmother, a half-brother and half-sister, and an Australian Air Force step-father called Digby, who taught us both to celebrate the joys of alcohol at an alarmingly early age. Rather like the Tuyns at Sizewell, the Youngs became a kind of alternative family for me, and I remember hours spent happily with Peter's mother Patsy and her own mother, known always as Gran. They had a healthy respect for the multi-medicinal properties of Gordon's gin, when taken in sufficient quantities as early as possible in the afternoon, and sometimes well before that. The family had once been closely connected with Brakspear's Brewery, and ran their homes as the best kind of countryside pubs.

After nursery school, Peter had enjoyed, if that is the word, a far more orthodox education than me, first at Summerfields in Oxford and then at Marlborough, but there was always something intriguingly subversive about the Youngs, and they were also, of course, highly theatrical. Indeed, my only glimpse of life at a British public school was when I went to see Peter and two other Marlburians who subsequently became professional actors, Michael Elwyn and Michael Pennington, in a 1958 school production of *Saint Joan*, which I still remember as being rather better than many I have seen since in professional playhouses.

Even on fleeting weekend visits to Marlborough, I realised that I would have been no better equipped than my father to survive at a British public school, so it was therefore with considerable relief that I always went back to the anarchy and comfort of Sizewell. Even that, though, had to end in the late 1950s, when with only about three pupils left, Harry could no longer afford the rent of the hall. He moved briefly to Exeter, then took over Les Volets Jaunes, a large chalet on the ski slopes above Chateau d'Oex in Switzerland, where he finally hit the mother-lode running a successful girls' finishing school.

Haleh, Richard and I naturally went wherever Harry did; he had got us through our minimal O and A levels in English and French at an amazingly early age, but there was now, at least for Richard and me, the distant hope of Oxford and the concomitant problem of all the subjects we had never studied. After a couple of happy if chilly late-1950s winters lounging around the girls' school pretending to teach them how to ski, an art you will be surprised to learn I never mastered for myself, let alone them, I took the Merton College advice of Robert Levens and tootled, a word beloved of my godfather Peter Bull, along the lake to Geneva where, to my amazement, I was accepted at the age of sixteen at the university to do a diploma course in teaching French as a foreign language. To this day I have never discovered why Geneva University took me in, or what they thought they were getting: I suspect I either filled in the forms wrongly, or else they were misread. Almost shockingly soon, I found myself in a large group of mainly Swiss Germans and Belgians in their late twenties, all training to be interpreters at the nearby headquarters of the United Nations.

It was surely as obvious to them and our tutors as it was to me that a chubby sixteen-year-old English schoolboy was not exactly par for the course, but I have always thought it said a good deal for Swiss imperturbability and *politesse* that, having accepted from me a minimal amount of local francs – twelve to the pound in those distant, jammy times – for the year-long project nobody ever asked what I was doing there, or why I wanted to do a crash course in teaching French to foreigners, which of course I didn't. All I wanted was something to impress Robert Levens back at Merton, and the following summer I was ceremoniously presented with just the thing: a gold-embossed diploma, the only prize I got out of my year in Geneva unless you count a heavy Swiss-French accent, which is still remarked upon and much mocked by French cab-drivers. To this day I have to remember that *septante*, *huitante* and *nonante* are only acceptable when counting to seventy, eighty and ninety in Swiss French rather than French French. After nearly half a century's bitter experience, I find that being taken for Swiss in France is nearly as bad as being taken there for Belgian.

But something else came out of my year in Geneva: the city had, apart from its famous Jet d'Eau, an amazing number of cinemas, many of which were arthouses way ahead of their time. Here, on lonely weekends (I failed to make any Swiss friends at all, though luckily my darling cousin Virginia Fass was another student), I discovered whole seasons of Chaplin, D.W. Griffith, the Gish sisters, Bogart and Bacall and, if I was very lucky, the movies were merely subtitled, not dubbed. True, that was a problem too, because since we were in Switzerland the captions had to be in the three national languages, French, German and Italian, and took up more than half the screen. Sometimes all you could see were the tops of the actors' heads, frantically – or so it seemed – bobbing about above an ever-rising tide of multilingual words.

It was in those back-street Geneva cinemas, at a time when I am sure many of my contemporaries were discovering more traditionally sexy pursuits, that I first began to think about the cinema as something more than a brilliant invention at which my father and grandmother could earn a living. The idea of programming films, of showing them in seasons dedicated to a single actor, director or even studio, seemed fascinating, and to this day I have always secretly hoped that – as seems to

have happened in so many other areas of my working life –
one morning the phone would ring and I would find myself
programming director of the National Film Theatre. Then
again, maybe at sixty I had better give up on that dream.

When I wasn't otherwise occupied, pretending to be a skiing
teacher in Chateau d'Oex or a trainee interpreter in Geneva,
there were still some joyous late-1950s holidays to be spent
with what Earl Spencer might call my 'blood family'. Robert
was still making an average of three or four films a year,
and every summer at that time the organisers of the Venice
Film Festival – now a rather more solemn, academic and
multinational affair – would invite armies of British actors
from Pinewood, Elstree and Shepperton to show off their
current releases and sign a few autographs. The rule of thumb
then was that the worse the film the more elaborate and
costly its initial publicity campaign. I seem to recall all of
us once living for about a week in a luxurious hotel in
Munich, trying untruthfully to persuade the local German
press that *Genghis Khan* was something other than utter,
albeit expensive, multinational rubbish.

My darling father, inscrutably cast as the Emperor of China,
had discovered during the shooting that if he Sellotaped his
pigtail to the crown of his head he could stay in bed for
an extra hour each morning. Meanwhile, James Mason and
the other more dedicated thespians were busily occupied in
Makeup, attempting to look rather more authentic. Pa was
never strong on authenticity: there remains to this day a
throne-room shot in the 1938 *Marie Antoinette* where, if you
look very carefully, you can see that Louis XVI is wearing a
pair of grey flannel trousers under his robes.

But my father, whose talent for spotting a freebie at a
thousand paces is one I have proudly inherited (I am writing
this on board the most luxurious of all cruise liners, the
QE2, by which, in return for half a dozen showbiz lectures
to unusually captive audiences, my wife and I are transported

free to places like Rio de Janeiro then flown home again in business class. In more recent times we have also made such loving friends and such generous hosts as Marvin Leipsig and Arthur Feuer, who live, conveniently enough, just near where the *QE2* docks in Fort Lauderdale.) I had worked out that every August the Venice Film Festival could, with a little ingenuity, be turned into a fortnight's all-expenses-paid holiday for the entire family.

In the view of about four generations of my family, Venice rates as the perfect holiday destination, especially if you are wise enough – as we always were – to stay at someone else's expense in a little hotel on the Lido called the Quattro Fontane. This had an open-air courtyard dining room to die for, and I trust it is still there; it was only about twenty yards from the Excelsior beach. Pa had only to nip across the road to the casino, and others of us intent on culture could catch the free Excelsior Hotel boat into Venice for a few frescoes, or maybe just an ice cream. Something for everyone of all ages, in fact. After about my fourth summer there I used to fantasise about lying on the golden sands and being transported back to the 1920s, when Cole Porter had first met Noël Coward on that very beach, Diaghilev and Nijinsky having only just left it, and a gay time was being had by all.

Even in my own time, we were not without celebrities: Vivien Leigh, Kenneth More, Emlyn Williams, anyone with an English movie to sell and a suntan to acquire ended up on the Lido in August as, rather more surprisingly, did the Duke and Duchess of Windsor. One summer they rented the beach hut next to ours. It made for a curious, neighbourly relationship: by 1957 the Windsors were a little past their prime and surrounded, as I recall, no longer by courtiers but several yapping dogs. She was always yelling at him about them, either because he had failed to anchor them adequately to the beach hut, or because she was, as I soon discovered, a fearful old bitch herself, whose daily delight seemed to be in destroying what little chance her husband had of attaining peace and quiet, or even a decent lunch.

He was infinitely sad, while she reminded me forcefully of Fanny Cradock, a celebrated tele-chef of the period who also took delight in reducing her husband Johnnie to a quivering wreck in public. But the Abdication was only twenty years past, and even a world war had failed to shake them from the public memory. The Windsors were then, rather like Elizabeth Taylor and Richard Burton a decade later, the most famous and scandalous people in the world. To have them as next-door neighbours, if only in a beach hut, gave us hitherto unimaginable social stature: people we had never met would drop in claiming to be old friends, so that they could peer over the beach umbrellas to see if the Windsors were really as old and sad as they appeared to be. It was like meeting some celebrated old variety double-act who had fallen from public favour yet were keen to recapture the glamour of their own past, without much help from anyone. Their show was still on the road, but they were badly in need of an audience and some decent reviews.

As the 1950s came to a close – were they really as magically eccentric as they seem now, or were we just younger and better at being happy? – there was still the problem of my Oxford entrance: with lunatic ambition, I applied now to Balliol and Christ Church, both of which turned me down by return of post. But I had somehow intrigued Levens at Merton as a kind of walking, or at any rate staggering, work-in-progress, and he suggested that, as time was still on my side, I might like to spend a term or two at a London crammer and get the Latin and Maths O levels that, with my newly achieved Geneva diploma, might swing me a place at Merton in 1960 to read Modern Languages – or, more accurately, French. Miraculously I would still be not quite eighteen.

So it was that I spent a happy six months or so at Stafford House in Kensington High Street, where I met my first adult love, a gorgeously funny brunette called Bay Kirkbride whose affections I had, alas, to share with a rather smoother, more dapper rival. I think he was an ambassador's son, and therefore considerably better than I at the social graces. Whether he was also better at sex I never discovered because, gentle reader, in those far-different days we never got our kit off, even at seventeen, and especially not in Kensington High Street.

But what I loved best about Bay and her equally enchanting mother Thea, who had once wanted to be an actress and was therefore, like her daughter, endearingly stagestruck, was that they lived at Long Crendon in Corner Cottage, one of those magical Oxfordshire homes that nowadays exist only in Merchant-Ivory movies, full of carpets and curtains and heritage and Helena Bonham-Carter. The Kirkbrides, too, like the Tuyns and the Youngs, let me join their family as a kind of honorary son. Looking back now I wonder how it was that, with a loving and happy family background of my own, I was adopted throughout the 1950s by all these other people. It wasn't as though I looked underprivileged, or in need of food or drink; neither do I think I had any other natural attributes of the orphan, or seemed unhappy with my lot. I must just have been the kind of boy whom people took in, and I only wish that at the time I had been a little more grateful, or even aware of the honour they were doing me.

There was still one more wondrous movie location on which to join Robert. His stage career had continued triumphantly after the Roussin hits with *A Likely Tale*, in which he appeared as twins, thanks to some brilliant backstage trickery and a double, but then lurched into an uncharacteristic disaster with *Fanny*. It was his one and only attempt to sing and dance on stage, though collectors of Robert's vintage moments can, of course, find him doing both in the final scene of Cliff Richard's first movie hit *The Young Ones*, and jolly uneasy he looks in it.

But the failure of *Fanny* to attract its original Broadway

audiences, and the fact that he was contracted to do it for a year, unusually depressed Pa: after one matinée he and I walked down the Strand towards Charing Cross for our usual restorative tea of Fuller's walnut cake (double icing, and where is it now, when we really need it?). I had agreed that if by the end of our promenade nobody had stopped Pa for his autograph, I would accept that his career was finished. It was, for me at least, an increasingly nervous walk, but as we neared the station an old lady obligingly came towards us, autograph book at the ready. 'Mr Laughton,' she said, as Pa started to sign, 'I did so enjoy you in *The Private Life of Henry VIII.*'

During this less than wonderful time, Pa also made a brave if doomed stab at cabaret, appearing at the Café de Paris late at night with Julian Orchard in a memorably bizarre entertainment, largely cobbled together from old Kingsley Amis poems and Robert's own stream-of-consciousness thoughts. Café habitués accustomed to Noël Coward, Marlene Dietrich and Josephine Baker sat over their champagne glasses in a kind of open-mouthed astonishment: 'Mr Morley,' said the coming attraction Sophie Tucker on his last night, which followed rather too quickly on his first, 'you have a great beginning and a great ending. All your act really needs is something in the middle.' Quite soon after that, the Café closed its doors, to reopen as a disco some thirty years later.

But there was better to come: Pa, Robin Fox and Ros Chatto now formed themselves into a West End management, and Robert discovered around his fiftieth birthday that he enjoyed directing plays for other people almost as much as he did playing in them; he had one or two considerable successes as both a producer and a director, not least with *Tunnel of Love* and *Once More With Feeling*. He also got himself an unusual job standing in for a vacationing Bruce Forsyth on *Sunday Night at the London Palladium*, a weekly variety show that regularly topped all the ITV ratings and involved my ham-fisted father in 'Beat The Clock', a complex sequence of audience-participation games, nearly all of which he jovially stymied, either by failing to explain the rules adequately, or being unable to work out which contestant had won and precisely what.

There was also the memorable Sunday night when, just before Christmas, he came out to introduce that week's star turn: 'Now,' Pa says cheerfully, 'this is really an amazing piece of luck. As you know, next week is Christmas and, believe it or not, our star guest tonight is . . .' consults note '. . . an American called Buddy *Holly.*'

At that time, Mr Holly was – to everyone but our non-musical family – just about the biggest pop star in the firmament, and sadly only a few months away from his sudden, violent death in an air crash. This was also to be his only appearance on British television. Although, of course, there was no videotape or telerecording, an alert member of his British fan club filmed it all from his television set on a grainy, flickery strip of celluloid. It is still shown religiously at all Buddy Holly conventions, where my father lives on as the only man who had never heard of him. Such is the nature of fame, I guess. As for *Sunday Night at the London Palladium*, Bruce Forsyth duly returned to his empire without severe competition, though not before the *Observer* had noted, 'Mr Morley resembled a performing elephant, albeit of genius, participating with the utmost reluctance in a cabaret staged by a house of ill-repute.'

Domestic matters did not improve that Christmas: my father set fire to the Fairmans chimney and crashed the family car on ice in the same week. From then until the day he died, he never again drove a car, unlike his mother-in-law Gladys, who insisted on driving her imported Californian Thunderbird at breakneck speed along the narrow roads around Henley. Eventually, able to bear it no longer, we reported her to the local police and got them to remove her car keys when in her early eighties.

Not, however, before she and Robert were driving across America from New York to California. Unlike my father, who regarded all travel as an excuse to strike up conversations with strangers in hotel bars and bus shelters, Gladys did not believe in stopping: if you were going somewhere with her, you drove day and night until you reached your destination. However, on this adventure Pa persuaded G that he really had to have a bath, a meal and a bed for the night before proceeding any further.

In Minneapolis, they checked in at a hotel and went down to the dining room where, to Pa's horror, they saw a notice on the glass doors announcing that the restaurant was closed for the annual dinner of General Motors, a local car manufacturer. Through the doors, large car salesmen could be seen chomping their way through T-bone steaks the size of Alaska. Pa was about to turn away in hunger and despair when Gladys sent for the head waiter. 'Now,' she said, 'you won't know me at all, but I am a very old English actress and, by an extraordinary coincidence, a lifelong friend of the General's, who I'm sure would not want us to go away hungry.'

As they were shown to a table, Pa attempted to explain to his mother-in-law that General Motors was not a man. 'Nonsense,' said Gladys. 'I happen to know that he served in the war, and with considerable distinction.' She believed what she chose to believe; all other facts were considered untrue. It is one of her many talents that I failed to inherit. My grandmother was not only a beauty, an actress and a manager, she was her own complete universe. Nothing else mattered to her or, perhaps, to us.

By now Robert had taken up a new career in journalism, initially thanks to a long-running travel and leisure column in the *Sunday Express*; he was also soon to pioneer the kind of restaurant column in which he would review not the food, about which he knew surprisingly little beyond that he enjoyed eating large amounts of it several times a day, but the conversation and general deportment of other people in the restaurant. For the late 1950s this was revolutionary, and led to several complaints not least from Gladys, in whom Pa was the first to find wonderful magazine copy. She regarded all forms of journalism as faintly vulgar, with the possible exception of favourable theatre reviews, and like many of my family she never understood how Pa and I could so eagerly have joined the enemy – conveniently forgetting that she was the daughter of one of the first-ever 'leisure' journalists, the one with his own food-and-wine magazine back in the 1870s.

The last of the great 1950s movie locations – by which I mean the ones that coincided with school or college holidays and therefore included me – was Vienna, where we went for *The Journey*, a film in which its director Anatole Litvak intended to commemorate – however idiosyncratically – the Hungarian uprising, only a few miles and a few months from where it had happened. Litvak, never a director to be restrained by quiet good taste or the fear of repeating himself, had seen in the tragedy the perfect old-style Hollywood strangers-on-a-bus movie, and cast it accordingly. He also found a way to reunite the two stars of the recently triumphant *The King and I*, Deborah Kerr and Yul Brynner, though this time, alas, without the songs. Yul would give his evil Russian army officer, and Deborah her usual British matron in overseas distress. In his first film, Jason Robards Jr was to be the handsome American army officer who comes to her rescue in the nick of time. Among the rest of an amazing cast were E. G. Marshall and Annie Jackson, as the doting parents of a child played by Ron Howard, later to become a distinguished film director himself. Then there was David Kossoff playing . . . well, David Kossoff, Anouk Aimée as the brave leader of the Hungarian resistance, and Robert as a portly British war correspondent loosely based on Richard Dimbleby.

As with *Beat the Devil* a few years earlier, the off-screen saga of the movie was vastly more intriguing than anything they captured on camera. Deborah, like Ingrid Bergman for years a model of wifely Hollywood rectitude, was in the throes of leaving her real-life war-hero husband Tony Bartley for the screenwriter and novelist Peter Viertel, who was also on the location with his great friend the *Herald Tribune* humorist Art Buchwald – who, had I but known it, was to be my columnist neighbour on that paper from the early 1970s to the present day.

The British press had already got wind of the Deborah scandal, and for several weeks Viertel, Buchwald and my father roamed the bars and restaurants of old Vienna, not an irksome task, attempting without much success to divert the gossip columnists from Deborah. The best thing to emerge from the fracas, apart from the fact that Deborah soon got her divorce, married Viertel and has lived with him happily ever after, was that Buchwald took to interviewing Robert, who was on good form: 'We British,' Pa told him, 'are really only ever happy abroad when the natives are also the waiters. We don't altogether enjoy them being at our tables, or in the same sea. We prefer them always to be one or two feet behind our chairs, holding the bottle of wine.'

Once again, looking back at these years from the perspective of 2002, I am appalled by how little we noticed of life around us. The Russians had only just left Vienna, the city still bore all the scars of its post-war quadruple occupation, and we were barely more than a decade down the line from *The Third Man*. Yet all we noticed was the affair between Deborah and Peter. Somehow world politics always stopped at the edge of a movie location, and we lived as if in a luxurious quarantine.

In the same retrospect, the best thing *The Journey* ever gave us was the lifelong friendship of Annie Jackson and her husband Eli Wallach, one of the the greatest of all American character actors. At the time of *The Journey*, Annie was as pregnant in real life as she was meant to be on camera.

When the picture had, as usual, overrun by several weeks, she announced to Pa that she was going home to have her baby delivered in a safe American hospital, even though her work in the movie was still unfinished. 'Of course you are, my darling,' said Robert, 'and when your case comes to court and you are being sued by Litvak for millions of dollars, I shall be only too happy to give you a character reference.' Annie completed the movie, returned home and gave safe birth.

Forty years later, at the end of the 1990s, I found myself in Sag Harbor, near the Wallachs' summer home in the Hamptons, where the enchanting local theatre was staging a version of my *Noël & Gertie* with Twiggy and Harry Groener. I soon found myself in the Wallachs' swimming-pool. That summer, the fashion in the ultra-fashionable Hamptons was to install a freshwater shower on the grass by your pool to cleanse yourself of chlorine. 'I'll tell you a funny thing,' I said to Annie. 'We in England are usually years behind you Americans in new-fangled plumbing, but we already have these shower things indoors in our bathrooms.' I had forgotten that Annie, like many Americans, doesn't deal in irony, and soon found myself on a compulsory tour of her many indoor bathrooms, each duly equipped with a shower and hot and cold running water.

I love the story – too good and plausible, I hope, to be apocryphal – of Annie and Eli waking up one morning in a Rome hotel to the ringing of the telephone. I have never known two harder-working or more consistently employed actors, and on this occasion Eli was completing one film when his agent had called with news of yet another Mafia godfather to be played in a Hollywood mini-series right away. 'You really wanna do that?' said Annie sleepily.

'No,' said Eli, 'but I gotta go for it.'

'You don't,' said Annie. 'You've worked every hour God made since we met. We now have enough money to live out the rest of our lives, and leave all the kids well provided.'

Eli, however, has never believed anything of the sort, and remains convinced, even after sixty years at the head of his profession, that a pauper's grave could well still await him. Annie decided she had to do something to convince him of his wealth so, uncharacteristically, she went out into Rome and bought herself a floor-length mink coat, then returned to the hotel to show Eli what they could indeed afford. 'Jesus, God,' said Eli, and reached for his agent's number. 'I gotta get to Hollywood right away. I gotta pay for that damn coat.'

The filming of *The Journey* finally ended with Robert, commendably straight-faced, delivering such memorable hokum as 'These Hungarians . . . we always thought them a bunch of gypsy fiddlers, and now they've taught the world a lesson in courage it will never forget.' The film also went in for massed peasants revolting and the Red Army, led by Yul on horseback, in sexy black leather.

Its best moment for me came on the afternoon they were shooting the final sequence. In this, Deborah had to escape the clutches of the evil Brynner and run down a hill, conveniently crossing the border into Austria, to where Jason would be waiting for her with open arms as the credits rolled.

That afternoon, however, Robards, as was his wont, had enjoyed a rather liquid lunch. Back on his marks to start the escape shot, he looked up and saw Deborah, quite a large lady, hurtling downhill towards him at full speed. Very slowly, while she was still several feet away, he fell over backwards into the snow and lay there immobile. It wasn't quite the ending Litvak had in mind and is, alas, nowhere to be seen in the final cut.

15
How Not To Be a Schoolmaster

Home from the Vienna Woods, I presented myself once again to a still wearier Robert Levens at Merton. By now, however, I was equipped with Harry's intensive education, the impressive-looking scroll from Geneva University, a couple of A levels and the missing O levels in Latin and Maths, which I had picked up with surprisingly little difficulty after a few months in Kensington High Street.

Looking as surprised as I was, Levens admitted that this might now be enough to scrape me a place at the college from the autumn term of 1960, which I think he called Michaelmas. He added that I would, of course, be subject to an interview, but that he had noted I appeared to have little difficulty in expressing myself – his implication being that, if anything, I had *too* little difficulty with that particular skill.

But we were still only hovering around Christmas 1959. I went home to my parents and announced proudly that I was to be the first member of my family ever to get into a university. Ma was suitably impressed, my brother and sister seemed unconcerned, but Robert was less than thrilled. In his view all education was a waste of time, and that I would voluntarily subject myself to three extra years of it seemed unfathomable. I would remain, he forecast gloomily, three years behind all my non-collegiate contemporaries for the rest of my life.

The only other time my father and I disagreed was over my divorce, and I fear we shall be getting on to that in due course. In all fairness, this was an especially difficult, dark time for my parents, not that they ever let us children in on the secret. The problem was my uncle John, Gladys's beloved and handsome only son, born in 1915 during her first marriage to my grandfather Herbert Buckmaster, and therefore Ma's younger brother.

Johnnie had grown up a golden boy, good-looking beyond even Gladys's wildest dreams, and an Eton scholar. He had been barely five at the time of his parents' divorce, and lacked the courage with which my mother had determined to make her own life and not have it disturbed by parental failure or inadequacy. Indeed, it was Ma who, after her parents separated, was largely responsible for bringing up Johnnie and taking good care of him, even though she was barely five years older.

But from the outset Johnnie was deeply disturbed, and this was at a time when psychiatry was still largely untried and untrusted in Britain, as were most chemical solutions to the schizoid condition. In retrospect it is clear that he had suffered from it virtually all his life. When it started is still a matter for conjecture: after Eton he set out to be an actor and a cabaret star, with a triumphant 1930s nightclub act as a mimic. He was, perhaps, haunted, though, by the fame of a distant and much-married but still dominant mother, and a military father who could hardly be expected to have approved of his choice of a showbiz life.

Modern analysis would probably suggest that Johnnie failed in his own desire to impress and live up to the conflicting demands of his parents, but there was a worse problem. In the mid-1930s he fell passionately in love, for the first and only time in his life, with Vivien Leigh, already at the end of her own first marriage to Leigh Holman. For a few magical months they were inseparable. Photographs of the era show them at nightclub tables and first-night parties, each as gorgeous as the other, one of the first of the golden couples. But then Vivien began work on a film with Laurence Olivier, and overnight Johnnie was ruthlessly cut out of her life. He never recovered from losing her, and spent the rest of the 1930s roaming aimlessly across America doing a little intermittent stage or nightclub work, but no longer focused on anything except his loss.

Then came his season with Pa in *Oscar Wilde*, and soon after that the war. Johnnie and his half-brother Jack Merivale, whom G had adopted as a step-son and who, ironically, lived with Vivien Leigh for the last ten years of her life, joined the Canadian Air Force. Johnnie had been only recently at the Algonquin in New York, doing a successful season in cabaret, but was under pressure from his father Buck to come home and fight like a man; G suggested the softer option of acting in California. His choosing to join the Canadians was a third way, but it soon became clear that he was mentally in no state to fight other people, and the rest of Johnnie's war was uneventful, ending up with Gladys, as she had always hoped, acting in a California and New York revival of *Lady Windermere's Fan*, which also featured Jack and, interestingly, Cecil Beaton – his only stage appearance.

In these post-war years, Johnnie's uncertain mental state of highs and lows was all too evident to everyone except my grandmother – who until the day she died resolutely refused to acknowledge that anything was wrong with her darling son – and, of course, unobservant little me. I vaguely remember thinking that my uncle seemed at times a little hysterical and moody, but in our family that was nothing new or unusual.

True, there had been one terrible occasion when David Niven called on Vivien Leigh, in one of her most disturbed Hollywood moments just after the war, to find her and Johnnie, both naked, locked into a California beach-house with nothing but several empty pill and vodka bottles for company, and making no sense. Niven got them through that particular crisis without any adverse publicity, sending for Larry from London to sort out the mess, as he was still Viv's husband. But the shit truly hit the fan early in 1952: Johnnie had just finished a successful Broadway run as the

Dauphin in Bernard Shaw's *Saint Joan*, and Gladys was in England restoring her career with the success of Nöel Coward's *Relative Values*. One cold February night, Johnnie had the worst and most violent of all his manic episodes: he fired an illegally owned gun into the windows of Saks Fifth Avenue. Luckily the shop was closed and there were few pedestrians on the snowy street. He was arrested and charged with felonious assault, as well as the illegal possession of two knives, which he was alleged to have brandished at the Manhattan cops as they were trying to pin him to the sidewalk.

Naturally the story ran in the English press and for Gladys, having to play a light comedy every night five thousand miles away from her golden boy, the strain must have been immense. She and Johnnie's father Buck, now reunited half a century or so after their bitter divorce, refused to countenance the concept of mental illness, least of all in their only son.

But for Noël Coward, in New York on his way to his regular winter home in Jamaica, the problem was more immediate: Johnnie had been committed by the police to the Bellevue Hospital for the Mentally Insane, a nightmarish Manhattan snake-pit where, as Noël realised at once, he might easily be killed or maimed by another loony inmate. To their considerable credit, and with no help from either Gladys or Buck, Noël with Jack Merivale and the ever-supportive Adrianne Allen got Johnnie out of trouble and Bellevue, by promising that he would leave the country immediately, never to return.

Back in London, Gladys reluctantly came to terms with what had happened to her son. As she wrote to Noël in Jamaica, 'I shall never forget, nor cease to be deeply, deeply grateful to you for all you have done. I am torn with anxiety and heartbroken by the knowledge of the unhappiness of my beloved John, but the Countess in your play is as merry as a grig eight performances a week . . . laugh, clown, laugh.'

And her acknowledgement of Johnnie's 'unhappiness' was the nearest that she came in her long life to admitting that she had a schizophrenic son. He spent the rest of his life in and out of the Priory in Roehampton, and other less salubrious psychiatric and nursing homes, usually in a heavily drugged state. By the time psychiatry in Britain caught up with Johnnie's condition, he was past caring, and had been so heavily sedated for so many years that he hardly responded.

During the 1950s, when the drugs were working, he was allowed out for family weekends, and I recall this infinitely charming, still wonderfully good-looking man wandering vaguely around the house as if he had somehow mislaid his glasses rather than his mind. Occasionally the pills wore off unexpectedly, and I have a distant memory of Johnnie charging down the corridor of some Brighton hotel, naked and clutching a carving-knife, while we were there on tour with Pa and a new play.

But that, too, escaped the attention even of the *Brighton Argus*, and the curious thing was that I don't think any of us found it especially frightening or even alarming: we were used to Johnnie and his odd ways, and only sorry that we couldn't be of much help. Sadly, although he remained on good terms with my parents, and brought us children line-drawings and water-colours of considerable talent, he refused resolutely to be reunited with his parents, whom he blamed for not dealing better with his condition.

Then, not long after Gladys died, Johnnie, who had seemed so peaceful for years with the drugs, found a knife and fatally cut both his wrists. He was dead before they found him, and not yet seventy.

How do you follow that? As usual in these memoirs: remain infuriatingly cheerful, and wonder vaguely if there was anything more that my immediate family could have done for him, and decide, on balance, probably not. For most of his life my mother was his guardian angel, and in the thirty years since she ended it she has scarcely mentioned his name, at least not to me. It's how we all survive, I guess, and there are many worse ways, several of which I seem at some point in my life to have explored before returning to base. 'The trouble with your family is that none of you seem to have any feelings,' said my second wife – 'present wife' would seem to tempt Fate. Oh, but we do, my darling, we do. It's just that we don't always trust them, and certainly not in mixed company.

Back to me in 1960, and an unusual problem: I had virtually the whole year to fill in, since the Oxford acceptance had come in December for the following October. At first, I decided to drift around in London: this was, after all, supposed to be the start of a new era of liberation, and I had the great good fortune to hang out with Robin, his wife Angela and what Lillian Hellman had already called the Little Foxes. You will now know them as the actors Edward and James and their brother Robert, an impresario of considerable talent and caution, but when I first knew them it was because of Robin, to whom you've been introduced, and Angela, whose two great claims to fame were that she was the daughter of the real-life Mrs Worthington in Noël's celebrated song, and Frederick Lonsdale the playwright. Shortly before the war she had married Robin, who went on to win the MC and become the most influential agent and fixer of his time. He it was who guided my father's post-war career as well as a host of others, from Paul Scofield's to Vanessa Redgrave's. My father was never quite the same after Robin died far too young of a particularly terrible bone cancer.

Robin was also chronically unfaithful, and perhaps the first man in Britain to be caught out by television. His wife Angela was attending a Harrow cricket match featuring her boys; Robin as usual had pleaded pressure of office work. The headmaster of the day, rather fancying Angela and knowing she secretly preferred tennis to cricket, told her of a television set in his study on which she could surreptitiously watch a good Wimbledon final. As she tuned in, the camera was panning around the Royal Box, and there Angela saw her beloved husband sitting next to Princess Marina of Kent, in such a way that she knew at once with whom Robin was currently being unfaithful to her.

The Foxes were a family like us who believed that least said soonest mended, and I spent some happy weekends with them, at their home in Cuckfield and also in Robin's London pad, conveniently situated at the corner of Burlington and Clifford Streets. Robin, Pa and Ros Chatto had their theatre management offices there too.

Given that Robert, the littlest Fox, was still at school, his elder brothers and I must have made an odd-looking trio as we roamed central London in search of something to do; the two tall, indescribably elegant old Harrovians and the rather sweaty, ungainly third party whom, for some kindly reason, they had decided to take under their well-dressed wings. Eddie and Willy – he changed his name to James on entering the acting profession and finding that there was already an established character actor called William Fox – were both, I think, destined then for the Guards rather than acting. They had managed to get what would now be called a vacation job serving as junior floorwalkers in Fortnum and Mason – a department store legendary to me for the morning on which the redoubtable Australian actress Coral Browne had walked in to be greeted by the floor manager: 'And what might be Madam's pleasure this morning?'

'Well, dearie, my pleasure would be a good fuck, but I've actually come in for a pound of grapes.'

The reason I remember Eddie and Willy at Fortnum's is that I used to go and meet them there after work. One evening around Christmas, we were all laden with Christmas shopping, and I suddenly found myself carrying all of their parcels as well as my own. 'You see, old boy,' drawled Eddie, 'my brother and I might be about to join the Guards, and Guards officers, as I'm sure you know, are never allowed to be seen carrying parcels in a public place.'

To my fascination and infinite jealousy, both the bigger Little Foxes were now enviably romantically involved – Eddie, as I recall, with the gorgeously long-legged Tracy Reed, and Willy with the young Sarah Miles, with whom, of course, he was to co-star in the film that made their names, *The Servant*. Conventional wisdom has it that Willy-James's next film, the Mick Jagger/Nick Roeg *Performance*, drove him into a world of drugs, from which he escaped into the clutches of the Mariners and several years as a door-to-door religious-books salesman. I have always had an alternative theory, though untested on Willy himself, that the trouble started for him rather earlier, around the time of *The Servant*, when it was reasonably obvious to all of us that Dirk Bogarde and Sarah Miles were both deeply in love with him, and that his father had more than a passing interest in Sarah too. Trying to sort out that little lot would surely have been enough to send anyone into the arms of God. Especially if you were also working with Joe Losey as a director and Harold Pinter as a screenwriter.

I have been lucky enough to stay reasonably close to all the Little Foxes, even though I have had to review them and, inevitably, not always favourably; but I am still haunted by their late father, and by the manner of his death. He was struck down far too early in what had seemed a charmed and relatively carefree life, at the height of his powers, soon after he had effectively created from behind the scenes both the Grade Organisation and the English Stage Society within which George Devine built his revolutionary Royal Court in 1956. Robin had always known how to hunt with the hares and ride with the hounds, without ever losing his seat and always dressed appropriately.

Early in the spring of 1970, while Pa was beginning to work on one of his greatest hits, the Alan Ayckbourn comedy *How the Other Half Loves*, Robin appeared in his dressing room looking haggard. Pa wrote,

As always, I was reassured and happy to be in my old friend's company, and we managed the ritual bonhomie and drank the usual champagne, blissfully unaware of the impending catastrophe. Somehow, though, he didn't seem himself, and a few days later I was to learn that my trusted friend and manager had terminal cancer. The shadow of his approaching death made life suddenly so very much colder for us all. In the evenings, after rehearsals, I would drive down to the King Edward Hospital at Midhurst for a picnic in his bedroom, bearing caviare and champagne and curious mousses from Fortnum's and drinking the champagne by his bedside. I don't think it helped him very much, but in times of crisis I find extravagance often helps me. Late one evening, I left him and walked along the corridor to where a nurse sat at a table, writing reports on her patients. 'I'm off now,' I told her unnecessarily. 'I gather the news on Mr Fox is rather good; they haven't found anything sinister.' She didn't answer for a moment. I had caught her, I suppose, off guard. Into her eyes came a look of disbelief, instantly checked by professional caution. 'Oh, yes,' she said. 'Mr Fox is really doing very well.' I never again had any hope at all.

But once again we are getting ahead of ourselves. Some time early in 1960, hanging around Fortnum and Mason waiting for the Little Foxes to finish their shift, fantasising that one day a book of mine would be stacked up all over the windows of the neighbouring Hatchard's – a fantasy that came true ten years later, and never has again – I noticed just across the road a curious sign: GABBITAS & THRING, it read, EDUCATIONAL ADVISERS. Something, sheer curiosity, I suppose, led me to climb the stairs to a Dickensian office presided over by a lady in spectacles, who bore a remarkable resemblance to Joyce Grenfell in the then-current St Trinian's movies.

'I happen to have a little time to spare before Oxford,' I heard myself say, 'and wondered if perhaps I could do a little supply teaching?'

The Grenfell lady looked at me doubtfully. 'You can prove you're going up to Oxford in the autumn?'

'Oh, yes,' I said proudly. 'I have it in writing from Dr Levens of Merton College.'

She seemed surprised, but impressed. 'In that case, there is nothing to stop you taking employment for the summer term as a junior master in a boys' preparatory school. In fact I have just the one for you, the Prebendal in Chichester, twelve pounds a week. You start at the end of April.'

Before she could change her mind I hurried back into Piccadilly, there proudly to tell the Little Foxes that, although I might have failed to land either Sarah Miles or Tracy Reed or a job in Fortnum's, I was now a prep-school master in Sussex. They seemed disappointingly unimpressed, and my father was little short of horrified that a child of his would actually wish to join the enemy *and* take its shilling. I, on the other hand, had discovered for the first time in my life that I was employable, and it was something of a relief.

The Prebendal School in Chichester stands in the cloisters of the magnificent cathedral, and I arrived in the nick of time for a quiet revolution. In the early 1960s British prep schools, especially those attached to venerable cathedrals and run by them, were not in the forefront of educational reform. Little seemed to have changed in those quiet, sheltered cloisters since Trollope had begun documenting them a century or so earlier.

But behind the scenes, change was indeed in the chalky air. At our first staff meeting, the headmaster, a cleric and possibly even a relic of the cathedral, began handing out the term's duties. Most of the staff were unbelievably ancient but, apart from me, there was one young junior master who seemed to have been born at some time within the current century.

'You, young man,' said the head, 'will, of course, be in charge of weekend games.'

'I fear not, Headmaster,' he replied.

There was a pause, which seemed to last for weeks.

'I beg your pardon?'

'I don't do weekends, sir. My wife and I are only recently married, and we have a young son. I intend to go home at weekends and look after my own child rather than other people's.'

It was a world-changing moment: suddenly we had a new young professional in our midst and the others, all apparently willing to abandon their private lives for three months at a time, had met their match. Years later, when my son was born and I had been bullied by the Catholic Mafia in Boston (where his mother and I had married) into agreeing that our children would all go to Catholic schools, I began to explore the possibilities of the same kind of change with the headmaster of Douai Abbey. 'I think,' I said nervously, 'that not being Catholic myself I would quite like to come and get my son every weekend and bring him home, just to make sure that he is, well, still my son.' The thought might have been 'not being interfered with by the monks' but that seemed a little irreverent, not to say sacrilegious. The old headmaster was appalled at first by the idea of these weekly returns home, but as various other parents followed my example, the school staff slowly became aware of the magical possibilities of weekly boarding, which I had inadvertently opened up for them. If all the parents could be persuaded to take their children away on Saturday mornings and not return them till Sunday nights they, too, could have a decent weekend's break. In all my puff – another favourite phrase of my godfather Peter Bull – I have never been responsible for any other piece of social engineering in which I could take more legitimate pride. Almost alone, I brought the concept of free weekends to the staff and pupils of one now-defunct boys' Catholic public school near Reading, where at least one monk was later charged with child molesting.

I can't say that either I or my son was surprised. I have

always taken the view that it is hard enough to bring up one's own children, so why on earth would one take on the children of others, unless there was some sort of other benefit?

At the Prebendal, I hasten to add, there was nothing queer going on – or, at least, if there was, it escaped my attention. Mind you, a good deal escaped my attention: I had never properly appreciated until then just how devious, brilliant and subversive a group of twenty or so ten-year-olds can be, especially when they sniff the blood of an untrained newcomer. *Lord of the Flies* was my bedside reading, Evelyn Waugh's Captain Foulenough my new hero, and I became rapidly obsessed by one of the late Giles Cooper's best radio plays, *Unman, Wittering and Zigo*, in which the last three boys on the alphabetical school register come to ghastly ends. Giles himself died, mysteriously and tragically, soon after writing that play by falling out of a fast-moving train, and I have always vaguely suspected that a very small boy was around to give him the fatal shove.

I am proud to report that nobody died during my term in charge of the juniors at the Prebendal, and a surprising number of the older ones even passed Common Entrance for which, quite wrongly, I took much of the credit. Three months passed in a haze of Sussex town-and-country life, of which I remember best the morning when a local oculist, Leslie Evershed-Martin, came into the staff room to find me. 'You're an actor's son, Morley, here's a collecting box. Go round the school and ask every boy to contribute sixpence to the theatre I intend to build in that field up by the roundabout.'

This was, I remind you, 1960, and the idea that Chichester could build itself a theatre on the sixpences of schoolboys, even assuming I could get the little beasts to part with them, seemed laughably idiotic. Luckily I didn't laugh, and we collected a respectable number of sixpences. It transpired that Evershed-Martin had seen a television programme in which Kenneth Tynan and Tyrone Guthrie, two of my all-time heroes, had walked around a theatre Guthrie had recently built in a relative Canadian backwater, Stratford, Ontario. What Guthrie could do in Ontario, Evershed-Martin reckoned he could do in West Sussex, and within three years the Festival Theatre was up and running, with Laurence Olivier as its first director. He, too, had said yes to Evershed-Martin, and within another year Larry had been offered the ultimate prize, directorship of the National Theatre. It is one of the lesser-noted historical truths of the twentieth-century British stage that, were it not for a Chichester oculist with no previous theatrical connection, we might still be awaiting a National Theatre, since it was only while Larry was at Chichester that the London company was finally established at the Old Vic.

16
A Merton Man

My last pre-Oxford summer was spent lazing around the Thames Valley and going on the overnight sleeper from Victoria to discover Spain with Peter Young and his splendidly theatrical grandmother, who taught us how to order champagne cocktails with sugar or salt around the rim of the glass, and staying for a week at Stratford where, in one amazing season, it was possible to see Olivier, Charles Laughton, Paul Robeson, Edith Evans, Sam Wanamaker and young hopefuls such as Albert Finney and Vanessa Redgrave, all on the same Shakespearian stage and often in the same production. It was the starriest of summers by the Avon, and I was there thanks to another star of the company, Robert Hardy, who had recently married my aunt Sally. Staying with them in a cottage just outside the town, I got up one morning to find a single glass eye staring at me balefully from the basin in the bathroom. It was one of the most frightening moments of my life, until I remembered that the veteran actor Esmond Knight was also staying in the cottage, and had lost one of his eyes in the wartime sinking of HMS *Hood*.

Merton College, Oxford, October 1960: season of fog and mellow fruitfulness, mist swirling across Christ Church Meadows, cobbled streets, dons in long black gowns, undergraduates on bicycles two by two, punting on the Cam – or was that Cambridge, and haven't we, anyway, done all this? If not, someone else almost certainly has, probably John Betjeman, or Max Beerbohm.

I was thrilled to be there, even though I only knew about three people: the don Robert Levens, who had steered me safely into his college, my old Sizewell friend Richard Burlingham, who went up to Pembroke that term, and my distant cousin Sarah Quennell, who was selling secondhand books at a shop in the Turl. She and I also had another distant cousin at Balliol, Gerald Cadogan, who later became a distinguished archaeological journalist on the *Financial Times*.

I also knew Peter Young, of course, who went up that term to University College, but this brief spell was about the only time in our adult lives when he and I were less than friends. A year or so earlier, I had fallen in love with a gorgeously English girl called Jill Norwood, whom I'd met through Bay Kirkbride in Long Crendon. It was, I think for both of us, a first serious – although, in those cautious days, not strictly sexual – affair and when it broke up, as these things do when you are seventeen or so, I was not made any happier by the fact that she moved on to Peter. Idiotically I had introduced them. It says something, I guess, that Jill and I are godparents to each other's eldest children, and although we meet too seldom, whenever we do I can always remember with absolute clarity the good times and then the heartbreak when she left me. Looking back, our affair – if you can call it that – seems to have been conducted almost entirely on railway stations and foggy winter nights, with one or other of us always *en route* to somewhere else on the Southern Region, changing at Reading or possibly Basingstoke. It wasn't quite *Brief Encounter*, or Trevor Howard and Celia Johnson, but I always thought we came damn close. Especially considering we were only teenagers.

But the new thrill of Oxford made even the break-up almost bearable, and it didn't take me long to grasp that I had ended up, by luck rather than judgement, in the perfect college. Although still famous for its oarsmen, Merton had developed a strong line in college and university theatre: the actor Oliver Ford-Davies, and the director, Sam Walters, later and still of the Orange Tree, Richmond, were running Floats, the college drama society. In my year there were two other entrants, Jo

Durden-Smith and Brian Winston: Jo became a distinguished journalist with strong Soviet connections and a gorgeous Russian wife, Brian a flamboyant and pioneering professor of film and journalism here and in America. Both were also defiantly stage-struck. Among the senior fellows, Nevill Coghill and Hugo Dyson were two magical eccentrics who gave the impression that they had only narrowly missed going on the stage themselves. Nevill was directing student summer productions well into his seventies, while Hugo, after whom I named my only son, played the old don visited by Dirk Bogarde and Julie Christie in *Darling*, a film made by John Schlesinger, another Merton man who had been taught by Dyson.

I was also more than lucky that my first-year college roommate was a tough, brusque and very funny north-countryman called Roger Laughton, later to rise through the ranks of BBC and Meridian ITV management to a media professorship at Southampton; although he had a healthy distrust of us theatricals, he went on to edit the university newspaper *Cherwell* and gave me my first regular columns as a film and theatre critic – for which, until this moment, I have never thanked him.

There were other Merton men – it was to be at least another twenty years before the college began to take in women and, indeed, a female Warden – of my generation who, shamefully, I can scarcely remember meeting there at all. This was perhaps because, as soon as was practical, I took to living in the Oxford Playhouse, either acting or just watching Frank Hauser's professional company, which included Sean Connery and Diane Cilento, in rehearsal and performance. It was therefore only in later years that I discovered that around the college quadrangles in my time were Robert Scott, later knighted for failing heroically to get the Olympic Games into Manchester, Howard Stringer, who became one of the most powerful figures in American television, and David Wood, the actor and children's playwright.

But it was in Brian Winston's rooms that I spent most

of my student time, for reasons that, as so often in my life, were closely connected with food. Brian's loving North London family took the view that the Merton catering system, which dated back to the thirteenth century or thereabouts, was scarcely enough to keep a good Jewish boy going. They arrived most weekends with a selection of kosher treats, which also kept me and several other near-starving Mertonians going. Unversed in kosher practices, however, I took to buttering bread with knives that had also seen meat, whereupon Brian would throw the offending cutlery out of the window, thus giving visiting American tourists the idea that the college housed a demented professional knife-thrower.

It was also in Brian's rooms, during my first Oxford year, that I met an enchantingly vivacious fifteen-year-old schoolfriend of his, Ruth Leon. Brian had taken on her personal education, but when you are eighteen and someone else is fifteen, you really belong to different generations. Now that I am sixty and Ruth is fifty-seven and we have been married for a decade, the age gap seems mysteriously to have vanished.

At this time, my father was also getting into catering diffi-culties: he and the redoubtable actress Molly Picon, for many years a leader of the Yiddish Theater in New York, were appearing together in the West End in a curious east-west comedy called *A Majority of One*, which was set at least partially in Japan. Their director, Wendy Toye, decided they should therefore be at least vaguely acquainted with the complexities of Japanese eating, and duly arranged a visit to the Japanese embassy in London. There they had been served the raw fish and were about to start on the tea ceremony when the ambassador enquired rashly of Miss Picon what she would like to follow. 'Just a very good doctor,' came the reply, and they were rapidly ushered out.

Most of my first two terms at Merton were spent unchar-acteristically working, and working very hard. The problem was this: if you only had one modern language – two was the usual minimum – they liked to punish you right away, so you had to spend two agonising terms studying Latin. Once you had managed that, and passed an Easter exam called Prelims, you could forget all about the Latin for ever, and spend the next two and a half blissful years doing nothing but French, which entailed about half the academic workload of any other Oxford student.

So, still watched over by Levens, I did six months of Latin, the only six months I ever actually studied in college; after that, when it came to French – a subject for which Merton disdained in those days to keep a tutor on the premises, which is probably how I got in – you were 'farmed out' to an amiable if uncharismatic professor in Keble, where they seemed to take in stray students rather as if we were bags of washing.

Once over the Latin hurdle, I discovered what I really wanted to do with my Oxford life, and that, of course, was to spend as much of it as possible in rehearsal. I started cautiously with one or two purely college productions, then joined the OUDS and made my début for them at the Oxford Playhouse as a spear-carrier in the Pirandello *Henry IV*. David Senton was in the title role: he was perhaps the best actor of my Oxford generation but decided nevertheless, as did Peter Young who was also a fine student player, that it was not likely to be a safe profession for later life. Luckily his son Oliver has inherited the paternal talent and taken to the stage.

Backstage at the Playhouse, I began to make the friends among the Oxford acting community who were to stay with me not just for our undergraduate terms but, in most cases, for the rest of my life. Also cast in that production was the actor and now concert singer John Watts, later to appear in a shortlived West End musical called *Troubadour*, which for some reason was financed largely by the Japanese. 'First Pearl Harbor,' I am ashamed to admit my *Punch* review began, 'and now this . . .' They opened shortly before one Christmas, and closed just after New Year, a run of about a fortnight, but on

1 January John had the wit to send me a postcard reading 'John Watts in *Troubadour*. Now in our second year.' He and I, and Annabel Leventon, have reunited in 2002 after forty years to revive my old *Noël & Gertie* on stage in London and the South of France – there is a lot to be said for old friends playing old friends.

Troubadour was set during the Crusades, and at one moment there was a battle scene involving arrows and a lot of dry ice. To fill out the crowd of extras, some students had been recruited from RADA, and told to ad-lib some suitably period comments. A Home Counties girl, complete with wimple and veil, happened to be standing downstage near where I was sitting in the stalls: 'These Crusades,' she said, in pained tones as yet another arrow whizzed past her through the dry ice, 'are spreading like wildfire.'

Also in *Henry IV* was Nigel Frith, the only one of us who has never left Oxford in the intervening forty years, save when his revolutionary musical version of *Hamlet* – complete with an unusually happy ending in which the Ghost returns to take Hamlet up to heaven – became a standing-room-only triumph all over Japan, with a noted Japanese female pop star in the lead. Nigel still lives by himself in what was the family home in Old Headington, writes epic Greek verse, teaches at one of the colleges and has filled his home with his own Gothic paintings, which, did I not know him and love him, I think I would assume were the early work of a serial killer.

From *Henry IV* at the Playhouse, which the university had conveniently just bought, thereby allowing us the run of the place during term-time, I went straight into the OUDS summer 'major', a revival of *The Shoemaker's Holiday* in the open air of Wadham College garden. There I made such other friends as Neil Stacy, a fine character actor, Richard Clayson and Andrew Garrett who, until Clayson's sadly early death, built harpsichords in partnership, Rupert Rhymes, who for many years was the taciturn power behind the throne of the Society of West End Theatre Managers, and above all Christopher Matthew, with whom I seem to have spent most of the rest of my life.

Chris and I went through several Oxford productions together, never taking them as seriously as we should, and hoping for the kind of small but flashy roles that would not entail too many arduous rehearsals, and would allow us to nip off to the pub or, better, the local Indian restaurant when not required onstage.

I find it oddly hard to remember Chris as anything but the man I still see almost every week and sometimes more often than that. After Oxford he, like me, did a little light teaching at a Swiss finishing school, went into advertising then out of it, made his name as the author of the Simon Crisp books and radio broadcasts, wrote several television scripts and finished up with the 200,000-copy bestseller we all dream about, in his case an A.A. Milne update called *Now We Are Sixty*.

Godfathers to each other's eldest children, now cautiously moving into grandfatherhood, co-conspirators in a lifetime of trying to make others pay us to do what we would probably have done anyway, Chris and I have always seemed to me so alike in our increasingly irritable and bemused attitude to the world around us that I am always a little shocked when others remark on our differences: Chris is gently religious, a novelist, a writer of television comedy and drama, none of which describes me at all. Yet I kind of know what we are going to like or dislike, almost before either of us gets round to reading or seeing it. What we share, I suppose, and have shared since Oxford, is a vague guilt that we have never quite got to grips with the times through which we have lived. He is into John Betjeman the way I have always been into Noël Coward, and there lingers at the back of our minds the idea that we might have been happier and more easily employable if we had been born into their pre-war world.

But we weren't, of course, and even had we been, I doubt

we'd have done much better. We are temperamentally misfit time-travellers, and the miracle is that we have found partners and children and even employers who manage to put up with us, even if we must often appear to them to be living on some other planet. And the good thing about all of that is, it gets better as you get older: an increasingly youth-oriented world now expects people like us of sixty or so to be a little dotty, and hard of hearing, and grumpy about what's on television, so who are we to disappoint them? Chris now writes a television column for the *Daily Mail*, a perfect space in which to sound off about the kind of people who appear on the small screen these days unless, of course, it's us playing daft daytime panel games with Alan Coren, or in my case filling up time in yet another instant tele-biog of some long-dead movie star.

And that was just the men. Also around the OUDS at this time (though not yet granted full membership – that would only come in Maria Aitken's generation a year or two later) were the actress Annabel Leventon, whom forty years later I had the joy of directing in a couple of Noël Coward plays at Jermyn Street; Joan Shenton, an enchanting actress and singer with strong South American connections who later ran an impressive medical television company; and the equally gorgeous Nancy Lane, who went on to become a Cambridge professor of science and an adviser to several prime ministers. I have always thought of her as a Canadian dancer with the best legs in the business, but I guess that's what you get for being time-locked. It has only just occurred to me that another elegant and distinguished Cambridge science professor, Mary Archer, now takes to the musical stage from time to time to sing with Kit and the Widow. There must be a thesis in there somewhere about Cambridge and scientific cabaret, especially if you also include Tom Lehrer at Harvard.

But in 1960 Oxford was still an overwhelmingly male university: no men's college – and they still outnumbered the female colleges by about twenty to five – yet took in women, and there was a curious generation gap. Those born in my year, 1941, were the first not to have been called up for national service, which meant that undergraduates a year ahead of us were often almost three years older, and therefore vastly more experienced; the memory of campaigns in Aden, Suez and Cyprus, where a near-contemporary, Auberon Waugh, had accidentally just shot himself in the chest, was still comparatively raw.

Moreover, the concept of the gap year was unknown, and many in my first year had come up straight from the sixth form to collide uneasily with men just back from firing at the overseas foe. Our time was also almost exactly that of John F. Kennedy in the White House – he was elected in the winter just before we all went up, and assassinated in the autumn immediately after we went down: the 1962 Cuban missile crisis was the outstanding political event of our Oxford years, unless you count the Profumo affair, which erupted during our last term, suitably enough in 1963 when, according to Philip Larkin, sex had only just begun with the coming of the Beatles.

Wildly apolitical as always, I dimly recall hearing of the Cuban missile crisis backstage at the Oxford Playhouse on a crackling radio during a matinée: young Americans, we were told, were heading for the Canadian border to avoid the draft, but that seemed a long way to go, and somehow I couldn't visualise Cubans sailing up the Thames in gunboats. So I carried on with the matinée, and have been rightly accused ever since of total detachment from the political world around me.

For a university that has, shamefully, to this day never allowed itself a drama department, Oxford was still, in my time, rich in actors; and, which was new, we also had some strong directors. Until recently, in the generation of Trevor Nunn and Peter Hall, that had been a uniquely Cambridge stronghold. But we could now boast two of world class:

Braham Murray, who went on to run the Manchester Royal Exchange for many years, and Michael Rudman, implausibly the son of a Texan oil millionaire, who ran Nottingham, the Traverse and Hampstead, and was Peter Hall's deputy at the National for several seasons, before establishing a strong free-lance career in the West End and marrying Felicity Kendal.

These were also, of course, the years of the satire boom: every Saturday night we would gather in the Junior Common Room at Merton to watch with amazement *That Was the Week That Was*, which mocked everything our parents and tutors held sacred. Most afternoons, after his history tutorials, Alan Bennett could be seen in his duffel coat trudging down to Oxford station to catch the London train for another performance of *Beyond the Fringe*, while his co-star Dudley Moore could still be heard from time to time playing jazz on a Sunday night in one of the colleges or the city's only real nightclub, a pub cellar just off Carfax.

Even I was dimly aware that there were other Oxford lives going on, but none of them seemed especially academic. The Union was the centre of all political activity, though I am ashamed to say I never joined, while the river was where you would find most other Mertonians in mid-training. Journalism flourished as never before, and I recently found in my mother's attic a prophetic edition of *Isis* from some time in 1963, one which hailed Peter Jay, Jonathan Aitken and Jeffrey Archer as future stars.

It took several years for us to realise that ours was an incredibly privileged generation: unlike our predecessors we had fought no real wars, suffered no long-term unemploy-ment, and even university grants were readily available and unrepayable. The colleges seemed then to operate a different system of student intake: now they go for the brightest and the best academically, but then they appeared to be trying to build a series of little village communities – every year they mixed academics with oarsmen, scientists with would-be politicians, locals with immigrants, the state-educated with public-school boys, in the hope of getting a real social mix across the university.

Sometimes the mix failed to work, and élitist or exclusionary groups remained just that: my great good fortune was that, educated somewhat eccentrically at home and abroad, I came from no recognisable social or academic background, and was therefore able to drift around the colleges owing no special loyalties of class or background to anyone.

My love life was also looking up: in the Taylorian, a curious building conveniently just across the road from the Playhouse where modern-language students from all over the university could find a library and occasional lectures, I fell in with a gorgeous French-Armenian girl called Francelle Carapetjan, and we spent several happy afternoons watching romantic French *nouvelle vague* movies in the two thriving arthouse cinemas around the city, the Scala and the Moulin Rouge.

While the Playhouse in my time became an increasingly student stronghold, presided over by its professional general manager Elizabeth Sweeting who patiently taught us the fundamentals of running a theatre, the larger New Theatre (now the Apollo) was still a number-one touring date, through which professional companies passed on their way into or out of the West End. Thanks to my parentage, there was usually someone I knew in the cast or backstage: when not required at the Playhouse, I could nip across to the New to see how the grown-ups put on plays – with rather larger budgets than any we ever had at the Playhouse.

Thus it was that I achieved a theatrical education and training at a university that had not intended to offer anything of the kind. What I learnt, somewhat painfully, at the Playhouse was that I wasn't cut out to be an actor. In any case, I had already decided that that would be a no-win situation: if, implausibly, I was to do well, critics would assume it was because of my parental background. If, on the other hand, I did badly, they would be surprised that I hadn't inherited the family gift.

But I now knew that theatre was all I was any good at, because it was all I understood. I began writing local-paper Oxford reviews, and occasionally got one into *The Times* – bylined in those days 'From Our Special Correspondent' – which made me feel as good about myself as I ever had. Even when I couldn't get into print, I found that in pubs, restaurants and college common rooms I could talk about theatre far more lucidly than I could about anything else, and fellow students were occasionally inclined to take my advice as to whether the current play at the New or the Playhouse was really worth buying a ticket for.

I had been up at Merton for almost a year when, sheltering in the lodge from a particularly vicious rainstorm, I found myself next to the elderly Warden, whom I had never met but now felt obliged to address in some politely social way. 'Very wet out this afternoon, Warden,' I ventured.

There was a lengthy, almost Pinteresque pause. 'All communication with the Warden of this college, young man,' he eventually responded, 'must be in writing.'

All the same, I got to know him a little better in the ensuing terms, and I was the one chosen to break the news to the old boy that one of his junior professors at the college had just run away with the cook. 'Tell him gently,' I was told, 'or this could be the cardiac arrest.' I tapped on his study door and broke the news as gently as possible.

There was another terrible pause.

'Just tell me one thing,' he said at last. 'Was the cook of the female persuasion?' I think it was quite soon afterwards that he eventually retired from the Warden's Lodge.

There were enough other eccentric dons to keep us all happy: Lord David Cecil, whose son Jonathan I have had the joy of working with in revue, was still lecturing on the romantic poets and had only recently enquired of one of his students, 'Tell me, I am getting so forgetful, was it you or your brother who was killed in the war?'

His lectures, like those of W.H. Auden, and Hugh Trevor-Roper and his arch-enemy A.J.P. Taylor, were always packed, attended by hundreds of us who were not studying their subjects but desperate for a starry performance at the podium, where Taylor famously spoke for an hour every week with no notes. Of the other starry academic eccentrics, my contemporary Michael York recalls having a college tutor who solemnly put saucers under all the electric points in his house every night, to trap and preserve any escaping electricity. Every morning he would equally solemnly empty the empty saucers.

Another of the splendours of Oxford theatre life was that it could be pursued even during long vacations: no sooner had the summer term ended than various college and university groups would set up tours, of which the best usually ended up at the Edinburgh Festival in August.

Thus I spent my first Oxford summer on that well-known centre of theatrical excellence, the bandstand at Budleigh Salterton, where a somewhat scratch company of undergraduates were treating those who bothered to stay in their deckchairs – in the usually pouring rain – to a less than wonderful *Romeo and Juliet*. My second year started rather better, with a production of *The Devil's Disciple*, which introduced me to such other actors of my generation as Ian McCulloch, who graduated straight from Oxford to a starring role opposite Vanessa Redgrave at Stratford, Michael Brunson, who followed me into ITN some years later, Peter Snow, another ITN contemporary, and Giles Block who became Peter Hall's assistant at the National Theatre and is now the splendidly termed Playmaster of Shakespeare's Globe.

Peter Fiddick, with whom I was to share many happy years of my Radio 2 *Arts Programme*, writing then in *Cherwell*, found me 'chubby and unconvincing' as Uncle William in *The Devil's Disciple*, and my performances that same term as the Steward, the Sea Captain, and Herr von Eberkopf in the Sam Walters *Peer Gynt* did nothing to change his opinion of my prospects as an actor. At the end of that term my luck altered drastically for the better, when it was announced that Peter Dews would be coming back to his old university to direct, in the following February at the Playhouse, an undergraduate production of both parts of Shakespeare's *Henry IV*.

After my father and Harry Tuyn, Dews was the third of those Falstaffian men who conditioned my early life and to whom I owe an unrepayable debt. At the time of our meeting Peter had just come off his greatest triumph, the BBC Television *An Age of Kings*, which was the first attempt, long before Peter Hall at Stratford, to unite Shakespeare's *Richard II*, *Henry IV* (both parts), *Henry V*, *Henry VI* (all three parts) and *Richard III* into one single weekly narrative sequence, with an all-star cast headed by Robert Hardy and Sean Connery. Shot in black and white five years before the advent of colour television, *An Age of Kings* is still, for my money, the best of all television Shakespeare, and although Dews went on to run both Chichester and the Birmingham Rep, where he established the career of Alec McCowen in *Hadrian VII*, this was undoubtedly his finest hour in a career that was clouded all too soon by ill-health. And that he was willing immediately after *An Age of Kings* to re-create two plays from the sequence with an all-student cast for virtually no money was only typical of his immense personal and theatrical generosity.

My luck was to be chosen as his assistant director and stage manager, and in an unusually frozen January, when it was possible even for me to walk up the Thames from my student lodgings on Iffley Lock to Carfax, we assembled some weeks before the start of term to begin the rehearsals, which were in effect a series of Dews master-classes in the art of acting Shakespeare.

At the auditions, he and I had assembled the best of Oxford acting talent: David Senton as the old Henry IV, Oliver Ford-Davies as Falstaff, Nigel Frith as Hal, Neil Stacy as Justice Shallow and a cast of around fifty others, including the young Michael Johnson, later York, as the treacherous John of Lancaster.

Dews made no concessions to student life – no essays, tutorials or sporting fixtures were allowed to interrupt rehearsals – and he did us the honour of treating us exactly as if we had been a regional rep company. It was about forty years later, when I took to directing plays, that I realised everything I had ever learnt about how to run a company had come from Dews, who had an extraordinary ability to direct by stealth, anecdote and insight rather than any more dictatorial method. He was a fund of theatrical anecdotes, many of which we still retell to this day, like that of the old and slightly deaf actor who found himself as the armourer to one of Wolfit's Macbeths. Daydreaming quietly at the back of the set, during the scene where Macbeth arms for battle, he suddenly half heard Wolfit bellow at him, 'Pluck off, Pluck off,' and duly hastened off the stage.

Virtually every Oxford actor found his or her way into these *Henry IVs* – even the 'citizens and soldiers' included Peter Young, Nancy Lane and the equally gorgeous Slade art-school student Ciaran Madden – and they were even, I think, the occasion of Dews' last ever stage appearance: one matinée I had failed to rouse John Watts from a deep slumber and Dews had to go on, irritably and in a somewhat ill-fitting costume, as young Mortimer, a performance of quite hilarious improbability for which he never quite forgave me.

If we all took any single lesson away from that Dews production, it was that the theatre was real and earnest, and if you were really keen to join it, then the sooner you ceased messing around with the rest of student life, even its academic demands, the better. There should and would be no time for anything else. I think it was this epic production, more than any other, that sorted out those of us who wanted a life in the theatre from those who were playing at being players.

Dews achieved a remarkable standard of undergraduate

acting by ignoring the university once he had drawn his cast from it; he expected a professional level of engagement and involvement, which he got from everyone, including even those with finals only a term away. It was a unique and extraordinary experience, and beyond all doubt the highlight of my university life; I was also lucky enough to get to know Dews' loving and lovely wife Ann, den mother to us all and in sole charge of haircuts.

In my second year, I also took part in a form of street theatre, organised on pavements and in car parks all over Oxford by Nigel Frith to perform his own verse drama of *Robin Hood*, in which I was all too inevitably cast as Friar Tuck. We finished up playing it that summer on the grass outside the Royal Shakespeare Theatre at Stratford, to the bemusement of tourists and RSC actors alike. That summer a number of us also got walk-on roles in a Dirk Bogarde movie called *The Mindbenders*, which was being shot around the deserted quadrangles. But the academic year ended with something still more spectacular.

The OUDS summer major that year was *A Midsummer Night's Dream*, staged in Worcester College gardens by Nevill Coghill, who had begun directing undergraduates and such professional visitors as John Gielgud and Peggy Ashcroft there before the war. This, sadly, was to be his farewell *Dream*, but he was determined it should still feature his greatest trick: walking on the water. Whether he was doing *The Tempest* (in which case it would be Ariel crossing to Prospero), or the *Dream*, where it was Puck to Oberon, Nevill had devised a simple but stunning finale. Some days earlier, you would wade into the lake with empty oil drums, and line them up just beneath the surface of the water. Then you would lay planks over them, just at the surface level, so that when, in artificial light as the plays ended, Puck or Ariel ran across the planking, they would appear to be walking on water.

All went well until I rashly invited my grandmother Gladys

Cooper to the opening night. Nigel Frith was giving his Bottom, I was Snug, with Chris Matthew as Snout. As G came backstage I rashly asked her what she had thought of the evening. 'Very nice, dear, though I had never realised Worcester Lake was so very shallow.'

Nevill lived on at Merton for several years, but he never did another production, and I don't think anyone ever bothers with walking on the water now. Somehow you just had to be there.

My second summer vacation from Oxford was again spent on the road, first as a guest with the Christ Church Players for a German tour of *The Rivals* with Andrew Geddes, later a circuit judge, who impressed the company when we reached Hesse-Darmstadt by taking us around his family castle, the kind of place, you felt, where Dracula would have lived if only he could have afforded it.

No sooner was that tour over than I joined another, this one of *Romeo and Juliet* in which I gave my Old Capulet, first at the enchanting if windswept Minack on the cliffs of Cornwall and then, rather more surprisingly, all over kibbutzim in Israel. That bit of the tour, however, was nearly aborted when we reached Venice only to find that the British Council money, what little we had been granted, had already run out, leaving us and some superb costumes – only recently created for the famous Zeffirelli *Romeo* at the Old Vic – stranded on Venice station.

All was not lost; we discovered a little ship that ran up and down the coast of Cyprus, from Venice to Haifa and back, on a weekly basis, and I duly presented myself to the captain. 'We English students from Oxford,' I explained carefully. 'We go Israel, do play. If you allow us put sleeping-bags on your top deck, we will do cabaret every night for first-class passengers.' The captain, about whom there was more than a whiff of James Robertson Justice, agreed, and we duly set sail from Venice.

The first night out, members of the company including Michael Emrys-Jones (later Elwyn), Michael York, Peter Young and I duly played for the passengers several songs and sketches that had, we thought, gone down reasonably well at previous college gatherings and an Edinburgh Festival or two. Next morning, the captain sent for me. 'Mr Morley,' he began, 'we little shipping firm. One boat, all we go is Venice to Haifa and back. We honoured to have English Oxford students on board. Feel free to camp on deck,' I don't think he meant it quite like that, 'and use the ship as though she were your own. Bars, restaurant, pool, everything. Only do me one great favour. Never perform cabaret again.'

We survived humiliation and Israel, where I remember kibbutzim already surrounded by armed guards shortly before the Six-Day War, and an extraordinary indoor theatre in, I think, Tel Aviv, where to our delight there was air-conditioning and running water – and padlocks on the dressing-room doors. I asked the house manager if it was traditional to lock up Israeli actors during the interval. 'Not really,' he replied, 'but, you see, we built all this for the Adolf Eichmann trial, and you are the first live show we've had in here since.'

Our experience on the kibbutzim was not without adventure: on arriving at one after an all-day journey, Peter Young and I were venturing to an outside toilet when a guard advised us to go by a rather less direct route. Any special reason? we enquired. Well, said the guard thoughtfully, only that a couple of men were shot to death last week on the main path. Needless to say, we went round the back.

When I returned, mercifully unshot, to the relative tranquillity of Merton for my third and last year, I made a half-hearted attempt to catch up on all the work I had failed to do in my first and second, but was soon back in the theatre where I had now become Secretary of the OUDS, a curious role that mainly involved booking distinguished guest speakers – in my time I managed to get John Gielgud, Peter Brook and John Osborne for no more than their train fare and a rather good dinner at a restaurant called the Elizabeth. My predecessor Neil Stacy had managed to bag Sir Donald Wolfit, and cherished a telegram from the great overactor: 'To arrange for my arrival you will kindly contact me at home. My telephone number is Hurstborne Tarrant 291, which number you will ring, and ring until there is a reply. Wolfit.'

The big production of my final autumn term was Michael Rudman's *Good Woman of Setzuan*, which introduced a new generation of Oxford players, among them David Aukin, later to manage both Hampstead and the National Theatre, and the future Python Terry Jones.

Meanwhile, my new-found career as a student critic nearly came to an abrupt halt when the *Daily Mail* picked up, in some indignation, on a student film review I had written of *The Young Ones*, hailing the especial brilliance not of the young Cliff Richard, but of the actor playing his father, one Robert Morley.

Looming ahead now was not only the ghastly prospect of Finals, for which even I recognised I was hopelessly ill-prepared, but what to do thereafter. Somehow the limit of my ambition had always been to go up to Oxford; once that had been achieved, I had run out of things I really wanted to do, and rather envied the academics who would be allowed to stay on in some research role. Clearly I would have to leave, but to go where and do what? I knew I didn't want to go back to teaching, after my somewhat uninspired term at Chichester, and I also knew it would be be a mistake to go into the theatre: I had not exactly set Oxford on fire with either my thespian or my directing talent.

I was also, with my usual appalling timing, just about to miss out on what was to become a golden age of student drama: the year after I went down from Merton, 1964, both Oxford (with the controversial anti-capital punishment musical *Hang Down Your Head and Die*) and Cambridge (with a Footlights revue called *Cambridge Circus* starring John Cleese among other future comedy stars) had shows transferring to the West End, a privilege reserved in my day only for the long-running *Beyond the Fringe*, which had been a fully professional affair from the outset.

I decided to do what everyone else I knew in our last year was doing, and apply for a BBC General Traineeship. Even then these were few and far between (sadly they no longer exist), but if you were lucky enough to get one, it led to a kind of fast-track broadcasting career, where you were paid generously for a three-year training in radio and television, and expected to end up if not as the BBC Director General then somewhere close. In my time, or just before it, both David Dimbleby and Melvyn Bragg had been, I think, among the lucky contestants. I got through the initial Oxford round, and was summoned to Broadcasting House where three rather ancient gentlemen considered my application form in some detail, asked me a few questions about current affairs and, stunned by my ignorance of the world at large, duly informed me that I could not have a General Traineeship, and I would oblige them by never again entering Broadcasting House.

Over the last thirty years, I have managed to enter first the BBC Television Centre and then Broadcasting and Bush Houses every week, and sometimes every day. I have been lucky enough to spend seven years on *Late Night Line-Up* (BBC2), ten on *Kaleidoscope* (Radio 4), five on *Critics' Forum* (Radio 3), and the last twelve as sole host of the *Radio 2 Arts Programme*, but somehow I still go through those heavy Broadcasting House doors rather furtively, as if expecting one of those old gentlemen (all of whom must be long dead) to lay a ghostly hand on my shoulder: 'Aha, caught you at last, my lad. What did we tell you about never trying to work here?'

But my luck was in. In my second year at Oxford I had befriended Peter Snow, one of the tallest men I had ever met and invaluable therefore for filling out the stage in

Shakespeare: he and another very tall Oxford contemporary, Gordon Honeycombe, would invariably turn up as earls, book-ending the cast line-ups like vast totem poles and adding an air of lofty distinction to whatever classic we were currently staging. Peter had distinguished himself in an earlier OUDS *Richard II*: when required as Northumberland to respond to the news that Richard is holed up in Pomfret Castle with 'a holy man', he managed nightly to utter the line 'Belike it is the Bishop of Carlisle', while implying with a heavy wink that the two men were doubtless even now engaged in some fiendish homosexual practice.

Peter was a year or two ahead of me and had picked up one of the first traineeships at ITN, the then relatively new commercial television-news company, which had been founded in 1955 by Geoffrey Cox, a distinguished New Zealander who had been a war correspondent on the *News Chronicle*. Cox, aided by such early recruits as Aidan Crawley, Robin Day, Ludovic Kennedy, Christopher Chataway, and his deputy editors David Nicholas and Don Horobin, had realised that BBC radio and television news were ripe for a challenge. Locked into pre-war ways, their newsreaders had only recently abandoned their dinner-jackets and it was clear that they were, in effect, actors, never writing or reporting events but merely reading them aloud, the only concession to the new medium being the occasional still picture or clip of movie newsreel. It was like watching a man reading the news on radio.

Such reporters as the BBC did employ were also hugely deferential: when greeting a minister or even the Prime Minister, the customary first question was 'Excuse me, sir, but is there anything you'd like to say to us about anything?' I was always vaguely surprised to find them on their feet rather than their knees.

Geoffrey decided to put an end to all that: not only would his newscasters – even the term was new – write and report the news, but they, led by Robin Day, would challenge politicians for the first time on air, questioning the veracity and blandness of their standard statements. It was a social and journalistic revolution, and it all began at ITN, operating out of one small suite of offices and an equally cramped studio atop what was then Associated-Rediffusion's Television House in Kingsway, with a staff of barely fifty.

After a brief interview with Geoffrey, I was offered a traineeship to start in the autumn after my Finals, and also a general newscasting and reporting job by the then relatively new commercial ITV station in Southampton, Southern Television. Thus encouraged to believe that there would be some sort of life for me after Oxford, I frantically started the final preparation for finals, and even acquired a weird confidence in the end result. Indeed, so sure were Chris Matthew and I of victory, that we decided our only problem would be intellectual exhaustion. This was easily solved: Chris remembered that he had an aunt in Paris, who would be happy to see us for a long weekend, during which we could gather our strength for the final exam onslaught early in June.

I recall two things only about that magical weekend: firstly, going to see Edith Piaf in one of her many farewell performances at the Paris Olympia and finding, to my horror, the house barely a quarter full. The French, however, knew a thing or two that we visitors did not: the first half of the evening consisted of derelict jugglers and very old comedians. There was then a lengthy interval, during which *le tout Paris* arrived in all its finery, just in time for the second half, which was indeed all Piaf. The curtain rose on an empty stage, and then, as the band struck up 'Milord', a spotlight far upstage picked out a little old lady dressed in funereal black, who hobbled slowly down to the footlights. As she did so, the audience stood and cheered. By the time Piaf reached us, it was to a full standing ovation as the years literally fell away from her, and she went into the first of twenty classic songs by Aznavour, Trenet and Marguerite Monnot, all of them, of course, her discoveries. As with Dietrich, Lenya and Garland later, I was just in time to see one of the great showbiz legends of the twentieth century, and once seen, never forgotten: you just had to be there, and I thank God regularly that I was. Those women, even in their final solo shows, were ultimately more theatrical than any more conventional players I have ever seen: they were the essence of showbusiness, of what Kenneth Tynan once called 'high definition performance'; and with them, the best of it died.

The other event of that French weekend was the Profumo affair, and his admission that he had lied to the House of Commons about Christine Keeler.

Somehow, returning to Oxford to be examined in Old French seemed irrelevant and anti-climactic, and our Paris weekend did not do much to improve our chances. Some weeks later, Chris and I were summoned for lengthy *viva-voce* examinations, at which a panel of dons questioned you in person about your written papers. The length of these panels convinced me not only that I was in with a good chance, but that they were probably undecided about whether to award me a first or a second. In the event, it transpired that they were trying to decide between a fairly humiliating third or a totally humiliating fourth. Luckily we just scraped thirds, like most of the actors of our generation – though not all: both Neil Stacy and Oliver Ford-Davies scored firsts. In the intervening forty years, I have occasionally been asked about my college or my university, but nobody, in private or public, has ever enquired, mercifully, as to what class of degree I achieved. I think they only get round to asking you that if you stay in the teaching racket.

17
Of Thee I Sing, Baby

Reluctantly, I now began to pack up my Oxford belongings, settle (at last) my massive Blackwell's book bill, and start on a round of farewell parties that involved the traditional Pimm's on the college lawns, and a strong sense of regret that I had to go down from the most magical place I had ever known. I went home, and then to spend a week or so in Southampton where Southern Television were still seriously thinking of employing me as a news writer and reporter. One of my earliest assignments was to script a clip of local newsreel that showed some small children playing Cowboys and Indians in a clearing in the local woods: 'No,' my script began, 'it's not the Wild West, it's the New Forest.' Rather more than thirty years later, my wife Ruth and I were back in Southampton, not only because my younger daughter was at college there but also because we were about to sail off as lecturers on yet another cruise. On this occasion, fog had delayed the sailing and we were put up in a local hotel. We turned on the TV, and some children were playing in a wood. Up came the newscaster saying, 'No, it's not the Wild West, it's the New Forest.' Not a lot changes in regional television news.

Although Southern made it clear that the job they were offering was to start there and then, I decided to turn it down – not something I would have been inclined to do later in life, but this was still a time of virtually full employment, at least for Oxbridge graduates, no matter how poor their degrees.

I felt that, having gone straight from teaching in Chichester to Merton, I was entitled to some time off, in what would now I suppose be considered 'a gap year', although admittedly I was taking it rather late.

ITN seemed almost too eager to agree to this, and promised that their offer of a traineeship could indeed be postponed for a year, while I went out into the world and acquired some 'experience'. I didn't tell them exactly what I had in mind, as I feared they might consider it rather too much of a holiday. What I had accidentally come across, glancing idly down the Personal Column of *The Times*, was a small announcement to the effect that the University of Hawaii was looking for graduate students on year-long contracts to work in their drama department in Honolulu. I had remembered from fifteen years ago those golden sands, those amazing sunsets, the warm Pacific and a kind of magical Hawaiian kingdom. I duly applied for the job. I suspect there cannot have been too many other candidates, because the air ticket came in the return post with the suggestion that I should fly out right away, it now being almost September and the start of the undergraduate year.

Also in the letter was a suggestion: although it would be possible to go out to Hawaii on a purely academic visa, the university recommended that I try for fully fledged immigration to the USA, as this would mean I could work my passage home the following summer, and take odd jobs in the college vacations, which were, as elsewhere, of considerable length.

Accordingly I presented myself at the American Embassy in Grosvenor Square, where only recently the likes of Vanessa Redgrave and several Aldermaston marchers had been arrested overnight for a marathon anti-American protest, and spent two days being medically examined and signing declarations to the effect that I was neither homosexual, black, nor intent on assassinating the President, which seemed ridiculous – until Dallas, whereafter it was never to seem quite so ridiculous again. Having passed with flying colours, I was summoned to the presence of one of the vice-consuls, who sat at a large desk in front of the American flag and a vast picture of John F. Kennedy. 'Mr Morley,' he intoned, 'I am proud to tell you that you are now a fully fledged American citizen. By next week you will be in Hawaii, and by next January you will be in Saigon.'

Even I, bleakly uninterested in world affairs as usual, had noticed that a war was brewing in Vietnam, and my enthusiasm for becoming an American citizen died so abruptly that I tore up the newly signed papers in his office, just after he had finished explaining that as an immigrant, one moreover of military age who had done no national service in his own country, I would be among the first to be called up. My lifelong and somewhat more courageous friend Peter Young, then also starting on a teaching assignment in California, took the full visa, was called up just as he was leaving the USA a year later, declined the offer of a boot-camp in San Francisco, and spent much of the rest of his life trying to get his name removed from the undesirable-aliens register at American airports where, needless to say, he is now warmly welcomed as a fine, upstanding possessor of the two best McDonald's franchises north of Barcelona.

All I can now recall about my first return to Hawaii (I have spent the rest of my life getting back there whenever I could) was that, despite far too much hotel-building on the Waikiki sands, the islands were much as I remembered them from 1949. My first day on campus, I registered, discovered I would be doing everything from acting through teaching to scenery building, and met, in the green room of the university theatre, a tall, dark, quietly beautiful girl from Boston called Margaret Gudejko. We were engaged within the year, married within two, stayed together for the best part of twenty-five, had three children and (so far) two grandchildren, who, after Margaret's and my uneasy and very unhappy divorce, have kept us, if not together, then at least no longer at daggers drawn. That, it has always seemed to me, is what children and grandchildren do best. Apart, in my case, from providing an annual excuse to visit Disneyland theme parks around the world.

We are, in fact, the perfect Disneyland family. When I was a child in the Californian 1950s, old Uncle Walt was just building his first playground at Anaheim: by the time my children were of travelling age he – or, rather, his heirs, since the old boy had just gone into the cryogenic deep-freeze of his choice – had started his colonisation of Florida, and by the time my grandchildren came along, there was a whole new EuroDisney conveniently sited just at the Paris end of the Eurotunnel. The only trouble with this one is that it's a little too small: when my grandson Barney and I were at the top of Magic Mountain and he looked over the side and saw a French family sitting down to eat, I had some difficulty in explaining that these were real French people having their lunch, rather than some amazingly lifelike new Disney animatronics laid on for our amusement. Concepts of real reality versus Disney reality are about as far as I have ever liked to go into philosophy or the art of the unknown.

But back to Hawaii: our first major production, in a new purpose-built theatre on the Honolulu campus, was to have been George and Ira Gershwin's *Of Thee I Sing*, the first musical ever to win a Pulitzer Prize in 1934 and ripe for a major rediscovery. The only problem was that it is set almost entirely in the White House, and its score centres on a president, John P. Wintergreen, using his marriage as a cynical election-winner. We were just about to open when, on 22 November 1963, news came from Dallas of the assassination of John F. Kennedy.

Needless to say, we never opened that show: instead, our first season featured a sombre *Hamlet*, a *kabuki* drama called *Benten Kozo* since many of the students in Hawaii were Japanese, then a rare revival of the play that had given me my name, *The Man Who Came to Dinner*, in which I played (none too well) the Noël Coward character, Beverly Carlton.

That production did, however, introduce me to the two best friends, apart from Margaret, that I made during this sunbaked year. The first was the actor playing the Man. In real life he was Dave Donnelly, for thirty or so years the diarist on the *Honolulu Star-Bulletin* and a man after my own heart – large, bearded, gregarious and a compulsive gossip, as befits his journalism. In his time Dave has been a disc jockey, a children's television host, an actor, director and writer, all without ever leaving Hawaii or his daily column. I can think of no other journalist in the world who has survived quite so well for quite so long in one single area of one single paper. When he goes, if he ever does, a lot of the post-war social history of the Hawaiian islands will go with him.

My other great friend was my future wife's room-mate on the college campus; they lived, at virtually no cost since they were still students and the university was generous, in considerable luxury in a purpose-built high-rise apartment block, which was about as far removed from the concept of British college digs as could be imagined: the beach was only a twenty-minute bus ride away, and the temperature seldom dropped below 90° in or out of the Pacific.

This girl (in those days we were still allowed to call them that) was local, determined on musical stardom, but oddly hard to cast. She wasn't an especially great actress, singer or dancer, nor especially tall, blonde or beautiful. What impressed me was her single-minded determination to make her name in showbiz – it was rather like being with the young Ethel Merman, whom in many ways she resembled, complete with the golden-foghorn voice and the utter dedication to her own future stardom at whatever personal cost.

Although she had been starrily cast in the aborted *Of Thee I Sing*, there wasn't much else on offer that academic year in Hawaii, although I do recall she and Margaret alternating roles on an island tour of Murray Schisgal's *The Typist and the Tiger*. When Margaret and I left Hawaii at the end of the summer term, she to go home to Boston, I to ITN in London, both of us to consider the now very real prospect of marriage, we stayed in touch with her on the backs of Christmas cards. One year she moved to New York, and was, I think, on the glove counter at Saks Fifth Avenue; another year she had reached the back of the chorus of a road tour of *Fiddler on the Roof*, and that was more or less where I thought she would end up, until the very late 1970s or early 1980s when she wrote saying that she had become a big star on the New York gay bath-house circuit.

Gay bath-houses not being a very English concept, I was still in some doubt about her stardom. She asked what it would take for me to believe her. 'Well,' I said, 'next time I am in New York,' where I was already reviewing Broadway for the *Herald Tribune*, 'I will book us a table for lunch at Sardi's,' then the great theatre restaurant. 'I will get there first,' I told her, 'and if when you come in anyone at all, from a waitress to the hat-check girl, seems even vaguely to know you, I will accept that you are a star.' As she came in, virtually the entire restaurant rose to its feet and I had to admit, there and then, that she had indeed become a star. Her name was, and is, Bette Midler.

Apart from Bette, and of course Margaret, the other stars of my Hawaiian year were the three men who ran the drama department: Earle Ernst, the great *kabuki* authority who, on behalf of the US Army, had rebuilt the Japanese theatre after the war; Ed Langhans, a considerable expert on seventeenth-century London theatre; and Joel Trapido, who was always the department's father-confessor. There was also Dick Mason, who designed all the sets and tried with increasing despair to teach me the basics of scenic construction, and Al (later Paul) La Mastra who became a celebrated Hollywood film and television editor.

Years later, working in California for the BBC, I went to stay with Al high in the Hollywood Hills. His house, as did – and do – most in that nervous neighbourhood, bore a sign reading, 'Beware: Instant Armed Response', and he warned me on arrival that if by any chance I left the house without him, and failed to deal correctly with the complex security system, men with guns and dogs would instantly come racing down the street and, in all probability, kill me on sight, assuming that I was an undesirable intruder.

Needless to say, the first time I left the house alone I set off the alarm by accident. Then I sat on the lawn for several hours while people passed me on foot and in cars. To them all I waved cheerily and indicated that I was English, and had therefore failed to set the alarm correctly. As it turned to dusk, Al returned and turned off the alarm; of the men with dogs and guns, I saw no sign. Since then, Los Angeles has never seemed quite so alarming, unless you count the health-food restaurants and the shopping malls, and the way that every time you go back they seem to have moved everything around, rather like an Ideal Home Exhibition being demolished and rebuilt every six months. The façades are everything: I am always surprised to find that behind the front doors there is often a real house, instead of just the lean-to back of a studio set.

Apart from the legendary Viveca Lindfors, who had started out in the same Swedish drama school as Garbo and Ingrid Bergman, gone to Hollywood for Errol Flynn and *Don Juan* before the war, and now came to us to give her *Hedda Gabler*, the other leading figures of my theatre year in Hawaii were Wally Chappell, who finished up pioneering children's theatre in the Midwest, and Randy Kim, who is Filipino and soon became one of his nation's leading actor-directors.

The rest of us did as little as possible: the heat was considerable, and the temptation to stay on the beach often irresistible. Indeed, I think I spent the major part of my graduate year under water, although occasionally I was shamed into taking part in fly-the-flag functions. There was still a British consul in Hawaii, although I seem to recall that he doubled up as the local head of what was then BOAC. Honolulu airport was air-conditioned and boasted a couple of good bars, so some nights we would just drive out there to watch the planes take off and thereby reassure ourselves that there was a world beyond the islands, not that many of us wished to rejoin it.

But in those days Honolulu was the major stop between Los Angeles and Tokyo, and if BOAC had an especially starry passenger – Sir John Gielgud, for instance, *en route* for the Australian tour of his *The Ages of Man*, or the newly paired Rudolf Nureyev and Margot Fonteyn on their way back to America – the BOAC consul and I would hurry down to the VIP lounge to place flowered *leis* round their necks and reassure them that we were, indeed, still flying the flag.

When it came to Shakespeare's birthday, we laid on an entire verse-speaking gala dinner at one of the local hotels, and there were similar celebrations for the Queen's birthday – it was perceived to be in the best interests of HM Government, and who were we to turn down a free dinner? Hawaii had once, briefly, been a British protectorate, and we weren't about to let the other foreigners forget it.

My other friends included Harry Dove, who had the Rolls-Royce franchise for the islands, and his wife Lorraine, who later married the great Henry James expert Leon Edel, another refugee who came to the islands for a short stay and remained for many years, totally seduced. We used to run a book on how long it would take visiting professors from the mainland to take off their ties and start teaching in shorts and sandals: Francis Fergusson, a distinguished theatre historian, managed the transformation in less than a week.

Then there was the great and good Norman Wright, who had been for many years all over America the travelling book salesman for the university publications, and was, in the local amateur theatre group, the best Willy Loman in *Death of a Salesman* I have ever seen: a lifetime on the road had taught him exactly how it felt to be out there riding on nothing but a smile and a shoeshine. He and his beloved wife Debbie had settled permanently in the islands, and Norm, who had started acting in the war with Maurice Evans' Pacific troupe for the US Army, can still be seen in minor roles on reruns of *Hawaii 5-0*, a series that started, alas, after my time in the islands, but gave useful employment to the locals for many seasons to come.

When it came to Christmas, I went to California to be with my grandmother Gladys, who was now filming as Mrs Higgins in the musical *My Fair Lady* with Rex Harrison and Audrey Hepburn, Wilfrid Hyde-White, Jeremy Brett, Mona Washbourne and, of course, Stanley Holloway: the last great gathering of the Hollywood Brits. All in all, the shooting at Warner Brothers kept Gladys happily on the payroll for the best part of six months, and as she was also now starring with David Niven and Charles Boyer in a triumphant and very classy TV crime-caper series called *The Rogues*, her twenty-year Hollywood career was ending on a high.

On the *My Fair Lady* set, where I spent a few days watching the shooting, all was not entirely smooth: Audrey clearly resented not being allowed to sing, Rex was his usual irritable and arrogant self, and the two great old rival queens, the director George Cukor and the designer Cecil Beaton, were hissing at each other like scorpions from either side of the lavish sets – not least because Cecil had done a lucrative deal with *Vogue* to sell his stills, which he regarded as rather more important than any of the scenes that George was trying to get in the can.

But in all fairness, it was Beaton, in one of his many diaries, who gave us the best picture of Gladys in her late seventies:

Our Mrs Higgins comes to Cukor's room at Warner's with a pot of marmalade, which she has made from the oranges in her California garden, and a sheaf of early photographs of herself, taken at the time when she was England's greatest beauty and the First Lady of the stage. These are to be used in connexion with a pre-Raphaelite portrait of her which is to be hung in Higgins' study . . . Gladys has a marvellous way of facing the onslaught of the years. No excuses. Her eyes may have lost some of their lustre, but none of their intensity. She does not give her past beauty a thought. She's too interested in everything else. She looks at you with seeing eyes. She breathes in fresh air. She radiates health, and her complexion is so burnt by the sun that it has become like a walnut. She tells me what she eats ('If you really want to know, hot water and lemon first thing. Then a huge cup of milky coffee and prunes for breakfast. Only yogurt for lunch. Then I cook myself a proper meal at night'). She's Spartan and self-disciplined . . . pressed to tell us her theories on acting, she pooh-poohed: 'Oh, I don't think about it. After all these years I just try to get out there and be heard and hurry through it all as quickly as possible and then go home.'

Although her loveliness made her the great picture-postcard favourite and a household name throughout England, Gladys has never had the easy, pampered life of a famous beauty. Adulation, and tributes in the form of jewellery or flowers, seldom came her way. At the height of her glory, her mother once came into her dressing room and said, 'You're too thin, dear, you're all nose.'

But, sensing something on the soft wind of the long California evenings, Gladys realised that it was now all over. The Hollywood Raj, that inspired collection of British actors who had colonised MGM and other studios so successfully since the coming of sound in 1930, had outlived its usefulness. There was a chill in the air, and G decided to go home to the family by the Thames in Henley. She sold the Hollywood house on Napoli Drive to an old friend, Marti Stevens, gave most of its contents to the University of Southern California and set off for home, giving one last Hollywood interview to the English journalist and novelist Gavin Lambert:

Colman, Aubrey Smith, Clifton Webb, the cricket eleven, they'd all gone by now and Gladys Cooper seemed to be the last of the colonial settlers in Hollywood; she knew it was all over, and I think she was keen now to get back to her family in England where she knew she could still get work in the theatre. She had no patience with decay or loneliness, or failure, and she was not one to stay around after the party was over. She'd really belonged to MGM at the height of its Anglophilia, and now that was all over and Hollywood had become a youth industry, the old colony simply couldn't survive and I think she was very wise to get out when she did – otherwise she'd just have ended up like Helen Hayes, doing parodies of herself on television for ever. Gladys was a very cool lady, and she knew when to stop something in her acting, as in her life. You remember that moment in *Rebecca* when she looks at Joan Fontaine and realises she's in the wrong dress? Other actresses would have gone overboard at that moment and ruined it; Gladys understood about restraint, and she also managed to keep her head well above the rubbish she was often given to do on the screen. She kept her head and her distance always, and that was what made her as an actress.

And as for G, so even for me: the Hollywood of my childhood in the late 1940s was now fast disappearing into the late 1960s, and although I often go back (I spent one memorable Christmas Day there with the bachelor actor and professional fish mimic Richard Haydn, author of *The Journal of Edwin Carp* and still to be seen in his last major role, that of Christopher Plummer's best friend in *The Sound of Music*: we managed to see seven movies in a day and not a single Christmas tree), it is no longer my home territory, if ever it was. Just occasionally, with the late Roddy McDowall or George Cukor or Coral Browne and Vincent Price, it was possible, even in the 1990s, to sit by a pool reminiscing about the studio days and the eccentrics who populated them. But since Roddy was the last of that generation to die a year or two ago, I seldom look forward now to going back: too many ghosts, not enough surviving friends. New York is different:

there, they live longer, work harder, and can still remember the day before yesterday.

Talking again of Coral, it was soon after her arrival in Hollywood as Mrs Vincent Price when she discovered that Charlton Heston and Vanessa Redgrave were about to open at a local theatre in *Macbeth*. Coral, who collected theatrical disasters the way others collect stamps, rang the box-office instantly: 'Coral Browne calling. I'd like to book two tickets for the opening night of the Charlton Heston–Vanessa Redgrave *Macbeth*.'

'Gee, I'm sorry, Miss Browne, we've been sold out for months. This is a very popular attraction.'

Coral slammed down the phone and dialled again. 'Hello, this is Mrs Vincent Price. I'd like two tickets for the Charlton Heston–Vanessa Redgrave *Macbeth*.'

'Gee, I'm sorry, Mrs Price, we've been sold out for months.'

She dialled a third time. 'Hello, could I just book two tickets for immediately after the interval of the first night of the Charlton Heston–Vanessa Redgrave *Macbeth*?'

By then, as she already knew, she could have had most of the dress circle to herself.

Back in Hawaii, I completed my year feeling faintly guilty at being paid four hundred dollars a month for what was clearly the best vacation of my life, then headed back to the real life and rain of London. It was the end of August 1964, and on the way home I stopped only once, to see the magical new Guthrie Theater in Minneapolis open with the George Grizzard *Henry V*, one of the last of the great Tyrone Guthrie's own productions.

18
And That Is the End of the News

Back in London, I rejoined my old friend Chris Matthew and we leased a flat from Amanda Reiss, whose mother Ambrosine Phillpotts was still my father's most faithful and long-suffering co-star, on the top floor above a launderette in Craven Terrace, just off Lancaster Gate.

This was a happy time, made happier because almost immediately I was allowed by ITN to become one of their late-night newscasters, not responsible for the major bulletins at five to six and five to nine (we were still several years away from *News at Ten*) but for broadcasting the five-minute bulletins we supplied on demand through the night to any of the dozen or so local ITV stations around the country who were our paymasters.

It was instant fame, made better for me when Chris overheard the manageress of the launderette boasting to a neighbour: 'We've had them all in here – Donald Houston, Sheridan Morley, Inia Te Wiata . . .' Mr Te Wiata, I should explain to younger readers, was a Maori tribal chieftain who, some years before Dame Kiri Te Kanawa, had come from New Zealand to take London by storm in a revival of *The King and I*, or possibly *South Pacific*.

Although I regarded myself as engaged to Margaret, who was still in Boston thinking about marriage and England, Chris was still on the romantic market, and inclined to bring girls home from his advertising agency for a little discreet canoodling on the Amanda sofa we shared. This could lead to embarrassment if I returned unexpectedly, so we devised a system whereby, as I closed down the late London ITN news bulletin, I would briefly scratch one ear to indicate that I was on the way home, or the other to suggest that I had a party to go to, and that Chris would therefore be undisturbed for another hour or two.

Looking back, I suppose these were the Swinging Sixties, but they seem, like so much other real-life reality, to have passed me by: the *Oz* trial, sex and the Beatles, *Lady Chatterley's Lover* being considered unsuitable for our servants, George Melly and John Mortimer standing for a new world of sexual and social freedom, Vanessa Redgrave being carted off to jail. I remember it all, but almost always through the safe perspective of an ITN television camera, or a strip of film to be rapidly edited and scripted for the next bulletin. Something about my year in America, or my peripatetic childhood, meant that I still saw myself as a perpetual outsider, unable to join the anti-American protests about the beginnings of Vietnam because I knew and liked too many Americans, and was planning to marry one. I felt oddly stranded, neither English nor American, neither a student nor a teacher, neither entirely grown-up nor still a teenager. I was twenty-four going on about sixty, already nostalgic for a world that clearly wasn't there any more, but that I could recover in old theatre programmes and crackly recordings.

It wasn't until thirty years later, writing the authorised biography of John Gielgud, that I understood my problem: 'If I go in through a stage door,' John once said to me, 'I know absolutely everything and everyone, but if I walk back through it into the street, I know nothing about anything.' That, above all, was why I came to love him. Once I was with him, walking down Piccadilly when we met Mrs Thatcher, then at the height of her premiership, whom we both knew slightly. In the course of polite conversation, John enquired where she was now living.

'Number Ten, Downing Street,' replied the Prime Minister, in some surprise.

'Oh, you women,' exclaimed John, 'are always so clever at

buying the right sort of property. I never seem to meet a really good estate agent.' Our meeting ended more or less there.

The feminist revolution also came and went without me: I wasn't a woman, had always lived in mixed-sex schools and colleges, and in my own world of theatre and cinema, women had always managed very nicely on their own resources. Having Gladys for a grandmother made one aware that not all women had to be downtrodden housekeepers or reluctant mothers, and already I had cast myself somehow as an outsider and an observer: ITN was the ideal excuse for not really getting involved in anything, and a starting salary of nearly a thousand pounds a year was then enough to live in reasonable central-London comfort. If the 1960s were a party, I saw myself as one of the hired entertainers or, at worst, having come along in some vague capacity with the caterers. The only motto I have ever found useful in life was given me by the redoubtable Carol Channing, who became an unofficial godmother to my son Hugo: 'Remember, kid,' she told me, 'people like us are never at the party. We are the party.'

Years later, I found myself at the newborn LBC London radio station, interviewing a not-yet Prime Minister Thatcher when she was still Minister for Depriving Children of Milk or whatever. 'It has been said, Mrs Thatcher,' I opened, rather pompously, 'that England is a great place to live if you are neither very poor nor black.'

There was a brief pause.

'Well, I'm not, am I?' she replied, and I knew even then that she was on her way. The rest of us stood and watched, appalled and largely impotent.

At ITN, I began to learn the rigours and the magic of commercial television news as it operated in the mid-1960s. The undoubted star of the newsroom in my time was Alistair Burnet, with whom I worked on the two Wilson elections of 1964 and 1966; he was far and away the greatest current-affairs broadcaster I had ever come across on either side of the

Atlantic, better than anyone in the business over here today, and probably only comparable to the American giants like Walter Cronkite and Ed Murrow, who saw the USA through war and peace for over forty years.

The most amazing thing about Alistair was his political memory: these were the days before computers, when even autocues were in their infancy, but on an election night, when on the only other television channel there was an army of Days and Dimblebys, we just fielded Alistair. No notes, no researchers, just a mine of information so that you could simply tell him of a Labour gain in Winchester, then watch him do ten minutes to camera on how and why it had happened there. It was like standing behind some great actor while he made it to the top of the mountain as Lear, and I have never forgotten the sheer excitement of watching Burnet hold together our somewhat tacky army as we went over the top and saw the BBC off the field.

ITN understood the virtue of being pirates: unencumbered by the old radio rules, or any sense that we had to be 'the voice of the nation', we went in for the quick kill, asked the questions the BBC still dared not ask, and got the results. We were Jack to the BBC Giant, with a fraction of their staff numbers and less than a tenth of their budget. When abroad, especially in situations where we needed back-up from local embassy officials, I was not alone, I think, in unashamedly claiming to be the BBC, because their writ, thanks to the World Service, ran considerably wider than ours abroad in those still early days. When I joined, ITN still had some months to go before its tenth birthday.

Because this was the pre-videotape era – although my mother managed to make some flickery home movies of me as a newscaster, by holding a cine-camera right against her TV screen – I have few records of my ITN newscasting life. Somehow, doubtless because of my bulk and general hamfistedness, I never got the more glamorous foreign assignments that made stars of Gerald Seymour, Peter Sissons and Michael Nicholson in various corners of foreign battlefields. Indeed, I think the furthest I was ever sent was to a deserted and soggy field somewhere near Watford, on the day it was announced that here would be built the new metropolis of Milton Keynes. I still feature in the new town's historical and promotional videos, looking somewhat unconvinced and watched over gloomily by a couple of stoically cud-chewing cows.

But I loved my time at ITN: Geoffrey was a generous and enthusiastic editor, the newsroom was run with tremendous efficiency by David Nicholas and Don Horobin, and I was thrilled to find Lynne Reid Banks on the typewriter next to mine, having already written the novel that would make her name, *The L-shaped Room*. Later Gerry Seymour became a bestselling writer of thrillers, some of which were based on his ITN experiences in Northern Ireland and elsewhere, and other budding novelists in the newsroom in my time included Iain Johnstone and Gordon Honeycombe.

Something about newswriting and newsreading seemed to lend itself to the contrast of fiction, as if all that reality had to be channelled into a text rather more permanent than a two-minute piece for the nine o'clock news, read as it usually was in those days by either Andrew Gardner or Huw Thomas, the latter a charming Welshman with a habit of grinning broadly whenever he read an item about any member of the royal family. This so endeared him to our viewers that when, some years later, ITN tried to retire him, he left seven crammed sacks of his fan mail outside the editor's office door as a none-too-subtle response. He survived on air for several more years. Years and years later, watching one of the great television comedy series of all time, *Drop the Dead Donkey*, I was not entirely amazed to discover that at least some of the cast and writing crew had spent a little time studying our old ITN, not least David Swift, who did a devastating impression of Reginald Bosanquet, the ageing, alcoholic, grouchy, chauvinist and increasingly embattled newscaster, who nevertheless we always loved best.

One of the real-life characters in the newsroom – who, for some reason, was never immortalised by *Drop the Dead Donkey* – was the chief studio director Diana Edwards-Jones, a splendidly noisy and very funny Welsh lady who took no prisoners and was herself a perpetual one-woman show, addressing her beloved cameramen in language that even I had seldom heard before. It occurs to me suddenly that, for someone who has always been accused by family and friends alike of unreconstructed male chauvinism, I have spent a large amount of my career working for and with very strong women: Diana at ITN, Joan Bakewell at *Late Night Line-Up*, Margaret Allen at *The Times*, Kathy Knorr at the *Herald-Tribune*, and a succession of superb arts editors up to and including Liz Anderson at the *Spectator*. And two distinctly headstrong wives, plus a couple of equally determined daughters, have all been good enough to live with my apparently prehistoric male conditioning. Then again, my father, not exactly a feminist, spent much of his career being managed and organised by yet another strong woman, Rosalind Chatto, while of the several showbiz biographies I have written, at least four – those of Gladys, Katharine Hepburn, Gertrude Lawrence and Ginger Rogers – have been about women who all had to make their own way in what was then a male-dominated showbusiness world. When I first took to directing on Shaftesbury Avenue a couple of years ago, it was with Vanessa Redgrave and her sister-in-law Kika Markham – not exactly the shrinking violets of their sex. Maybe I am not as unfeminist as I have always thought, or maybe it is just that opposites attract. We'll get back, I fear, to the self-analysis in another decade or two.

Throughout my three years at ITN we remained camped – not a happy word, since it was the least gay environment in which I have ever worked – on the top floor of Television House in Kingsway, of which the lower floors were occupied by Associated-Rediffusion, a curiously feeble ITV company that then held, rather tenuously, the London weekday franchise, but seemed to make most of its money from hiring television sets to those who declined to buy one – presumably in the hope that they might just disappear like penny-farthing bicycles. Or else get a bit better, which was, at least in the case of Associated-Rediffusion's nightly output, a forlorn hope.

Associated-Rediffusion was not, even then, at the cutting edge of ITV network production: that was where you would find Granada, for whom we supplied a mid-afternoon newscast, just as they were opening up their 'Granada in the North' programme sequence, fronted in those days by Michael Parkinson or Mike Scott. Granada had no great love for ITN, reckoning that, as the producers of *World in Action* and much else, they could deliver a better news service than we were managing and, more importantly, one devoid of toffee-nosed southern presenters – or 'those bloody ITN wankers', as we were unaffectionately known by the likes of Bill Grundy and Brian Inglis of *What the Papers Say.*

As the duty afternoon and late-night newscaster – a polite way of letting me know that I would be lucky to make it to the main bulletins, except in the occasional case of illness or other staff emergency – I was often caught in the Granada versus ITN crossfire, especially as it was their mean trick sometimes to cut to us in the London studio about ten seconds before we were ready to go on air. This guaranteed shots of me combing my hair or, much worse, picking my nose, which was then the cause of much caustic comment by Parkinson, though luckily I never had to hear it, since it only went out in Manchester. Sometimes in Manchester or any Granada territory to this day, people in rail or bus queues – I spend a lot of time hiking and hawking my one-man show as cheaply as possible around the lesser-known theatres of the area – will point and burst out laughing, whereupon I know that they are recalling one of Parkinson's ruder insults of nearly forty years ago.

He, however, is a man I have always respected, not only because I spent several happy months with him on a daytime TV antiques quiz called *Going for a Song*, for which I originally signed up on the assumption that, with a title like that, it must be vaguely musical, but also because he gave my father and occasionally me work on his chat-shows here and in Australia, and again because he wrote the best and most perceptive of all Pa's obits a decade ago. One night, when his show still went out live, I was watching Mike interviewing Morecambe and Wise: 'And what,' he asked them at one point, 'would you two have been if you hadn't become great comics?'

Eric reflected for a moment or two. 'Mike and Bernie Winters,' was his considered response.

Granada apart, I loved ITN and might have stayed there for ever. As happened to me a few years later at BBC2, I got in by pure luck soon after the beginning of a television revolution, and because ITN was so small and experimental, we trainees (another was Richard Whiteley, which explains my appearances on *Countdown*) were able to learn vastly more, and vastly more quickly, about the art of television news than we would ever have managed at the already much more bureaucratic and formalised BBC.

By now, Amanda Reiss had returned to claim her flat in Craven Terrace, so Chris and I moved to Chelsea – or, if we are being brutally honest, to Parsons Green. There, our old Oxford friend Ian McCulloch had a top-floor flat he needed to sub-let, as he was off to Chicago to play in a Shakespeare summer festival for Peter Dews. We arrived to find the flat in a state of bachelor chaos. Chris, always tidier than me, did a major spring-clean, and placed the accumulated rubbish in a neat plastic bag by the back door. In the morning, we woke to find the bag back on our top landing with a still neater note: 'The top flat in this building,' it read, 'does not have dustbin rights.' A few hours later, the postman sweated up the stairs with a registered letter for Ian. 'Alas,' I told him, 'Mr McCulloch has just left for Chicago.'

'Chicago, eh?' mused the postman. 'I'll come back about four, then, shall I?'

The other joy for me of these ITN years was the coming of *Dateline*, a late-night news magazine programme which, I suspect because it went out close to midnight, I was allowed to write and even front on those evenings when Reggie Bosanquet had promising parties to visit. After a year or so, however, rumours began to spread around the office of a major ITN breakthrough: Geoffrey had been fighting the Independent Broadcasting Authority for almost a decade to get not just a couple of ten-minute bulletins each evening but a full half-hour of news at ten, and finally this looked likely to happen, in which case, as I rightly guessed, my beloved *Dateline* would have to go.

I had already been lucky enough to work on the two Wilson elections – and, indeed, the funeral of Sir Winston Churchill: as *Dateline* went out at precisely the right time of night, we were the first to cover live the lying-in-state at Westminster Hall. There was not to be another until that of the Queen Mother almost forty years later, and it was clearly an event of historic significance. For *Dateline*, my instructions were to remain in the studio, and simply voice-over the various royal and political celebrities who were to be found that night walking round Sir Winston's coffin. 'There,' I heard myself say, 'you see Sir Anthony Eden, and Prince Charles, and there,' I added, 'is, of course, old Queen Mary.' Coming off the air some minutes later, I said to our studio manager that it was a funny thing, but I had thought old Queen Mary had been dead for some time. 'She has been,' clarified the studio manager, 'but apparently our outside-broadcast unit went down, and they had some old newsfilm of George VI's body lying in state at the same place, so we used that instead. It looked much the same.'

Did we receive a single phone call of surprise or complaint? Did we hell. Either we had remarkably few viewers – as usual – or those we had couldn't be bothered to reach for the phone. In those pre-Mary Whitehouse days, television companies received few viewers' complaints: people were still just amazed by the invention.

Just before my ITN time, another amazing discovery had been made about viewing tastes and reactions: on the dreadful night of John F. Kennedy's assassination, ITN had used its panic-button control to interrupt all other ITV stations with the news from Dallas, after which it networked solemn organ music over a picture of the late President. BBC1, the only other channel in operation at the time, broke the news as a roller caption over an ongoing Harry Worth comedy half-hour, ending, 'More news at nine.'

The result? BBC television received over five hundred letters of complaint about the tastelessness of their scheduling on such a night; at ITN we received several thousand asking how we had dared interrupt *Coronation Street* with news of some dead American, of whom the writers knew little and cared less. That was also the night when, at Associated-Rediffusion, the critic Milton Shulman found himself producing a live chat-show, which had to deal, inevitably, with the assassination. Most of the obvious panellists were celebrating the first-ever BAFTA awards dinner, and in those days, of course, unreachable by mobile phone. Milton finished up in some desperation with Eli Wallach, who was conveniently working around the corner in a play, and a catastrophically drunk George Brown, then Foreign Secretary. Eli took offence at George's state on such a tragic occasion, and nearly succeeded in strangling him on live television. I have always regretted missing that programme. The dispute over coverage of the Queen Mother's death in 2002 was nothing new.

My working life at ITN was reasonably happy, but for once I was rather more focused on my own private life. My first ITN

Christmas, 1964, I was allowed to read – and, indeed, write – the lunchtime news just before the Queen's Speech, an honour bestowed on me largely because all the other newscasters had sensibly filled in their names on the holiday chart before me. But this was also the Christmas when Margaret came from Boston to meet my family and decide whether she really wanted to marry me and settle in a foreign country. As she wrote later: 'It was Boxing Day morning, when I met Robert Morley for the first time. His first words to me were "Good morning, my dear. Would you like toast or a bath?"'

Margaret and Robert formed an immediate alliance, I think because she understood him instinctively better than many of us who had known him longer. When in due course my sister Annabel married and settled in Australia, Margaret became for both my parents the daughter they had lost abroad. Towards the end of my father's life, it was she who went racing with him, she who was ready to have lunch at a moment's notice in whatever new pub or restaurant Robert fancied trying in the Thames Valley. She also gave my parents three beloved grandchildren (the only non-Australian ones they had in Pa's lifetime), saw my father happily into his middle eighties, and is still close to my mother. Margaret and I came to a bitter eventual divorce, but for the way in which she has consistently and unselfishly looked after my two parents, three children and now two grandsons, I shall always be in her debt.

We decided to marry, naturally, in her native Boston, in July 1965, but this was easier said than done. I have never had any religion, was christened but never confirmed, while Margaret came from a long line of Irish Catholics. Peggy, her mother, who is still splendidly alive, worked almost all her life for Polaroid in Boston, but has spent every one of the last forty or so Christmases crossing the Atlantic to inspect her three grandchildren, and now two great-grandchildren, and to present them with the latest in Polaroid cameras. Margaret was her only child, but at the time of our wedding her family was run and dominated by Peggy's own mother.

Known universally as Ma, she was a wondrous and formidable old bat, who seemed to me the oldest woman alive, who had fled Ireland at the time of the 1916 Troubles. She had settled in Boston, given birth to almost a dozen children of whom Peggy was the youngest, outlived at least two husbands, and now ruled her large family, few of whom had ever escaped her or Boston, with a rod of Irish iron. It was she, since Margaret's father had died tragically of alcohol poisoning in a distant hotel room a year or two earlier, whom I had to approach for her granddaughter's hand in marriage. She gave it with surprising alacrity, considering that I belonged to the 'dirty English', who had driven her into lifelong exile in Massachusetts, and that I was proposing to steal her beloved youngest granddaughter and take her to another country. But she seemed to approve of me, and she lived long enough not only to push our firstborn, Hugo, in his pram, but until the weekend that our first daughter, Alexis, was born in 1971: Ma waited, on her Boston hospital deathbed, until they brought her the news of yet another great-grandchild, whereupon she peacefully passed away, in what I think were her late eighties.

But in those days, to marry into the Catholic Church, especially in Boston, which was its American headquarters because of the Kennedy connection, was no easy matter: it had just got its golden boy into the White House, the first-ever Catholic there, only to see him brutally murdered. (At the time it was still widely assumed that Bobby and Teddy would carry on the succession of Bostonian Catholic President Kennedys in the White House.) A non-believer who wished to marry a Catholic was required to undergo several weeks of instruction, if not conversion, and ITN were only prepared to grant me a couple of weeks off the following summer to fly to Boston, get married, have a honeymoon and return to work in London.

I presented myself at the local Catholic priest's house in Arlington, where my first mother-in-law still lives, only to be told that my quest was hopeless, that I would have to stay in the area for at least another month before any wedding could be arranged.

This, I knew, would be considered a sacking offence by ITN, but then a miracle happened, which I do not suggest had anything especially Catholic about it. As I was disconsolately leaving the vicarage or whatever was the Boston Catholic equivalent thereof, the old priest suddenly asked where I had been to school. 'Sizewell Hall,' I replied, 'in Suffolk. You won't have heard of it.' But then I recalled that Americans say 'school' when they mean 'college'. 'And Oxford,' I added proudly. 'Oxford University, Merton College, nineteen sixty to sixty-three.'

'An Oxford man?' echoed the priest. 'I have never married an Oxford man. What time did you say on Sunday?' So I owe to Oxford my first wedding, as well as many of my lifelong friendships and most of what little I know.

My parents and sister came to Boston for the wedding, my brother wisely decided he had better things to do with his fourteen-year-old life, and there were several friends from Oxford, even one or two from Hawaii. My best man was Peter Young, *en route* back to a life and career in England, and one of the guests was the pioneering American chat-show host Jack Paar, who just loved to cry at weddings, preferably those of total strangers.

We spent our honeymoon in New York, where predictably I blew all our wedding-gift dollars on a large collection of theatre books, then sailed for home – at least, my home – on the SS *France*, a large, luxurious cruise liner where they upgraded you from a cabin to a suite if you could prove you were on honeymoon, which, of course, we could.

In London, I went straight back to ITN, leaving Margaret to settle into our small flat above a paint wholesaler's just beside

Paddington station. We rented it for all of nine pounds a week from, though we did not know it at the time, my old New York childhood friend and Oxford contemporary Johnnie Lahr's first mother-in-law.

Thoughtless and too often at work – a lifetime pattern, I now see, that started here and has never made me the best of marital material – I did far too little to explain London to Margaret, and at first she had few friends, all mine rather than hers. But she behaved, as always, with a clenched New England dignity, only once breaking down when she had been to an extremely chic silver shop, Mappin & Webb, to exchange a hideous wedding present given us by a distant cousin. Just before she entered the shop, her eye lit on a large sign above the door: 'By Appointment'. Entirely understandably, she returned to the flat and telephoned for one.

But she adapted quickly to London, my antisocial working hours and even some of my antisocial friends, and soon found a position at Longman's as an editorial assistant. One of her authors there was Kenneth Tynan, of whom she would return with news and office gossip about his flagellatory sex life, which astounded us in those distant, innocent days, especially as Ken had, I kept noting rather priggishly, only recently arrived as drama adviser to Olivier's first National Theatre company. After all, this was only a year after Philip Larkin had announced the coming of sex itself.

Looking back on the early years of our marriage, I think I was a fairly terrible husband: clumsy and nervous in bed, unenthusiastic about anything that didn't directly concern me or my career, unable to see life through any eyes but my own. I loved Margaret, in my own way, very much indeed, but we had met a long way from our homes, when we were in our early twenties and living away from our families for the first time. These are not excuses or, indeed, regrets for a marriage I would not have missed for the world, the one that gave me all of my children and grandchildren, but I remember several friends telling me that we were never going to make it, coming from such different backgrounds and educations. That they were proved right was largely my fault, and although I found Margaret a publisher for her first few novels, I fear her career was never high enough on my agenda – a complaint that is echoed loudly to this day by my second wife. I have enough trouble in maintaining my own career to focus on those even of the people I most love.

And now something else was going on in my life: one of the joys of ITN, and indeed of my later life at the BBC, was that the television programmes I wrote, edited or hosted seemed to happen late at night, which meant not being on call till about lunchtime. Already workaholic and spending far more than I earned – some things never change – I began to freelance as an interviewer for *The Times*.

As my journalistic life took off so, too, did our marriage click into place with Margaret's first pregnancy. As the flat in Paddington was clearly too small for three of us, we took out a £9000 mortgage (the largest cheque I had ever seen, let alone signed) on a brand-new Wates house on the edge of the woods just above Dulwich College. In a matter of weeks, I had acquired a mortgage and prospective fatherhood: a time, surely, for consolidation and playing it safe. At precisely that moment, however, with no other job prospects, I took it into my head to resign from a somewhat surprised ITN.

19
Hugo and the First Noël

What on earth made me resign from ITN aged twenty-six, with the aforementioned mortgage, a now-pregnant wife and no other job prospects? Two things, possibly three: the word around ITN was of the imminent coming of *News at Ten*, the half-hour networked bulletin that for years had been the dream of all who worked there. Even I could foresee that this would mean the end of the local London late-night news headlines and *Dateline*, where I had achieved my around-midnight fame, if such it could be considered.

It wasn't until I was talking to my old Oxford theatre and now newscasting colleague Peter Snow, during one of our lengthy Holborn pub lunches on one of those days when the news agenda seemed a little light, that he clarified my problem and my future. 'The trouble with you, Morley,' he said amiably, 'is that you lack any interest in current affairs.'

I saw, and none too soon, that he was absolutely right: I have always been bleakly uninterested in politics or news, tend to travel abroad only in search of a good beach or better yet a five-star hotel pool near an equally good restaurant, and am often hard-pressed to name the current foreign secretary. When asked to do so, which is now seldom, I always recall the great Tom Stoppard story. While trying to escape the life of a cub reporter in Bristol some time in the early 1960s, he was told of a vacancy on the foreign desk of *The Times*, and that getting the job was the only tricky bit. Once behind the desk, newspapers and television companies, in those happy days, were so overstaffed that one could continue to write novels, plays, biographies, whatever, in a nice warm environment with a tea trolley, free postage and not a lot else to do. There was, however, the interview to be over-come. 'I wonder, Mr Stoppard,' said the then editor Sir William Haley, 'with your interest in foreign affairs, if you could just name for me the present Foreign Secretary?'

'If you look at my letter, Sir William,' replied Tom, 'you will see it says "interested", not "obsessed".' He did not, I think, get the job, but I hope it is true that years later he met Harold Pinter at a party where they engaged in this exchange. 'I wonder,' said Pinter, 'if you'd have any objections to a tentative plan I have heard of, by which the Comedy Theatre would be renamed the Pinter?'

'No,' said Tom thoughtfully, 'no objections at all. But surely it would save considerable trouble and expense, Harold, if you just changed your last name to Comedy?'

My other reasons for leaving ITN were that I still belonged to that charmed 1960s graduate generation for whom there always seemed to be more jobs than applicants, at least in journalism, and that I had already found something I enjoyed doing still more than writing or reading television news.

Give or take a few profiles for *Isis* and *Cherwell* while I was up at Merton, and a few more in the *Honolulu Star-Bulletin*, my serious career in print journalism, if such it can be called, had started at *The Times*. While still an undergraduate I had sometimes been used, in the footsteps of Michael Billington, as 'Our Oxford Correspondent' by John Lawrence, a revered and wonderful old arts editor at Printing House Square. Such was his longevity at *The Times*, where rumour had it that he had joined the paper as a copy boy soon after the First World War, that he eventually finished up in charge of the Obits page, where it was reckoned he would be well connected to his often equally aged subjects. He was, however, now getting just a little deaf and absent-minded, and had recently run an obituary for the then Duke of Norfolk, the old boy who had triumphantly stage-managed the Coronation and was, if you looked closely, still just about alive.

Not exactly thrilled to find himself dead across an entire page of *The Times*, His Grace rang in some indignation to complain. John, for his part, had always believed that *The Times* was sacred, and therefore could not err. 'Before we start this very interesting conversation, Your Grace,' I heard him bellow down the phone to Arundel Castle, 'I would like to establish just one thing. From precisely where are you now telephoning?'

John always knew from precisely where I was phoning, usually some God-forsaken callbox in the Midlands or North to which he had sent me as a third-string, under Billington and Irving Wardle, drama critic, to pronounce for seven guineas per review on some local rep. There were still no bylines, but I loved the prestige of it all, and rapidly came to the conclusion that a drama critic was what I most wanted to be.

Accordingly, I wrote to every drama critic in London, and even some who were not, asking how in God's name one got a job like theirs. Only two bothered to reply: the veteran *Daily Telegraph* critic W. A. Darlington wrote courteously to wish me luck, adding rather disenchantingly that the last man to have written to him asking how to become a drama critic had then been killed on the Somme.

Rather more helpfully, Ken Tynan wrote back telling me to 'review everything: your life, your lunch, your family, your girlfriends, your journey to work, and one day they will let you review plays'. Not for the first or last time, he was dead right.

For now, however, with time on my hands since the move to our new house in Dulwich, I was able to focus, albeit too briefly, on being a father. The arrival of Hugo was the most exciting thing that had ever happened to me, even though, strictly speaking, I suppose it really happened to Margaret. He was born, as was our first daughter three years later, in a nursing-home just off Harley Street, where they indicated the imminent arrival of a baby by carefully removing the rich Persian carpets that lay under every bed and had presumably done so for a couple of hundred years. Somehow I found the old-fashioned nature of the place irresistible: it was like going into a very old country-house hotel that had fallen on rather hard times, but was still managing to deliver babies on a daily basis.

I suspect I was a hopeless father, clumsy and terrified of breaking this living doll we were given within a day or two to take home to Dulwich: I remember just watching him for hours, terrified that he might stop breathing or turn purple or fall out of a window, which of course he never did. Hugo was extraordinarily self-possessed from the day he was born, and has remained so these last thirty-five years. He and my brother were perhaps the only two babies I have ever known to arrive on earth looking unsurprised by their great adventure.

Hugo's arrival made us a family instead of just a marriage, and coincided almost exactly with my decision to start a new life in print rather than on the air; while watching him I soon dreamed up a scheme to keep me in work at *The Times*, albeit on a freelance basis and not, alas, as a drama critic. John Higgins, to whom I owe the rest of my career at *The Times* and a lot else besides, inherited me from the finally retiring John Lawrence, and over a Garrick lunch – the first I'd ever had, though by no means the last, without my father – I sold him the idea for a sequence of *Times* Profiles of Great Exiles.

Ever since I had lived in America and Australia something had interested me in the idea of exile and exiles, people who go abroad for one reason or another then find that they cannot come home, but remain painfully aware that they cannot feel altogether at home anywhere else, and I came up with a shortlist of five: the Duke of Windsor, Somerset Maugham, Noël Coward, Charlie Chaplin and Alfred Hitchcock.

My dream, of course, was to get back to the Hollywood of my childhood, or at least Switzerland and the South of France, which was where my exiles seemed mainly to be living now, but John soon made it clear that overseas travel was not within his budget: I would have to catch them all on their next appearances in London, which I did, except the Duke of Windsor who gave me the excuse for a sunny weekend in Paris. With one notable exception, all my exiles were angry old men, irritated by the England they had left, unhappy in their new-found lands, and unable to understand fully the changes that had overtaken their homeland in their absence and, worse, without their permission. They all seemed stranded, like ancient mariners, somewhere between their country of birth and their country of residence.

The exception, of course, was Noël Coward. I went first to meet him at the Savoy Hotel, where he was staying in his usual River Suite while filming Otto Preminger's *Bunny Lake Is Missing* with Laurence Olivier and a young Hollywood star who, during that first interview I did with Noël, put his head round the door of the suite: 'Just to introduce myself, Mr Coward,' he said, charmingly enough. 'I'm the star of your new film, my name is Keir Dullea.'

Noël, having reached a semi-colon in one of his long answers to me, looked up briefly: 'Keir Dullea,' he said, not unkindly. 'Gone tomorrow.'

A man who could do that on a reflex, without pausing for breath, then continue the original sentence exactly where he had left it, had to be someone special and I went away to write, for *The Times*, a profile that duly appeared unsigned under Coward's own title *Blithe Spirit*. All I had done was to act as a stenographer, writing down as much as I could – I have never managed shorthand – of Noël's lengthy monologue about the theatre, the cinema, Hollywood, Switzerland, the Savoy Grill, Gertrude Lawrence and much else besides.

'I am,' Noël told me, on that first adult encounter – we

had met when I was a child with my grandmother Gladys who was playing his *Relative Values,* also at the Savoy, in about 1952, but I seemed not to have made much impression on him then – 'one of the two greatest living British playwrights. The other, of course, is Terence Rattigan, and there's possibly young Shaffer coming up on the outside rail, but nobody else that I can see . . . I was the first living playwright to be staged by dear Larry-boy at his National Theatre,' where Olivier had recently presented an all-star *Hay Fever* with Edith Evans, Maggie Smith, Lynn Redgrave, and Derek Jacobi among others under Noël's own direction, 'and quite right too . . . I am England, and England is me. I was brought up in Teddington, Middlesex, an ordinary, middle-class little boy. I didn't gnaw kippers' heads in the street, as Gertie Lawrence quite untruthfully always insisted she did, but nor was my first memory the crunch of carriage wheels in the drive, because we didn't have a drive . . . but I am not modern, at least not in the Royal Court sense: I am not angry, nor do I have any desire to educate or reform the human race, even if I could . . . all I want to do is to entertain, which, of course, is why I am now so unfashionable among critics, although luckily the public still loves me . . . Like darling Johnny G, I am deeply uninterested in politics, especially as for tax reasons I now live abroad . . . I don't think it much matters whether England is run by Socialists or Conservatives: it's the individual people of all classes who really matter, and a duchess in distress can be just as moving as a bereft charlady: it is who we are that matters, not what we are, and we English are a curious lot – lazy, very witty, full of humour, very reliable and often as merry as grigs, whatever Wesker and Osborne tell us . . . I've been in the critical wilderness, man and boy, for about forty years, but I have to say I've often been very happy there, and done very nicely, thank you. I've made my way across sixty years from Teddington through

Clapham Common, Battersea, Pimlico, the West End, and on to America and now Switzerland, and had a very good time doing it.'

I wish I could say that I knew then this hour-long encounter would make my name as an arts journalist, but in the first place *Times* Profiles were then unsigned, and second it wasn't until I saw my Coward piece heavily quoted in *Time* magazine and elsewhere that I fully realised its significance. Noël had just come in from the cold, and this was the first time that he had talked at any length about himself or his work since the climate had turned in his favour with the National success of *Hay Fever* a few months earlier. It had been performed, as he said, 'by a cast which could have read the Albanian telephone directory out loud and made it rivetingly exciting'.

These late 1960s were the last of Noël's many turning-points: despite the success of *Hay Fever*, when I began writing about Coward he was still regarded by many, albeit wrongly, as an exiled relic from some pre-war world of lost glamour, much as we now regard perhaps Ivor Novello or Frederick Lonsdale; I was told by publishers and editors that if I wished to make my name as a theatrical journalist, I would be well advised to lay off Noël and get back to the newer star writers of the Royal Court revolution. But almost all the other would-be young critics of my generation were already doing that and, in an uncharacteristically astute professional moment, even I could recognise a gap in the market. The interest in my profile suggested to me that Coward might well be worth another look, and in the five years that elapsed between that first interview and the publication of my (and his) first biography, *A Talent to Amuse*, I saw Noël go from considerable neglect to a knighthood and sudden status as the Grand Old Man of British theatre.

In several letters, cards and cables that I cherish, he is good enough to credit me with at least partial responsibility for this last of his many transformations, but I am well aware that, as usual, Noël did it all by himself: I was just lucky enough to be the duty engineer who plugged him back into the circuit.

In return, Noël became godfather to my only son, and although he died when Hugo was barely three, I still have a wonderful picture of the two of them, Hugo on Noël's knee, looking, in Coward's own phrase, 'like two very old Chinese character actors' with nothing separating them but seventy years.

My obsession with Coward started that mid-sixties morning in the Savoy, and has not wavered in almost forty years. Many other biographies of him have been written since, and I am well aware that mine, coming as it did in Noël's lifetime from the typewriter of the pre-Aids generation, is now not just dated but outdated. All the same, it got my career and even my finances off the ground and, for that and more, I shall always be grateful to Noël. As for the title, *A Talent to Amuse*, I found it buried in a song from his 1930 *Bitter Sweet* that seemed to me unusually autobiographical, and is now used often to define its lyricist. When I found it, both the show and the song had been unheard for about thirty years:

> For I believe
> That since my life began,
> The most I've had is just
> A talent to amuse,
> Heigho, if love were all . . .

Who on earth made me think I could be a biographer? One woman. She was a literary agent called Jackie Reynolds, who eventually worked at Curtis Brown. To my amazement, she had written to me at Oxford, having read some of my undergraduate reviews in *Cherwell* and *Isis*. When I was just nineteen, she told me that if ever I thought of doing a book, I should come to see her.

Almost ten years later I did, and she negotiated my first biography with Heinemann. Shortly thereafter she introduced me to another agent, Mike Shaw, a contemporary at Oxford whom somehow I had never met. I only understood the reason for the introduction a few months later: Jackie was dying from cancer and wanted to be sure I was well looked after. And so I have been, these last thirty years or so. Characteristically, she never said a word about the cancer.

Of all the books written about Noël since – many not by me, though several are – the best by far for contemporary perspectives is Philip Hoare's 1995 *Noël Coward*, an amazingly successful work considering that Philip, by my reckoning, was barely born at the time of Noël's death, and had none of the advantages of personal acquaintance or friendship – not that these are always helpful to a critical biographer, as I discovered. By far the best critical study is that produced by my old friend John Lahr, with whom I made a three-hour BBC television documentary about Noël on the occasion of his 1999 centenary – the last of that length that will ever be made, I suspect, about anybody for arts television in Britain or anywhere else.

As the sole literary executor of Noël's estate, I have been in the happy position, over three decades since his death in 1973, of watching over, in partnership with his lifelong lover Graham Payn, his posthumous reputation, encouraging what books, productions and television documentaries would do him some good, and sometimes even managing to deter others that would clearly have harmed his memory. Now we are lucky enough to have been joined by both Dany Dasto and Alan Brodie, who bring to the Coward table their own expertise, and manage wonderfully to make Graham and me feel less alone on the night watch.

But the position of executor is not that of censor, and nor

should it be: often, all I can do is offer advice to be taken or rejected, yet I retain more pride in my work for the Coward estate than in many of the other, often better-paid assignments that I often ludicrously convince myself I can manage to undertake. Reputations are precarious and time-sensitive, shifting with an imperceptible change in the national mood: I have lost track of the number of journalists, directors and documentary-makers at home and abroad whom I have tried to guide towards what I believe to be the truth about Noël, and away from their inaccurate beliefs about where he came from and what he stood for.

Briefly, Noël was the playboy of the West End world, jack of all its showbiz trades and Master – hence the nickname – of most. He was a gay, subversive workaholic from South London, whose greatest creation was himself: the urbane, sometimes wealthy, always witty and wise entertainer, apparently without a care in the world even though he often had rather more than his fair share.

The boy actor of the First World War was the café-society singer-songwriter of the twenties, in which decade he also wrote the first play overtly about drug-taking and secretly, of course, about homosexuality, *The Vortex*. In the more complex thirties he became the cynical philosopher and passionate opponent of Chamberlain and Munich, but when war was declared he turned again, this time to the super-patriotism of *In Which We Serve* and then to the bitter-sweet, archetypally clenched, understated English romanticism of *Brief Encounter*. In the fifties, rejected by his beloved England, he discovered America, playing his own songs to the Nescafé society of Las Vegas with the same energy and enjoyment he had played them to the café society of pre-war London. In the sixties he came home to film *The Italian Job* with Michael Caine, having started filming in 1917 for D.W. Griffith with Lillian and Dorothy Gish. In the seventies he was awarded a long-deserved knighthood, and died in his beloved Jamaica, leaving his last poem unfinished by his bedside:

> When I have fears
> As Keats had fears
> Of the moment I'll cease to be,
> It gives me comfort to dwell upon
> Remembered friends who are dead and gone –
> And the jokes we had, and the fun . . .
> How happy they are, I cannot know,
> But happy am I, who loved them so . . .

With the exception of John Gielgud, who was once his understudy, I cannot think of anyone more obsessively involved with the history of twentieth-century British theatre, nor anyone quite so prolific within its many disciplines.

After that first meeting at the Savoy, I began to see Noël on his increasingly frequent journeys home from Jamaica and Switzerland, where he had made his homes. On one hilarious occasion he took me back to the Savoy to meet a couple of legendary American party-givers, the lawyer Arnold Weissberger and Arnold's discreet but long-time gay lover, the agent Milton Goldman. They invariably travelled with Arnold's mother, a fearful old lady: 'Did you meet the mother?' Noël asked, as we left the party. 'I don't believe a word of it. Mother, indeed. They hire her from the Sears Roebuck catalogue to make them look respectable.'

Another time we were crossing Leicester Square, when outside the Odeon we saw a poster advertising a rerun of a successful adventure film from J. Arthur Rank. 'MICHAEL REDGRAVE and DIRK BOGARDE,' read the poster, 'IN *The Sea Shall Not Have Them.*' Noël stared at this for a moment. 'I fail to see why not,' he murmured. 'Everyone else has.'

I had already started to think it odd that there was no biography of Noël, and that his own two autobiographies had been long out of print; they, moreover, did not cover the years 1930–39, nor those since 1945. I suggested to him that it was time someone wrote his remarkable life story, and that on balance he might do worse than me. In my innocence of publishing customs, since I had never written a book, I also suggested that, as it was his life we were talking about, he would, of course, be entitled to a sizeable cut of the proceeds, were there to be any.

Noël explained to me the tradition whereby biographees did not (then, at least) get any of the cash, and agreed that my 'curious fascination' with him and his work probably qualified me to write his life. As, however, I had never published anything longer than a thousand words, he proposed that I send him a couple of trial chapters about his childhood. If he approved them, he would open his files and give me two lists of telephone numbers: 'Those of my friends, and those of my enemies. Start with the enemies and you'll get a better book, dear boy.'

Once he had read the trial chapters and handed over the keys to his mother's trunk, which was full of letters and scrapbooks dating back to about 1910, he had only one reservation. He was hoping, he said, that I would write a critical biography, since fan books were unadulterated rubbish and a waste of bookshelf space, but he wanted no mention of his homosexuality. This was still the late 1960s: Gielgud's arrest and Lord Montagu of Beaulieu's prison sentence were still fresh, raw memories in the gay community, and the changes instituted by the Wolfenden report were as yet barely discernible. In his last play, *Song at Twilight*, written at this time, Sir Hugo Latymer, the character he wrote for and to some extent about himself (although at the time he always claimed it was Somerset Maugham), says to the old flame who wishes to 'out' him: 'Even when the actual law ceases to exist, there will still be a stigma attached to "the love that dare not speak its name" in the minds of millions of people for generations to come . . . It will take more than a few outspoken books and plays and speeches in Parliament to uproot moral prejudice from the Anglo-Saxon mind.'

That, around 1969, was Noël's position on what was not then known as gay outing; his was a position maintained by the likes of Dirk Bogarde (about whom I also wrote a book) well into the 1990s. At the time I started on his biography, Noël made it clear that his private life was to remain just that. Nowadays this is not a condition I suspect many of us would accept, but thirty years ago it seemed merely a reflection of the current sexual climate and, as such, unobjectionable. Besides, Noël made it clear that the ban was purely professional and pragmatic; when he died, he said, he hoped I would revise my book and tell the truth about his homosexuality, since he was not ashamed of it. But for the time being, he was still living on his royalties – we shared the inability to save money – and he could ill afford, therefore, to alienate an audience of his admirers, which was not, he reckoned astutely, made up entirely of trendy, young *Guardian*-reading liberals.

On the contrary, he said, his fan-base was largely comprised of old ladies in the Home Counties, with whom years ago he had reached an unspoken 'don't ask, don't tell' pact. Deep down, he thought, they all knew he was gay, and he knew that they knew that he knew. It was just easier if no one said anything. Why alienate a whole section of his constituency, just as he had begun to claw his way back into favour with his fellow countrymen after years of vilification as a tax exile?

It was not, of course, only the tax demands and a lifelong inability to balance his books that had driven Noël abroad in the mid-1950s: within a few months of the Gielgud arrest for homosexual soliciting in the Coronation summer of 1953 – in his *Diaries* Noël writes with unusual vitriol about John's 'sheer stupidity' in being caught – he and several other high-profile gays had moved abroad, aware of the attempt by the British establishment to start a witch-hunt against famous homosexuals, which had horrible echoes of the McCarthy persecution of suspected Hollywood Communists on the other side of the Atlantic at this same time.

All the same, as my book neared its end, I decided to make one last attempt to persuade Noël to let me tell the truth about his private life. It had not been particularly scandalous since, like Gielgud, he usually chose low-profile partners who would not disturb him at the typewriter or in rehearsal. However, he had long relationships with such near contemporaries as Ned Lathom, the producer Jack Wilson, and the actors Alan Webb and Louis Hayward, before he had settled down happily after the war with Graham Payn. I felt that this explained partly who he was and what he wrote.

Graham, Noël's secretary Lorn Loraine and his near-lifelong assistant Cole Lesley were my greatest allies and witnesses while I worked for nearly three years on the book, and I spent some long, pleasant weekends with them and Noël at his chalet above Les Avants in Switzerland. Certainly Graham and Coley had slowly come round to the view that perhaps the book ought somehow to deal with the private as well as the professional life.

Noël, however, remained unconvinced, until at last I thought I had found a way of changing his mind. In the late 1960s, the drama and television critic T.C. Worsley, a figure of impeccable *Financial Times*, Garrick Club and MCC credentials, courageously published a slender memoir called *Flannelled Fools* in which he revealed a lifelong addiction to the rough trade in homosexual encounters. Empires did not totter, membership of the Garrick was not withdrawn, and at last – or so I thought – we had the breakthrough to convince Noël that the sexual-tolerance climate was changing.

I took Worsley's book out to Les Avants on my next weekend visit, and Noël took it with him to bed on the Friday night. On the Saturday morning, Coley, Graham and I were gathered expectantly around the breakfast table. Noël duly appeared, in what I always thought of as his dressing-gown from *Private Lives* – it may have been since he threw little away – and tossed the Worsley memoirs across the table at me. 'I have read your little volume,' he said dismissively, 'but there is, I fear, one thing you have all overlooked. It is the difference between me and dear Cuthbert Worsley, and it is this. Nobody would care if Cuthbert Worsley had revealed that he slept with mice. About me, they care.' The subject was never mentioned again.

A Talent to Amuse was published in October 1969. Although I have written – alone and sometimes with Margaret or Ruth or others – something like thirty titles in the intervening thirty-odd years, a first book is like a first child: not automatically or necessarily the best or the most beloved, but the one whose arrival you always remember with the greatest clarity. 'No man,' my father wrote in his best play, *Edward My Son*, 'ever really deserves to have a child,' and, in a curious way, I think I have always felt like that about books too. What was so magical for me about *A Talent to Amuse* was that in those far-off days you published on a Thursday (or, to be precise, Heinemann did), got almost all your reviews that day, and the rest on the following Sunday, leaving only the magazines to follow. No long drawn-out straggling over the next few months as happens now, no frantically having to peer at multiple listings in minuscule type in the hope of the odd recommendation, but a short, sharp shock, not unlike childbirth or the opening of a play. You knew at once what you had got, and what we had got was a huge hit. On publication day, Michael Foot wrote in the *Evening Standard* of 'a major new biography and a major new biographer', and we were off. A week later, Heinemann ran an ad in which my name appeared above new publications by Enid Bagnold, J.B. Priestley, A.J. Cronin and James Leasor. I mention all this not only to boast – which, dear reader, of course I am doing – but also to underline something both miraculous and a little sad: because this was my first book, I thought it was always like

O.U.D.S
TRINITY TERM
1961

The
Shoemakers'
Holiday.

A Midsummer Night's Dream

JUNE 1962

OUDS productions programmes
for *The Shoemakers' Holiday*,
1961, and *A Midsummer Night's
Dream*, 1962

The Wild Duck, Oxford Playhouse, May 1962. The author, as yet
unbearded, is standing centre right. Others who appear in the text and
are seen here include Peter Young, Nigel Frith, Michael Elwyn,
Christopher Matthew and John Watts.

The first wedding: Margaret and I getting married in Boston, 1964 and our three children, Hugo, Alexis and Juliet, sometime in the mid-1970s

One of the few father–son teams to belong to the *Punch* table: Robert
and I in 1985, towards the end of the good times there

Ruth in Venice early in our relationship, photographed unusually well by the author

Me and my brother Wilton in Australia, where he was kindly, if
unprofitably, staging my *Noël & Gertie* in the late 1980s

Me with my brother and sister when both were long-time residents of Sydney

Me and my parents, still at Fairmans forty or so years after they
started our family there

Life upon the wicked stage: shows that I have written, narrated and/or directed over the last decade, and there are an alarming number of others. If you are a lifelong critic, the least you can do is get criticised

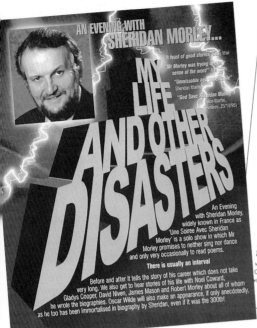

AN EVENING WITH SHERIDAN MORLEY...

"A feast of good stories" *Daily Mail*

"Mr Morley was trying to *give* sense of the word" *The Times*

"Unmissable and *enjoyable*" *Sheridan Morley*

"God Save Sheridan Morley" *Alice Martin*, *Antibes, 25/10/95*

MY LIFE AND OTHER DISASTERS

An Evening with Sheridan Morley, widely known in France as 'Une Soiree Avec Sheridan Morley' is a solo show in which Mr Morley promises to neither sing nor dance and only very occasionally to read poems.

There is usually an interval

Before and after it tells the story of his career which does not take very long. We also get to hear stories of his life with Noel Coward, Gladys Cooper, David Niven, James Mason and Robert Morley about all of whom he wrote the biographies. Oscar Wilde will also make an appearance, if only anecdotally, as he too has been immortalised in biography by Sheridan, even if it was the 300th!

BACK IN LONDON FOLLOWING SELL-OUT TOUR!

Law & Disorder

MICHAEL LAW & SHERIDAN MORLEY

with songs and stories concerning the likes of Cole Porter, Noel Coward, George Gershwin and virtually any other composer/lyricist you care to mention.

Directed by Ruth Leon

Produced by Alan S. Bennett

"Sheridan Morley is in his element ... the songs are impeccably performed by singer-pianist Michael Law ... a touch of genius!" *London Evening Standard*

NOEL COWARD TONIGHT

SHADOWS OF THE EVENING
RED PEPPERS

a double bill of plays by Noël Coward not seen in the West End for 30 years

May 9 - June 9
JERMYN STREET THEATRE

JULIAN SCHLOSSBERG
MASK PRODUCTIONS   REDBUS   MARK S. GOLUB   BILL HABER
by special arrangement with
THE LUCILLE LORTEL
THEATRE FOUNDATION, INC.
present

TWIGGY and HARRY GROENER in

IF LOVE WERE ALL

The Noel Coward -
Gertrude Lawrence
Musical

An Entertainment Devised by
SHERIDAN MORLEY
with The Words & Music of
NOEL COWARD

Scenic and Costume Design
TONY WALTON

Lighting Design	Sound Design	Wig Design
MICHAEL LINCOLN	DOMONIC SACK	PAUL HUNTLEY

Assistant Choreographer	Casting	Production Stage Manager	Technical Supervisor
JEFFRY DENMAN	STUART HOWARD/ AMY SCHECTER, CSA	DENISE YANEY	ROB CONOVER

Associate Producer	General Management	Marketing	Press Representative
MEYER ACKERMAN	EGS	THE RICHARDS GROUP	JEFFREY RICHARDS ASSOCIATES

Musical Direction & Arrangements
TOM FAY
Choreographer
NIKI HARRIS
Directed and Adapted by
LEIGH LAWSON
Album Produced by
BRUCE KIMMEL

VARÈSE SARABANDE
SPOTLIGHT SERIES

Twiggy, Harry Groe

Ruth and my three children on our wedding day in July 1995

My mother (*right*) and Ruth's mother, Rosie, on our wedding day

this and always going to be. Only now do I realise that it was as good then as it was ever going to get.

Admittedly, the success of *A Talent to Amuse* was hugely boosted by the Noël Coward seventieth birthday celebrations, which followed a few weeks later. Referred to long afterwards by Noël himself as 'holy week', these included a televised charity banquet at the Savoy, a National Film Theatre season of his forty or so movies as actor, director or writer, and the announcement from Buckingham Palace that he had been granted a knighthood in the New Year Honours.

Noël went proudly to lunch with the Queen Mother at the Palace, only to be handed a note from Her Majesty regretting that she was bedridden with flu, but hoping that her two daughters would make up for her absence. They gave Noël, from their mother, a pair of gold crested cuff-links. On the verge of his seventh decade he had at last been taken back into the heart of the establishment of the land he loved. It was truly wonderful to behold. Although he lived for three more years in tranquil Swiss and Jamaican semi-retirement, interrupted by a couple of movies and several more revivals of his early plays, they were, in his own words, something of an anticlimax.

Nineteen sixty-nine was an especially flu-ridden winter, and Noël missed the gala launch lunch for my book at Foyle's; he rang me that morning to apologise that he was briefly bedridden, and added that he was sending along an understudy whom he had encountered the previous evening at the Savoy: 'An old friend and neighbour from Switzerland,' Noël said, 'whom I think you might rather like to meet.' For some vague reason, I expected a lawyer or perhaps even a bank manager, and the venerable, white-haired, elegantly suited gentleman who took the chair next to mine at the top table looked perfect casting for the role. His name, he told me, with infinite courtesy and charm as we sat down to eat, was Charles Chaplin. He made a brilliant little speech about the Noël he had known for half a century, then drew his signature tramp on the title page of my own copy of the book. You can't ask a lot more than that of an understudy.

Margaret and I continued to go out to stay with Noël for the occasional Swiss weekend, and whenever Noël was in London he would trek out to Dulwich to inspect Hugo, his last godson. The last time he and I met was a few weeks before he died, on his final visit to London early in 1973: we were talking idly about *A Talent to Amuse* and he suddenly said, 'Something wrong with that book of yours.'

'Now you tell me!'

'Well, it's only that you paint me as a rather isolated figure, which to your generation I suppose I am, but I started out as half of a double-act with Gertie, and somehow I thought we'd end up together, still acting in plays of mine well into our eighties.'

But if you want to make God laugh, as Noël also once remarked to me, you tell him your plans. What had happened, of course, was that Gertie had settled in America during the war, married her theatre manager Richard Aldrich, and returned only once to London, in 1948, in a not very successful drama by Daphne du Maurier called *September Tide*. Then she had gone out, for the only time in her life, to Hollywood, to make a catastrophic film of Tennessee Williams' *The Glass Menagerie*, in which she played the mother of Jane Wyman with an accent not so much Deep South as deep South Wimbledon. But while she was there she saw another film, Rex Harrison and Irene Dunne in *Anna and the King of Siam*, and recognised instantly that here was the basis for a great stage musical. She bought the rights, took it to Rodgers and Hammerstein and the rest, of course, is Broadway stage history. Gertie's hope had been that Noël would play the King, but his hatred of long runs, dislike of long New York summers and lifelong unwillingness to sing the songs of others made him turn the role down, just as later he turned down Higgins in *My Fair Lady*.

It was Noël who recommended to Gertie, and Rodgers and Hammerstein, a new young friend of his, who doubled as a pioneer daytime television producer and nightclub lute-player and singer: his name was Yul Brynner. *The King and I* ran triumphantly through 1951 and into the long, hot summer of 1952, when Gertie's voice and her health became increasingly shaky. Rodgers and Hammerstein asked Noël if, for the good of his friend and their show, he could persuade her to leave the cast. Gertie refused: she had never given up before, and she wasn't about to start now. Besides, she had one great dream left. She wanted to come back and play *The King and I* at the Theatre Royal, Drury Lane, in the Coronation summer of 1953 – a royal return home after all those years abroad. She feared that if she left the show on Broadway, she would forfeit that chance.

So she played on through that long, hot summer and then, in late September, Noël went racing at Folkestone near where he was living, backed a couple of winners, came off the course, bought an evening paper and was stupefied to read, 'GERTRUDE LAWRENCE DEAD'. It was cancer, and she was just fifty-four. Although he lived on for another twenty years, I believe he never again wrote a truly great song or script: it had all been about her. When he wrote her for the last time it was as Elvira in *Blithe Spirit*. And why is Elvira a ghost? Because they were already separated by the war, by the Atlantic and by her marriage.

Sure, he was lifelong gay and she was lifelong impossible, but I had no trouble in subtitling my eventual *Noël & Gertie* 'a love story', because that is exactly what it was, albeit of an eccentric kind. At our last meeting, idiotically, I asked him if, twenty years after her death and thirty after she had settled in America, he ever still thought about Gertie: 'Every morning when I wake up,' he said, 'and every night when I go to sleep,

I see her on that *Private Lives* terrace in France: she never goes away.' That was just about the end of the last conversation we ever had. 'No doubt,' as they say in the play, 'no doubt anywhere'.

20
Alexis and Late Nights and Line-Up

A Talent to Amuse made my name as a theatrical biographer, but it wasn't going to be a pension, even if at twenty-eight I had been looking for one. There were now many other books I wished to write, and Charles Pick at Heinemann was benevolent enough to let me start with one about my grandmother Gladys Cooper. But the advance was hardly going to keep a family of three, even in a small Wates house in Dulwich, and I wondered just how daft I had been to resign from ITN. Margaret had had to give up her publishing job to look after our baby, and although she soon became a novelist and ghost-writer in her own right that, I need hardly remind you, is not usually a route to sustained wealth.

On the credit side, however, and this again is something that would not have happened in the more frantic and fragmented contemporary publishing world, the success of *A Talent to Amuse* seemed to have made me a mini-celebrity in my own – rather than just Noël's – right. I began to turn up in newspaper profiles, usually headlined, humiliatingly, 'Children of the Famous'. In one of these, fractionally more encouragingly headlined 'Fame Without Father', I was featured and photographed alongside Jonathan Dimbleby and Tarquin Olivier, so I reckoned that was probably roughly OK. I have this vague terror that, in another thirty years, we shall all reappear under 'Where Are They Now?'. That's assuming we make it to ninety.

In the meantime, I carried on profile-writing for *The Times* and reviewing London theatre for such specialist magazines as *Theatre World* and *Plays & Players*. The money was derisory even for 1970, but the profiles allowed me to lunch at *The Times'* expense with the likes of Arthur Miller, the young Peter Hall, Harold Pinter, George Devine, Julie Christie, Olivier, Redgrave, Richardson, Gielgud, Guinness, Marlene Dietrich, Katharine Hepburn, Spencer Tracy, John Osborne, Richard Burton, Elizabeth Taylor, David Niven, Douglas Fairbanks, Diana Rigg, Maggie Smith, Joan Plowright and countless other stage and screen stars, directors and writers here and in America, where I went with Margaret and Hugo to visit her Boston family whenever we could afford the air fares.

Many of my early interviewees have long since died, of course, but of those who were in my generation or younger, I am surprised to find, looking down the lists, how many I have continued to write about regularly over three decades. I can't claim, and wouldn't expect, to have remained friends with them all, and some indeed were never going to be friends of mine in the first place, but I take some sort of pride in that – allowing for icy patches of a year or five – I have remained close to a number of them, even though I have not always been able to review them with admiration. Some of those about whom I published my worst critical insults have even allowed me to direct them recently in plays, while others have been unforgiving to an extent that seems out of proportion to the offence.

The truth is that, unlike America where drama, film and even book critics are supposed never to be seen even talking to anyone they might have to review, the British theatre is a small and incestuous place. Maintaining a lifelong feud with someone you are likely to find at the next table in a crowded Joe Allen's requires an unusual dedication to hostilities that has always been beyond my capabilities. Also, none of us is getting any younger, and if there was anyone I had meant to cut I would forget who or why. It is hard enough trying to keep up with your friends, let alone maintaining non-relationships with enemies.

Purely by being in the right place at the right time, I was

also lucky enough to cover in these years the birth of Olivier's National Theatre, the coming of Chichester, Nottingham, countless other new regional theatre companies, and Peter Hall's ongoing triumphs at the RSC, which he had moved to the Aldwych as their first ever London home. This crucial concept was tragically abandoned by his successor Adrian Noble in 2000, and I now look back on the late 1960s as a golden age in drama. It happened through Jennie Lee's unprecedented, and to this day unmatched, achievements as the sole arts minister worthy of the title that this country has ever had.

Then, just as I was despairing of ever again having a regular job with a salary, a desk, a free telephone and maybe even luncheon vouchers, my luck kicked in again. The BBC had just opened their second television channel, called BBC2. Its main claims to broadcasting fame seemed to be tennis and the original *Forsyte Saga*. It did not immediately record large numbers of viewers, because in order to receive it you had to get a bloke to clamber on to your roof and turn your aerial round – many householders with dodgy tiling did not fancy this, especially as they also had to have a set capable of receiving 625 lines instead of the 425 on which BBC1 and ITV were transmitted.

There had been, since BBC2 first went on the air, a programme called *Line-Up*, which was originally intended to act as a ten-minute trailer for that evening's viewing. On the first night presenter Denis Tuohy had proudly announced the arrival of the brand new channel, only to disappear abruptly from the screen because of a massive Shepherd's Bush power cut, which blacked out the rest of the inaugural evening and much of West London. The following night, he opened the show and the network sitting beside a candle. For a while you could only receive us if you lived in selected parts of Hampstead or Bristol, preferably on a hill. The joke around the BBC Television Centre was that it would have been cheaper and easier to phone all of BBC2's viewers rather than try to broadcast to them.

But this was the first new television channel to have opened in Britain since ITV a decade or more earlier, and a maverick group of journalists and broadcasters, who wanted to do something a little more exciting and unpredictable than was currently going out over on the older channels, became involved. One of these mavericks was an ex-*Radio Times* journalist of considerable charisma called Rowan Ayers, who had become the deputy controller of BBC TV Presentation, and was therefore directly responsible for creating *Line-Up*, as well as all the trailers on both networks.

Rowan was – indeed still is, in a long Australian retirement spent mostly on boats with gorgeous women – a man of immense charm and Machiavellian cunning who, after years in the BBC, had learnt how to play the Corporation game while getting away with a surprising number of subversive activities. It was in his time that the *Radio Times* had begun, albeit subtly, to criticise the programmes it was supposed only to be announcing and celebrating.

This interest in reviewing, rather than merely previewing, led to Rowan's next breakthrough: he persuaded the first Controller of BBC2, Michael Peacock, that *Line-Up* should cease to be an anodyne trailer at the beginning of the evening schedules (there was then little daytime television) but move to the end of the nightly programming and expand itself into a late-night review show, hence *Late Night Line-Up*.

The original presenters were Nicholas Tresilian, Denis Tuohy, Michael Dean, Tony Bilbow and a young journalist recently come from advertising to start her television career at Southern, Joan Bakewell. She was forever haunted by Frank Muir's remark on the show one night that she was 'the thinking man's crumpet'.

Joannie was and is a good deal more than that, and it was she who, almost alone, pioneered a serious role for women in

British television. Until then they had been used almost entirely as dolly-birds, actresses, models or hostesses. Joannie proved that a woman could be seen to think on television, which may not seem strange now, but back in the late 1960s was about as radical as you could get.

As for me, my lifelong good luck kicked in somewhere around the beginning of 1968, when Rowan simultaneously lost two of his original presenters: Denis Tuohy was promoted to *Panorama* on BBC1, and Nick Tresilian opted for the life of a West Country farmer, returning to the media only in the late 1990s when he became the magnificently sonorous voice of late-night concerts on Classic FM.

This left Rowan with something of a problem, since *Late Night Line-Up* went out seven nights a week with several interviews and even short films in the mix, all of which required at least four presenters at a time when he was left with only three. My television career had existed thus far only on ITN, but by some weird chance Rowan had seen some of it and rang to ask if I would be interested in 'trying out' for an interview show, which, miracle of miracles, would also let me go some nights to a West End theatre, then return rapidly to the studio and review live on air whatever play or musical I had just seen.

Of all the jobs I have ever had in forty years of television, that was about the most enjoyable: live television reviews of first nights had long been a feature of New York broadcasting, and I was proud to introduce them over here, even if the idea only survived for a couple of years. The problem was essentially geographic: while in New York television is strictly local, in Britain most of it is networked nationwide; it was soon decided that even BBC2 viewers in Scotland, Wales or Cornwall would have precious little interest in a play opening that night several hundred miles away. It was only in the early 1990s, under the aegis of Melvyn Bragg, that I managed to get a regular weekly *Theatreland* going for those LWT viewers within the M25, and even that came to a sharp end after about four series when it was discovered that, however cheap we were to transmit, the rerun of yet another old Hollywood movie would be cheaper still, and probably attract better figures even among insomniacs.

So much for broadcast theatre, though in all fairness there is another problem: if you do a movie show on television – and in the years to come I did many – the film clips are free, and the picture opens simultaneously all over the country. None of that holds true for theatre programmes, where if you wish to be truly topical you have to film the clips yourself on stage during the last rehearsals, when actors least want a camera near them. And, of course, you are still talking about a local event of supposedly little interest to viewers outside the region. It was only when I became a stage director myself in the mid-1990s that I realised why television cameras are about as unpopular in a rehearsal room as they would be in a maternity ward where a birth is about to take place.

Rowan's idea of a try-out for *Line-Up* was to throw me straight into a live interview with John O'Hara, the crusty and magnificently irritable American author of *Butterfield 8* and the original *Pal Joey* stories, among much else; the theory in television on both sides of the Atlantic was then, apparently, that if you could survive an interview with O'Hara, anyone else would be a doddle.

As it happened, I was given only a few hours' notice of the interview to be done live that night, and realised only while driving to the studio late in the day that I knew little about O'Hara the man, or even his work: *Pal Joey* I knew only as a breakthrough Broadway musical, the one that had made Gene Kelly a star and the first to have a heel as hero, and *Butterfield 8* only as a film that had recently won Elizabeth Taylor a long-deserved Oscar. But from somewhere deep in my showbiz memory, I dredged up one more fact about O'Hara: when a friend of his, one of the greatest of all American composers, had died tragically young of an undetected brain tumour just before the war, O'Hara had said, 'They tell me George Gershwin died today, but I don't have to believe it if I don't want to.' The quote had always stayed with me, and I used it to begin our interview. O'Hara seemed pleasantly surprised that it should have been remembered, especially by an English journalist not born at the time of Gershwin's death. We spent a happy half-hour or so talking mainly about George and 'his lovely wife Ira', as one American radio announcer had memorably introduced the brothers.

Even though we never got round to discussing the book that O'Hara was meant to be promoting, the interview was reckoned good enough, and that night Rowan offered me a six-month contract at, I think, £150 a week, more money than I had ever made before on a regular basis.

So, now I had two families: the one at home in Dulwich, where Hugo was getting to be more fun by the day and Margaret had started on her first novel in the little time he allowed her, and the one at Television Centre, where *Line-Up* became my working life for the next six years. We were a tightly knit group, and you will have to forgive another cast-list. Joan was undoubtedly our star, because the press had caught up with the feminist or, at any rate, feminine revolution she was spearheading on the box. There was also Michael Dean, a hugely amiable New Zealander with a line in wry satire, Tony Bilbow, a bespectacled workaholic who has written episodes for just about every radio and television soap opera ever invented, and then such 'part-timers' as Phil Jenkinson, who still runs his own movie archive and fronted with me or Tony almost all of our weekend film programmes, and a man called Brian King who, sadly before most of us had the chance to get to know him, took his own life after a marital breakdown.

There were many other producers, researchers, film-makers and writers in the years I spent with *Line-Up*, and I hope they will forgive me if I only write about the ones to whom I became especially close: Barry Brown, the *Film Night* producer who went on to invent the BBC1 movie programmes fronted for many years by Barry Norman, with both of whom I have spent many happy hours around Wardour Street and Hollywood; Barry Crook, a burly Australian who now runs jazz festivals in his native land; Jim Smith, who had an affair with Joan Bakewell that was the gossip focus of the office for several months, until she started a still more intriguing liaison with Harold Pinter. I discovered this inadvertently and then managed, by the skin of my teeth (I'm a compulsive gossip), not to reveal it until it all came out in Michael Billington's Pinter biography – not least that Harold's *Betrayal* is to some extent modelled on the years he spent with Joan.

I found out when she and I were chatting alone in the office one afternoon about whom we would most like to talk to of the 'impossibles', people like the Pope, Garbo, Jackie Kennedy, Chaplin and Mao Tse Tung, who famously would never give interviews. I mentioned Harold as being almost in that league, and said how much I would like to talk to him on the programme. 'What time,' asked Joannie sweetly, 'would you like to go and see him?' I'm not exactly quick on the uptake, and it wasn't until some days later, thinking the whole thing through, that I reckoned that she could only organise such unprecedented access at such short notice to the great man if she was very close to him indeed.

Later, I got to know Pinter a little, and he has been more than helpful as a witness in several of my biographies and on radio and television programmes about the theatre and, of course, himself. Only once did I experience the renowned Pinter chill, and for once it was not really my fault. I was driving his wife and my old friend Antonia Fraser – we have shared the same superb literary agent, Michael Shaw at Curtis Brown, for about thirty years – home one afternoon, after one of the many literary panel games we used to play on Radio 4.

Knowing of my obsession with Coward, she remarked that Harold was directing a National Theatre production of *Hay Fever* with Maria Aitken, and if I would care to come in for a cup of tea, he would be sure to welcome my advice on how to deal with the play. God knows what made me think she was right, but I regret to say I held forth to him for about half an hour on the meaning of *Blithe Spirit*, Noël, comedy, ghosts, whatever. Only when I looked up to see the most basilisk stare I have ever encountered did it occur to me belatedly that Pinter was not perhaps desperate to hear my thoughts on *Blithe Spirit* or, indeed, anything else.

We happy few at *Line-Up* were immensely privileged: David Attenborough, who had inherited the channel from Peacock, decided that it would be healthy in the midst of BBC2 to have a small band of anarchic and irreverent pirates, who would question and even criticise everything the new channel was trying to do. Our brief stretched across all the arts, so we were allowed to discuss any topic that had occurred on television than night and often invited such turbulent critics as Milton Shulman to come in, have a drink and a sandwich and watch the evening's output, then go live to air and rubbish it unmercifully.

This made our little corridor at Television Centre something of a plague zone: whenever we went into the bar, which was often, other department producers would shrink away from us, unable to believe that on their own network we were encouraging critics to attack whatever they had spent months and fortunes in preparing. We were the enemy in their midst, and I regret to say we enjoyed every angry moment of it, as did David, who said that *Line-Up*, the cheapest programme on his schedule and, since it often went out around midnight, sometimes the least watched, was also the one that caused him more paperwork and indignation than any other.

Eventually the battle reached the BBC governors, to whom all the other BBC2 producing departments complained that we were 'seriously undermining and belittling' the BBC's own output. A particular source of grievance was that we had allowed Nicholas Tomalin to rubbish an expensive costume series called *The First Churchills*, having seen only the first episode. Attenborough defended us valiantly and we went on to make more than two thousand programmes, almost all live and unrehearsed. Bernard Levin once noted that we had become 'inseparable from and symbolic of the very concept of BBC2'. Immodestly, I think I could now add that we had invented the modern television arts-reviewing chat show in all of its better, later manifestations like *The Late Show* and *Newsnight Review*, not that there are many left now.

Our broadcasts were, if not historic, intriguing: I remember going from our tiny studio, hitherto only used for weather forecasting, to the large one across the corridor where they were wrapping up all twenty-six episodes of *The Forsyte Saga*. I brought Kenneth More, Nyree Dawn Porter and Eric Porter (unrelated; now that they are both dead I can reveal that she got her OBE by mistake – someone in Downing Street had said, 'Better give it to that Porter character in the *Forsytes*,' meaning, of course, Eric, and by the time the confusion was realised it was too late to retrieve it, so Eric went unhonoured to his grave) back to our studio for a farewell interview, and was amazed by the reaction. Nothing to do with the interview, alas: unlike the serial, we had begun some tentative but pioneering colour transmissions, and were therefore able to show amazed viewers for the first and only time the most popular characters, and more importantly their costumes, in something better than black and white.

Another milestone was achieved by the producer Mike Fentiman, yet another flamboyant buccaneer in an office unusually full of them, and Tony Bilbow: instead of inviting one of the usual armchair critics into the studio, they decided to go out one night into a local pub, and broadcast some live reaction to that evening's programmes. Again, almost thirty years later, nothing unusual in that – but Fentiman was the first to do it. *Line-Up* seldom gets the credit for the number of television breakthroughs we achieved, albeit always late at night and to relatively small audiences.

Later Fentiman established an entire access unit at the BBC for viewers to make their presence felt on air and even behind the camera, again a milestone in British broadcasting for which he has never been adequately credited, and other spin-offs included not only all the pre-Barry Norman movie-review shows, but also Mike Appleton's *Old Grey Whistle Test*, some pioneering alternative comedy, and a hilariously terrible Sunday-night show, with which I got landed for a while. Since our weekly budget had run out by then, this consisted of screening old repeat clips and pretending they had been 'specially requested' by viewers, whose names and addresses I am ashamed to say we often had to invent, much after the fashion of Letters to the Editor in newspapers.

On the other hand, our luxuries included no regular ending time: we could run the good interviews well into the small hours, and cut short the boring ones after twenty minutes or so; us presenters were allowed a degree of involvement in the casting of the shows, and the nature of the questions, that is now almost unheard-of in an infinitely more cautious television industry. *Line-Up* had almost as many presenters as producers, and we managed therefore to remain a force in the office, I hope for good, rather than being used as bland, actor-like frontmen and women; exactly as I had found at ITN, a new channel was allowing us a freedom and an editorial control that has now long since been denied those who merely front the shows.

I recall vividly another *Line-Up* programme for what happened just after it: I had been interviewing the stage and television dramatist Hugh Whitemore and, as was our custom (also long since abolished), we retired immediately after the show to a hospitality room in the basement where stacked trolleys of alcohol and sandwiches were demolished and replenished. The trick was not to let the guests in there before the show: some nights we lost the battle, and the occasional interviewee could be seen sliding gently off his (it was usually a man) chair and on to the studio floor in a deep, often noisy sleep as we went on air. But that night we had all remained commendably sober, and after the show we were joined as usual by Rowan and his then partner, the gorgeous and wonderfully named Gay Search. (After they broke up, she married another *Line-Up* producer, Tony Laryea, and when their children grew up became a considerable star of his television gardening programmes.)

Anyway, Whitemore was muttering on about the difficulty of finding new subjects for plays, when Gay suddenly began to tell us a story. She had been in real life the neighbours' child in the Kroger spy case, one of the family living across the road with whom the police insisted on billeting themselves for several months while secretly filming the activities of the Russians. Her best friend at school was the Krogers' daughter, just as their mothers were best friends, and as Gay described what it was like to have to betray those you love in the name of your country, Whitemore began to see that here was the making of a marvellous drama. The result was *Pack of Lies*, which Michael Williams and Judi Dench played in the West End for several months.

I began to know that we were winding down, having run out of topics after six years of seven shows a week – breaking only for Easter Sunday and Christmas Day – when I came in one hot August Saturday and asked Jim Smith what was to be our topic of the night.

'Meat.'

'I'm sorry?'

'Meat. There's nothing new on television tonight except a documentary about farming in Argentina, so I've invited three local Shepherd's Bush butchers round to have a look at it, and then I thought we could discuss the various cuts of meat you can get. For about forty minutes.'

Before it all came to a grinding halt, however, one other *Line-Up* night sticks in my mind. It must have been some time in the summer of 1973, just after Noël Coward had died and I had discovered from his will that I was to be his literary executor. One of my immediate tasks was either to update my own biography to take account of the last five years of his life, or to find a new authorised chronicler who could start again, freed now from the obligation to keep anything secret.

I decided on the latter course, and struck gold: a biographer called James Pope-Hennessy had just won the Hawthornden prize, then I think the highest award available to British biographers, for a life of Robert Louis Stevenson. I recalled that, as a young man, he had a brief affair with Noël. Perfect casting. I introduced him to George Weidenfeld, got him a sizeable advance and then, somewhat enviously, went to his flat in Notting Hill Gate to hand over all the papers that I had been unable to use, relating to Noël's homosexuality. We had a pleasant lunch at a nearby Italian restaurant, whereupon I drove up the road to White City for that night's *Line-Up*. Then I went home to sleep.

By this time we had left Dulwich and moved to a house called T'Gallant beside a farm in Waltham St Lawrence in Berkshire, not far from where my parents were still living in Wargrave, and my aunt Sally and her husband Robert Hardy in Henley-on-Thames. The reason for the move was the arrival of our second child, to our delight a daughter, a sister for Hugo. Margaret and I had settled on Alexis as her name, because of our devotion to a now sadly forgotten American actress of tremendous elegance and stylishness called Alexis Smith. Lexi, as she soon became known to all of us, was born, like her brother, in the Victorian nursing-home in Harley Street. I duly popped off to register her birth, one of the few useful things a father can do at such times, only to be told that we couldn't possibly christen her Alexis as in Britain that was a boys' name, derived from the Russian. Chickening out as usual in the face of authority, I grudgingly agreed that she should be named 'Alexandra (Alexis) Joan' – after my mother. About ten years later, Joan Collins began to play a female Alexis in *Dynasty* on television, and the problem went away. But there was one spooky coincidence, as Barry Humphries would say. When Lexi was in her early twenties, I was hosting some cabaret shows in New York for Don Smith; Alexis Smith herself appeared on one, so I was able to tell her that we had named our first daughter after her. A few months later, I went back to New York only to hear that Alexis Smith had died; when I returned to London, Lexi rang me with some family news. She was about to get engaged to a lovely man called Reg, she said. (He is now, of course, the father of my two grandsons.)

'What's his other name?' I asked.

'Smith,' she replied. So Alexis Smith lives on.

But back to Pope-Hennessy: I did that night's *Line-Up*, drove home to Berkshire and was sound asleep when at about four in the morning the phone rang. It was the night sergeant at Notting Hill Gate police station, asking if I could get there right away. Reluctantly I got dressed, drove the forty or so miles back to London, and entered the station to be greeted by a lone cop. 'Thank you for coming in so late, sir. Did you by any chance know a man called James Pope-Hennessy?'

'Did? We had lunch across the road only yesterday.'

'Yes, sir, I'm glad you told me that. Yours is the last name in his diary. We found him at about midnight, strangled to death in his own armchair. I hesitate to ask, sir, but is it true that Mr Pope-Hennessy rather liked being tied up?'

'Er, yes, possibly, but not, I think, by the neck.'

'I see, sir. Only routine, of course, but could you give me an exact account of your movements after you left him at lunch yesterday?'

'Yes, I drove straight to the BBC Television Centre in White City, parked the car, and then with Joan Bakewell I wrote and presented *Late Night Line-Up* on BBC2.'

'Did anybody see you, sir?'

You couldn't make it up, honestly, but it seemed to me one of the most apposite questions ever asked about *Line-Up* in those early days. As for James, it was later established that he had indeed been murdered by one of his 'rough trade' acquaintances, and Noël's secretary, Cole Lesley, eventually wrote the next Coward biography, quite brilliantly.

The other great thing about *Line-Up* was, as with ITN, the office hours: because the shows were late-night, we weren't expected to turn up for work until just after lunch, which meant that, on a full salary, I could still devote my mornings to other work, heedless of what it paid. Thus I went on interviewing for *The Times*, writing reviews for any magazine or paper – usually the *Stage*, to which I still contribute: it's the only place, if you want to be read by actors – that would let me. I even did some Radio 4 work, initially not the arts programmes that have occupied me on Radios 2, 3 and 4 almost ever since, but as the narrator, Mr Soppy, in a comedy series called *The Soppy Legends* written by and starring two wonderful eccentrics, Rob Buckman (now a distinguished doctor in Canada) and Chris Beetles, who runs a highly successful art gallery in St James's.

Rob and Chris had been comics since their medical-school days – a tradition had developed where doctors turned into entertainers or writers when not on their ward rounds: 'Richard Gordon' Ostlere and Jonathan Miller had started it, and when I went on to *Punch* with Miles Kington, I discovered him and yet three more doctors moonlighting as a singing group called to this day Instant Sunshine.

I think Beetles and Buckman really wanted Kenneth Horne, a genius of a straight man in radio comedy, but as he had just died they had to make do with me. For reasons known only to BBC accounting, we recorded the series in Manchester, trekking up every Sunday on the early train to be greeted by the same mournful Jamaican ticket collector at the barrier. Week after week, Beetles would solemnly inform him, 'We've come about the Jokes,' and I would spend the rest of the day giggling at their considerable comic invention.

We lasted on Radio 4 for a couple of series, whereupon I was sent for by a traditionally strait-laced Controller. 'Mr Morley,' he said wearily, 'if you seriously wish to make a career in radio arts broadcasting, you really must stop fooling about in comedy.' The choice was taken out of my hands when Beetles and Buckman decided to move on to other projects, but I have seldom found radio quite so hilariously enjoyable, either as a listener or a participant.

In the mid-1970s, I had hosted *Film Night*, still then under the *Line-Up* umbrella for a year, but had come badly unstuck one night when I rashly laid into a more than usually appalling Hollywood action adventure. The revenge of Wardour Street was swift and sure: they withdrew their free clips from our next few programmes, leaving me to sit there with an autocue and some stills but not a lot else: less than ideal conditions for a film programme. No more clips, they said sweetly, until I promised not to attack their productions. Nor would they allow any of their visiting Hollywood stars to be interviewed by me.

Were they doubly hurt because these same producers had been gainfully employing my father and grandmother in many movies over many years, or was that my usual second-generation paranoia? Either way it was clear that the situation could not be allowed to continue, especially as I decided for once to take the moral high ground by refusing to give in to what I announced in the press was 'distributors' blackmail', secure in the knowledge that I still had a contract under the *Line-Up* umbrella. Sure enough, after a couple of no-clip programmes, Rowan gave the show back to its original host, Tony Bilbow, and I returned happily to the nightly interviews.

Barry Brown and another BBC2 producer, Iain Johnstone, with whom I had also been at ITN, then began to redevelop the format for Barry Norman on BBC1, and the rest, of course, is television-movie history.

Not only did *Line-Up* leave all our mornings free, but the schedule also meant that we each hosted about three shows a week, leaving three nights clear for theatregoing. I got my first regular review column on the *Tatler* early in the seventies, and then, as *Line-Up* started to fade, an even better position as the sole London drama critic of the *International Herald Tribune*, which I have maintained to this day, more than a quarter of a century later. I also published other biographies and movie and theatre books, including even an early collection of notices I had written, which I called *Review Copies*.

One of my earliest international star interviewees, initially for *The Times* and later for the first-ever Capital Radio arts programme, *Aquarius*, which Susannah Simons and I inherited from Humphrey Burton, was the formidable Marlene Dietrich. I had first met her in California with Gladys after the war, and later in Switzerland with Noël, a memorable occasion when she announced that all she expected now of her old friends was that they should last through lunch. She had arrived at Les Avants swathed in the famous floor-length white fur coat, although it was August, clutching a long-playing gramophone record. Noël's hands were shaking, so he gave it to me to put on the record-player and we all stood there listening to the traditional applause. It seemed to be lasting rather longer than usual, right through the first band of the LP. There was then a short pause, after which band two started with more applause, but still no music. By this time we were seriously staring at our feet. 'Ze furst band,' rasped Marlene, 'vos my applowse in Denmark. Now ve hear my applowse in Sveden.' If Noël hadn't started to giggle, things might have gone better over dinner that night.

A few years later, I was with Marlene briefly on one of her

last concert tours in Britain. These usually took place not in the West End but in theatres like Richmond or Wimbledon, which she could hire by the week, thereby avoiding the need to share the profits with any management. The fans were still out in force but Marlene herself, having fallen off a stage in Australia, was now in pain and more than usually irritable. Once, backstage, I asked her who she really trusted: 'Nobody. Except the girl from Interflora I pay to run down the aisle every night with the flowers. Then I put the flowers in a bucket backstage, she collects them the following night and runs down the aisle with them again. They last the whole week. Clever, no?' And, of course, frugal, as she always was.

Many others, including my old friend Alexander Walker, had already written brilliantly of her movies, so I decided on a book about her post-war stage life, curiously unchronicled. Seen live in concert, Dietrich was, I reckoned, the greatest feat of theatrical engineering since the invention of the trap door. An old German lady with a slight limp, she would come down to the footlights swathed in acres of white fur and a sequined gown that held her together like armour, and take your breath away. Then she would receive her applause as of regal right, coolly sifting and apparently checking it for the correct volume and duration. She took no prisoners, held no hostages: it was patently not wonderful for her to be seeing us, or to be in our wonderful country again, and she wasted no time telling us anything different. Hers was one of the most icily unsentimental stage acts ever achieved: she was a musical Mother Courage. Like Lenya, she looked as though she had been trained in a school of asexual Teutonic drum majors; like Garland, she could suddenly find a catch in her throat that would break your heart; like Coward, she put a premium on crisp diction. Yet she was all her own invention, unique and irreplaceable, a sharp reminder of what could be achieved by the chemistry of the human spirit alone. Even I, in a long and lucky life interviewing stars, have never known a greater one.

I published a book she did not initially care for, principally, I suspect, because of the reference to the 'old German lady with a slight limp'. But a couple of years later, around the end of the 1970s, one or two other unauthorised biographies appeared, which she liked even less. Then she sent me a sharp note: 'I have read your book again, and maybe it is not so bad. Kindly send me to Paris at your own expense 200 copies for me to give friends for Christmas. I do not wish to pay postage either.' And so, of course, I did, and she didn't: few of us ever dared say no to Marlene.

At the end, she lived alone in her apartment at 15 Avenue Montaigne in Paris; what is not so widely known, however, is why she became a recluse. For years she had employed a maid to whom she was utterly merciless, and finally the maid decided to seek revenge. One night, a year or two before she died, Marlene was giving a dinner party for the likes of Charles Aznavour, Charles Trenet and Sacha Distel. Having yelled all day at the maid about the preparations, she then went to have a bath. The maid crept downstairs, sat by the elevator and, as each guest arrived, regretted that Madame had, alas, fallen suddenly and strangely ill, and would therefore be unable to receive them. Upstairs, meanwhile, Dietrich sat alone, like Miss Havisham, at the carefully decorated table, and decided that her friends had mysteriously deserted her. She almost never again left her bed.

During these *Line-Up* years, I had been tempted away from Heinemann, my original and kindly publishers, to George Weidenfeld, who was buying up authors as if they were going out of fashion – which, of course, most of us eventually did. He was another of the mogul father figures I have always sought out and cherished: vast, flamboyant, apparently unbelievably wealthy, and unconsciously as funny as any of the Kordas who shared his middle-European background. One night we were having dinner at the flat he and his beloved Annabel still inhabit on the Thames Embankment by Cheyne Row. 'I have good idea for you, Morley,' he said benignly. 'You write me life of Oscar Wilde.' I went over carefully to his gold-plated bookcases, took down my Wilde biography, which he had published a couple of years earlier, and silently handed it to him. 'I told you was good idea,' George said simply, and we carried on eating.

I had written my Wilde biography because my father had been the first actor to play him on stage and screen, and because George Weidenfeld, buying in Paris a job-lot of photographs from the turn of the century for some other book, had happened upon something quite remarkable. Among the photographs was one taken just below the Eiffel Tower, showing Wilde, in the last months of his life, immaculately dressed and with a showgirl on either arm, not to mention a golden watch-chain around his sizeable stomach, a top hat and cane. All previous biographies had emphasised that in these months Wilde was dying alone and unloved in abject poverty. As so often the camera told a different story, and I wrote the book to revise the then conventional wisdom about his death.

Yet another book I researched and wrote during the *Line-Up* years was *Tales from the Hollywood Raj*, about the British acting colony in California, which led me on to the first biography of David Niven, which I started to write at his sons' request around the time of his death.

Before I had got very far with that, though, my own golden professional life had come to an abrupt end: the enduring appeal of *Line-Up* was the regular income, the time it gave me for other projects and, perhaps above all, the club-like atmosphere. Having always been a loner at schools around the world, I now relished jobs in a community of people who rapidly became friends as well as colleagues. I was lucky enough to achieve that three times – at ITN, *Line-Up* and then at *Punch*. I have never achieved it since, and I miss it in this era of computers and home-working. The community of journalists was always what made my career such fun for me, and it died with the great exodus from Fleet Street to Wapping twenty or so years ago.

What brought about the end of *Line-Up* was David Attenborough's decision, after several years as Controller of BBC2 and then of all BBC television, to go back to his beloved wildlife: 'I find I prefer the animals in the jungle,' as he once told me, 'to the animals now inhabiting the Television Centre.'

His successor was an ex-Radio 1 Controller called Robin Scott, who had no liking for our programmes, and was determined to make his own life easier by cutting off what was still a prime source of internal complaints. Within a few months *Line-Up* and its now myriad satellite shows were off the air, and Robin sent for each of us presenters individually to consider our futures. I've no idea what he said to the others, although I know that soon Michael Dean returned (luckily not for ever) to his native New Zealand; Tony Bilbow went back to writing soap operas; and Joan Bakewell went off to seek her fortune on BBC1 – where instead of sidelining her to religion they should have made her the prime arts correspondent and sent her into battle against Melvyn Bragg and his *South Bank Show*. They never did and, without a recognisable arts face, the BBC never retained its supremacy in the field, leaving *Omnibus* and *Arena* to drift around the schedules without a host until eventually they became as confused as the crew of the *Flying Dutchman*.

As for me, Scott said amiably, I could choose between hosting *It's A Celebrity Knock-out* or, if I was very lucky, *Come Dancing*.

I tried to explain gently that I had not achieved even a third-class degree in Modern Languages from Oxford to embrace quite such a fate, but his eyes had already glazed over, and I found myself suddenly at White City tube station without a job or even a golden handshake: my ongoing six-month contract was, even after six years, still just that and about to expire.

True, I had the *Tatler* and the *Herald Tribune* and the beginnings of yet another Radio 4 arts programme, this one I think called either *Scan* or *Options* and run by the redoubtable Rosemary Hart. She kept me happily employed on *Kaleidoscope* all through the 1980s and beyond. I had also just started up, for Joy Boatman, the first-ever weekly theatre programme for the BBC World Service, *Theatre Call*. But even with all of that and a sizeable advance to write the life of David Niven and edit, with Graham Payn, *The Noël Coward Diaries*, both for Weidenfeld, the loss of *Line-Up* left an ugly hole in the middle of our finances. What was more, there were about to be five of us.

21
Juliet and Times *Remembered*

I think Margaret and I both knew right away that Juliet would be the last of our children: neither of us was getting any younger, I was a shamefully absentee father, and now I had the additional alibi of having to spend a couple of hours at least on the M4 every day. Although I had vague dreams of living in the country and writing my books in a gorgeous study, the truth was that we could never have afforded to exist on my books alone. It was the journalism and the broadcasting that paid the bills, and for those I still needed to be in London every day and most nights.

Juliet was born a week before Christmas 1975, in the amazingly modern and computerised surroundings of a sparkling new maternity ward at the Royal Berkshire Hospital in Reading, a bewildering change, at least for me, from the old Victorian nursing-home in Marylebone. She was, of course, the best Christmas present any of us had ever been given.

Because she was the baby of the family we all spoiled her rotten, although, oddly, it was Hugo and Lexi, then eight and five, who did most of that. They had their own living doll for Christmas, and watching the three of them growing up together was for me, and I hope for Margaret, the best of times in our then already rather distant and distanced marriage. Neither of us was unfaithful to the other, until everything else had fallen apart a decade or more later, but I think we already knew that temperamentally, emotionally, in our interests and desires, we were no longer a marriage made in heaven. What kept us together, of course, were the three children we so loved, always have and always will.

Waltham St Lawrence, the village in Berkshire where we had settled, reminded me of the nearby Wargrave of my own childhood where my parents still lived. Then it had one shop, one pub, and was still relatively untouched by the sprawl of new houses that was already turning Wargrave into a small town and Henley into almost a city. Perhaps without being fully aware of it, I was now trying to re-create for my family the life I had so enjoyed with Robert and Joan forty years earlier, admittedly on a rather more limited income.

Margaret and I had always been lucky with our neighbours: in Dulwich, they had been Claire and Michael Hamlyn, she the daughter of a legendary *Daily Mirror* editor who, back in the thirties, had been the first to go briefly to prison rather than reveal sources, and he a night and then foreign editor on *The Times*; in Waltham, they were the Bedwells, she a great friend to Margaret and he a stockbroker of tremendous joviality, Mr Pickwick come to life. They had three daughters who were only a little older than our children; throughout our ten or so years there, we got on so well with them that we put a gate into the hedge so that the children could play together without having to go out into the road. I often wonder if it's still there – I know the Bedwells are.

Whether it was an illusion, or we were just lucky in a Berkshire backwater village of admittedly considerable affluence, these late seventies also seemed a time of safety. I can never recall worrying, as perhaps I would now, where the children were when they were out of our sight, and I think Margaret, who was with them much more than I, gave them the kind of childhood that my brother and sister and I had enjoyed, of carefree living against a background of safety and solidarity.

The only time I can recall the real world crashing into our living room was when, one Boxing Day, we gave our annual drinks party and invited a new neighbour, Humphrey Atkins, who had just taken over from the assassinated Airey Neave as Mrs Thatcher's Minister for Ireland. It was at the height of the

Troubles, and he brought with him two amiable Special Branch detectives – amiable, that is, until Lexi, still only about six or seven, began experimenting with yet another new Polaroid camera from her American grandmother. She took a shot of Atkins, whereupon the two detectives, acting on reflex, pinned her to the ground and ripped the film out of the camera. Not an easy thing to explain to a small child.

The only other problem I recall with the children, which must indicate either how distant, unobservant or just wildly optimistic I'd always been, was taking Juliet aged about two to open a nearby fête. I bought several raffle tickets, only to find when drawing the lucky numbers that we had won the star prize, a teddy bear considerably larger than Juliet. Inspired by some daft *noblesse oblige*, I decided we couldn't take it home, and drew another ticket for someone else in the crowd. Juliet did not speak to me for several days, and now, twenty-five years later, frequently reminds me in times of trouble about my heartlessness on that occasion. What I have always loved about long-standing family feuds is their sheer eccentricity: my old friend Chris Matthew has never entirely forgiven his brother for furnishing a bed-and-breakfast establishment in the wilds of Scotland with tables that once belonged to their mother, while my beloved aunt Margaret did not speak to my father, her only brother, for a considerable time after she discovered that, on the blackboard outside her Kent farmhouse advertising her usual eggs, chickens and ducks for sale, he had added 'Robert Morley Autograph Five Shillings'. I have always believed it is the family that preys together that stays together: you need a good grievance if you're going to keep in touch with relatives. Somehow love alone is never quite enough.

But the only real problem with T'Gallant was how to pay for it and the children's necessarily private education: I had agreed with Margaret that they should go to Catholic schools. We had a fairly large mortgage, a couple of cars and a magical local nanny called Carolyn, and although Margaret was wonderfully willing to take over the research and writing of a marathon *Great Stage Stars* reference book I had rashly taken on, there was not going to be much money in it. Something would have to be done if we were to continue living, as I always have, in a style way above my likely ability to pay for it.

It was at this point that one of our erstwhile Dulwich neighbours came to my rescue: Michael Hamlyn was now night editor of *The Times* under William Rees-Mogg, and had noticed a vacancy in the office for a deputy features editor. The paper was still in the old Printing House Square opposite the Mermaid Theatre in Puddle Dock, and I duly went along for the interview. Thanks I suspect largely to Mike, although characteristically he never claimed the credit, I got hired.

I should have been a lot more grateful and thrilled than I was: after more than a decade in television and radio, I still had no Fleet Street qualifications for the job, no editorial experience since leaving Oxford student magazines, and had certainly not worked my way up through the ranks. And although I had been writing for *The Times* since my student days, some long and gossipy lunches with John Higgins at the Garrick were hardly the background I needed to run the feature pages of a major daily newspaper when my boss was away.

Which, luckily, she seldom was. Margaret Allen was another of the strong women to whom I have owed my career and sometimes my life, and sharing an office with her was what I most enjoyed about my eighteen months on the staff of *The Times*. She was the first woman ever to have achieved features-editor status on a major broadsheet, and she had blasted her way through what was still a very male and dusty office like a creature from some other planet, as she tried desperately to drag a hopelessly antiquated paper into at least the first half of the twentieth century.

But this was the only one of my relatively few office jobs that even she could never truly make me at home in or, indeed, the right casting for; the rest of the staff, and especially the subs, regarded me quite rightly as an outsider from broadcasting who lacked the *Times* ethos and was unlikely ever to learn it, and my chances of being taken seriously were seriously damaged on my first day when Nick Tomalin, who was soon killed in the Israeli Six-day War, came to take me out to lunch dressed in full leathers and crash helmet and on his beloved motorbike. As luck would have it, we nearly ran over Rees-Mogg as we skirted the fountain at the entrance to Printing House Square, and I have always thought that from the start he had me marked down as a dangerous terrorist in his midst.

To say that I was a round peg in a square hole at *The Times* would be putting it mildly. True, just down the corridor I had John Higgins as a major ally, and in the literary department I fast befriended Ion Trewin, who later because a distinguished publisher at Hodder, then Weidenfeld, and started me on my ten-year stint as John Gielgud's authorised biographer, and his successor Philip Howard. I also managed, after a rough beginning, since he did not suffer fools gladly and took me for one, to make a friend and ally of Louis Heren: he had started on the paper as a copy-boy in the thirties and gone on to be its greatest Washington correspondent. Undoubtedly he was also the best editor *The Times* never had.

My problem was that I wasn't working in either arts or books where I would have been happy, had there been a vacancy; instead, I was over on features, where what we seemed mainly to do was publish endless articles by Bernard Levin. As it happened, I had admired Bernard as a drama critic on the *Daily Express* and then the *Mail*, where he wrote overnight 800-word reviews of considerably greater brilliance than anyone before or since Tynan. For *The Times*, however, he was writing political columns of vast length and, to me, unfathomability, columns which, under his contract, we were not allowed to cut or alter. My job was therefore effectively that of a printer rather than an editor, charged merely with getting Bernard safely onto the page.

In those days Peter Jay and Charles Douglas-Home were the two rising stars of the paper, and the rest of us wasted considerable hours taking bets on which of them would finally get to be editor. In the event, just after my time, Charlie did, but then died young of cancer, while Peter went to be ambassador in Washington, and then Robert Maxwell's assistant.

Maxwell had been one of my last interviewees at *Late Night Line-Up*. He and my father had already crossed swords as the result of an *Any Questions* programme on which Pa had defined him as 'the six-foot Pole you wouldn't touch anybody with', and he had demanded a half-page national newspaper retraction. When the BBC refused to pay for it, and Pa said he couldn't afford it, Maxwell characteristically paid for the apology himself.

Some months later, he came into my *Line-Up* studio on the day a Department of Trade enquiry had announced that he was unfit to run a public company. Maxwell pretended he had not heard the verdict, although I had on my lap a copy of the *Evening Standard* that I could hold up as proof to the camera. 'How does it feel to be branded a crook?' was my first question.

'Say that again,' said Maxwell, so I did. Without another word he rose and walked slowly out of the studio. It was the first time anyone had done that, and he knew very well we were going out live and had no other guests. I spent the next half-hour talking to Michael Dean about the cricket scores, before we brought the non-show to a close. Years later, John Nott repeated the trick to rather wider publicity.

But I was, though I tried never to admit this to either of my beloved Margarets, still bitterly unhappy at *The Times*: I hated the ten-to-seven office life, especially because it often interfered with my theatregoing and love of long, alcoholic lunches. I hated publishing columns by others instead of writing them myself. Above all, I hated working on a section of the paper that I could never bring myself to read for pleasure, concerned as it was with politics, economics, industry or foreign affairs. I guess that the real truth is I knew I was never going to be a star at *The Times*, and couldn't deal with the relative anonymity still required of its deputy editors.

But I was lucky to be with Margaret Allen, who kept me sane and laughing with her sheer theatricality, then in very short supply on the paper, especially after we moved to the wasteland of New Printing House Square up the Gray's Inn Road, now an impressive glass skyscraper but then a dingy brick building from where it was all but impossible to get to a decent restaurant or even a good pub. At least the old Mermaid Theatre was across the road from the old *Times* building.

My one triumph on the paper happened purely by chance soon after I had arrived, and won me my only ever front-page, lead-story byline. Margaret, who soon saw that I was likely to prove worse than useless around the office, generously handed me a freebie to Jamaica, one of those travel jaunts paid for by the local tourist board in the hope of some good publicity and much enjoyed by journalists everywhere until, in the new morality of the 1990s, it was decided that there might perhaps be something vaguely corrupt about them. I had never been to Jamaica, was eager to see the house at Blue Harbour where Noël had lived and died, and on this press trip found some convivial travelling companions, not least Godfrey Smith, the everlasting Atticus of the *Sunday Times*. On our last night in Jamaica, we were given a formal banquet by the tourist board and I found myself sitting next to the then Prime Minister. This must have been about 1973 and, making polite conversation as one does, I asked him what kind of day he had just had. Quite eventful, he said. He had just resigned, having been unable to get any of his reforms through his parliament.

'Have you told anyone?' I asked.

'Just my wife,' he replied. 'I think I'll do the announcement tomorrow morning.'

'Would you mind terribly if I rang my paper in London and told them?'

'No,' he said amiably. 'Go ahead.' With some difficulty I found a phone, got through to London and luckily Mike Hamlyn at the night desk, to whom I told the story. Mike, who knew, as an old friend and neighbour, of my precarious relationship with current affairs, asked if I had got the story right. I beckoned the Prime Minister to the phone to confirm the details and, bingo, there was my world exclusive, on page one of the following morning's *Times*.

A few years later, lightning struck twice. I was in Monaco, interviewing Prince Rainier for my biography of his old friend and neighbour David Niven. Although there was my tape-recorder on the table and it was clearly running, Rainier suddenly drifted off Niven into thoughts about the recent car-crash death of his wife, the future of Monaco if his son Albert didn't hurry up and get married, the troubles he was having with his headstrong daughters, and a whole range of topics about which I had never heard him speak before in public. He also confirmed for me the magical story about him and Niven getting very drunk one late night at the Palace. At one point Rainier asked David who, of all the many actresses he had slept with, had been the best in bed. 'Grace . . .' Niven started to reply '. . . er, Gracie Fields.'

When I got back to London and listened to the tape, I realised what amazing material I had accidentally collected. I rang Rainier and asked if he had really meant to say all this for the record. 'Why not?' he replied. I opened my *Punch* window and shouted across Tudor Street to the then features editor of the *Daily Mail*, whose window was also open on an unusually hot London morning. Would he like a Rainier exclusive, and what might he be inclined to pay for it?

'A thousand if you can have a thousand words here in half

an hour,' was the bellowed reply, so I did. Thus ended a happy and profitable weekend on the Riviera. I wish journalism like that had happened to me rather more often, but I suppose one shouldn't be greedy.

While I was at *The Times*, although I think it was strictly against my contract, I continued to write showbusiness pieces for non-conflicting publications, and began to get a series of light-hearted articles into *Punch*, which was then being edited by Bill Davis, aided and often abetted by Alan Coren and Miles Kington.

Margaret Allen had the grace not to complain about this, or perhaps she never noticed it: she was unlikely to have been a *Punch* reader or supporter, given that she had only recently come to the end of a long and often tempestuous relationship with Davis, by whom she now had a grown-up daughter. Then something happened: Bill Davis offered me a permanent job as the first-ever arts editor of *Punch*.

This was the beginning of a dream come true: the money was better than it was at *The Times*, though not a lot, and I insisted that I should also be the drama critic of *Punch*, thereby displacing the admirable Jeremy Kingston, who soon found another home at *The Times* where he has been ever since. We have also, thanks to Jeremy's considerable generosity of heart and spirit, remained friends, which is just as well considering how many nights of the week we find ourselves in neighbouring press seats.

When I talked it over with Margaret Allen, dimly aware that I was leaving her after less than two years to work for the man who was not exactly her best friend at the time, I was struck yet again by her cheery generosity. She had noticed that all I seemed to care about was the theatre, and that as I was unlikely to displace the eminent Irving Wardle at *The Times*, I had probably better move on. With her blessing, I went down the corridor to submit my resignation to William Rees-Mogg, who blinked at me owlishly across the desk, reminding me of all the history tutors I had vaguely known at Oxford. He seemed flatteringly surprised that I was leaving him but, then, he had always seemed somewhat surprised that I had joined him in the first place. '*Punch?*' he murmured. 'Why would you want to go there? I wonder.'

I explained that the money was a little better, and that they were offering me the job I had always most wanted, as a drama critic: that much he seemed to understand, but the money issue appeared to surprise him. 'Is money a problem?' he asked benevolently.

'Well,' I replied, 'I do have a mortgage, and three children of school age, and my wife is a novelist, and . . .'

'Curious,' William responded benignly. 'I have never really found money to be much of a problem.'

'No, sir,' I said, 'but then how many people own, as you do, several hundred acres of Somerset?'

'Most of my friends,' he answered, and we parted on as good terms as we had ever really achieved.

I continued to write, somewhat spasmodically, for *The Times*, even sustaining an arts diary there for about a year under Mary Ann Sieghart, but have never set foot in Wapping – not so much out of principle, just that I have never been invited. My *Times*, I fear, is all in the past but, then, in some curious way, it always was, even while I was there: only in Wapping did it really begin to come to terms with the twentieth century, and even then not entirely happily, but I suspect I would not have much cared for Wapping either. Besides, Margaret left soon after I did, and without her behind the features desk, *The Times* would undoubtedly have been even less enjoyable than I'd found it.

My only real triumph in that resignation was recalling William's final gloomy prognostication that *Punch* was probably on its last legs and might well disappear from the bookstalls: in the event it was *The Times* that, shortly after my departure, went into the year-long union lockout, while we at *Punch* remained proudly on the streets, even if we had to print in France for a while due to a similar union dispute.

Even in my *Times* time, there had been the occasional one-day strike by the printers, a shock to us and older readers since even through world wars and the General Strike, some copies of the paper had always been available, at least to Downing Street and Buckingham Palace. At the time of the first one-day stoppage, which caused a temporary nervous breakdown around the building, I happened to pick up a phone in Charlie Douglas-Home's office when he was still home-affairs editor. His uncle, the recently retired prime minister and foreign secretary Lord Home, was on the line from his Hirsel in Scotland to complain that his *Times* had not arrived that morning. Sheepishly, I explained about the lockout and the general absence of the paper: 'Young man,' said Alec benevolently, 'I am not speaking of other people's copies of *The Times*. I am speaking of mine.' Another world was about to come crashing down.

22

Critical but Not Serious

I joined the staff of *Punch* as arts editor and drama critic early in 1977, and stayed there until the magazine was effectively destroyed by United Newspapers in 1989; twelve of the best years of my life in journalism, on a magazine that also provided me with a home when my own began to collapse.

The resident team was then, as always, very small. Bill Davis, as editor, was yet another of the flamboyant mogul figures for whom I seem always to end up working most happily: like Alexander Korda for my father, Rowan Ayers and George Weidenfeld for me, he was essentially what would now in America be called 'an enabler', a man talented not so much in himself as in his ability to galvanise others for projects that often seemed loony at the outset. His enthusiasm was intense, his bad temper always shortlived, his attention span and memory both astonishingly brief. Whereas Weidenfeld would solemnly invite you to write books he had already published by you, Davis would send over an article you had written for him a few years earlier, and ask for a minor rewrite or update. His theory was that readers, like him, never remembered anything for longer than the time it took them to read it, and I have an uneasy feeling he was probably right.

If I write about him now in the past tense, it is only because he seems to have settled abroad and given up the life of London journalism, but he is very much alive, and his faithful, brilliant assistant Caroline, with him I think for as long as any of his wives if not longer, still cheerfully rings for a rewrite of some old *Punch* piece, destined now for some curious medical magazine or giveaway hotel glossy. Bill is immensely theatrical, and should probably have been the ringmaster of a great circus, which, in a way, is what he always was for *Punch*.

I know that others on the resident *Punch* team sometimes found him more troublesome than I ever did (Miles Kington, in frustrated rage, once rammed his foot through the pedestal of Bill's solid mahogany desk), but they had to work with him considerably more closely than I. Mercifully Bill had precious little interest in the theatre – like many *Punch* editors before him, not least Bernard Hollowood, he had come from a background of financial journalism in and about the City, and was not known for his jokes (which is not to say that he wasn't often very funny) – and I was left alone to run the back of the magazine while he, Alan, Miles and David Taylor, the most single-minded and hard-working of us all, dealt with the front.

I gathered a wonderful arts team: Benny Green on television, Dilys Powell on film, Barry Took on just about everything else, except, of course, theatre, which I kept jealously for myself and went night after night to plays accompanied by Bill Hewison. He had been the *Punch* art editor for many years and also caricatured actors from a seat in the stalls; he produced overnight drawings of the cast that often told you far more about the play than anything I could manage in the accompanying thousand words.

Writing now about these *Punch* years is wonderfully nostalgic but also sad; they were not that long ago, yet so many of those who were there have now gone, often years before their time. Alan, Miles and Bill Davis are, happily, still around, but Bill Hewison died just as I started to write this chapter; we've also lost Geoff Dickinson, for years his deputy cartoon editor and a brilliant comic artist, and Benny Green. David Taylor also died prematurely after losing two of his children to early deaths, as also, in the last few years, did many of those who joined us for the weekly *Punch* lunches and sent in occasional material: Willy Rushton, John Wells, Robin Ray, Auberon

Waugh, Barry Took – the list goes on and on. We, their survivors, meet far too often now at the funerals of those we so loved and admired.

But at the time, and until the (very) bitter end, *Punch* was, for me at any rate, just about perfect. My best friend Christopher Matthew came in as a property correspondent, a column he regarded (much as my father treated the food column we gave him) as a welcome opportunity to sound off about more or less anything that crossed his mind or his typewriter, and my admiration for the veteran Dilys Powell increased by the week. She was already well into her eighties when Harry Evans unwisely offloaded her and her great theatrical contemporary Harold Hobson from the *Sunday Times* into a kind of semi-retirement. Within a minute of hearing the news, I was on the phone to Dilys.

All my life I had regarded her as the greatest film critic in the business, and she happily agreed to come to *Punch* 'for as long as I last, dear'. In the event she lasted six or seven years, well into her nineties, seeing every movie ever released, then writing about them in an often incomprehensible scrawl, so that I had (willingly, I admit) to go to the same press screenings as she did, just to work out what she was trying to say.

Early in the 1930s, Hollywood directors as legendary as John Ford and George Cukor had realised that Dilys was the first critic on either side of the Atlantic seriously to appreciate the meaning and importance of film, and even her most hostile reviews were shot through with a blazing love of the screen such as I have never elsewhere encountered. She hardly ever wanted or took a holiday, though she did once ring me in some agitation from a callbox on Paddington station: 'I have just fallen under a train, dear, and they seem to think I have broken my leg in about three places. Would it be awfully inconvenient if I had a week off?'

Sure enough, about a week later, she was back at the press showings of all the movies, albeit in a wheelchair. What also amazed me about Dilys was her agelessness and unshockability on the page: she would review the revival of a 1930s movie musical and some new semi-pornographic Polish underground movie from precisely the same perspective – was it any good, regardless of its subject or the age of its target audience?

When she died, her long-time admirer and colleague on the *Sunday Times* George Perry organised a memorial service in St Martin's-in-the-Fields. Having seen one or two actors, notably Rex Harrison, memorialised there to embarrassingly thin houses, I begged George to play safe and go for the considerably smaller Actors' Church in Covent Garden. He declined, and as usual I had underestimated Dilys: that vast Trafalgar Square church was packed to the doors with a thousand or so of her admirers. Many took to the pulpit to remind us that, apart from her sixty years in the cinema, she had also been (as I knew) a distinguished Egyptologist and (as I did not) that she had been for many years deeply involved in espionage for MI6. Nothing should ever have surprised one about Dilys.

Some time later I spent a couple of years as the film critic of the *Sunday Express* for Eve Pollard, another larger-than-life editor whom I always looked forward to meeting over a gossip-packed lunch, which is not something I can say of all my editors, many of whom I was careful to avoid, certain that if they put a face to the name they would fire me.

When Eve left the *Sunday Express* and I was instantly fired by her successor, I have to confess a certain relief: although in the theatre I have always been foolishly convinced that I was the best reviewer around – with the possible exceptions of Ben Nightingale and Michael Billington, and in America John Lahr – in the cinema I always felt oddly miscast, aware, as Dilys never was, that most films were made for someone who was not me, but considerably younger and sexier. Also, as I soon discovered, if you tried to work every day as both a film and theatre critic, something my good friend Clive Hirschhorn uniquely achieved for thirty years on the *Sunday Express* just before my time there, you only ever saw daylight or your family and friends at weekends.

Multiple lives like Dilys's are always fascinating: a few years later when Benny Green's funeral was held at the Golders Green crematorium, there were at least four large, distinct groups of mourners – the journalists, the jazzmen, the cricketers and the musicologists, with all of whom Benny had managed tirelessly to lead a long and prolific life simultaneously, while averaging five thousand words a day on the typewriter and countless weekly radio broadcasts. Just thinking about him makes me feel like a time-wasting underachiever.

Leslie Grade's was another memorable funeral at Golders Green. For some years he had been my father's agent (with Robin Fox and Ros Chatto) and was, of course, the brother of Lord Lew and Bernie Delfont. The two surviving brothers were coming out of the crematorium afterwards, and we were talking on the steps as the next funeral party was moving in. 'Come on, Lew,' eventually said Bernie, one old ex-vaudevillian trouper to another. 'I'm not staying for the second house, even if you are.'

My life at *Punch* soon settled into a cheerful routine: I would drift in just before noon, on the grounds that as a drama critic I was a night-worker, and listen happily to Bill booming down the corridor about some wildly implausible project that would usually turn out to be a great success. One might encounter Alan Coren in the corridor dressed as an Arab sheikh to do some lunatic survey, or the young Tina Brown (for whom Coren and I had both been to speak at the Oxford Union and rapidly decided to lure on to the magazine as soon as possible), dressed as a bus conductress for some equally unlikely Davis-inspired caper.

At other times you would suddenly hear comic songs drifting down the corridor, and discover Kington in his office with his beloved double bass, which sometimes I think he found better company than any of us, plus his three friends who with him made up Instant Sunshine.

Then again there were the *Punch* outings: Bill believed fervently in leading his often recalcitrant team and several followers on day-trips at home and abroad, and although I could spend the rest of this chapter recounting them, the reports can still be found in the relevant back numbers of what we survivors now refer to as 'the real *Punch*', to distinguish it from the magazines that followed under the same title, but bore no resemblance to the one we loved and published.

The outing I best recall was a local one: some time in the late seventies, Robert Carrier had opened Hintlesham Hall, almost the first of what are now known as country-house hotels, just off the A12 somewhere in Suffolk. As usual a coach was to transport the *Punch* team from Tudor Street, thereby allowing considerable pre- and post-prandial drinking for all but the driver *en route*. As I had to be somewhere else that evening, I decided to drive myself. 'You can't miss it,' said Bill, giving me a vague map, 'but the whole point is that it looks just like a real country house, so don't expect any signs.'

Following his directions, I motored down a stately carriage drive to an impressive front door. As nobody else was around, I decided I must have overtaken the bus. I rang the bell. A lady opened the door.

'I think I must be the first.'

'The first?'

'Yes, the other forty will just be arriving.'

'Forty?'

'Yes, for the *Punch* lunch, as arranged.'

'Well,' she said thoughtfully, 'I do have a chicken . . .'

I had come to the wrong stately home: Carrier's was just down the road.

Talking of social disasters, I have just remembered another: when I was living, in my first marriage, on that new Wates estate in Dulwich, we were happily surrounded by other journalists – the Hamlyns next door, of course, and along the road could also be found Julian Haviland of ITN and others. Then, somewhat to our surprise, one of the semi-detacheds in our row was sold to a non-journalistic family – the father was in the diplomatic service. We were a close-knit community, much inclined to use each other for babysitting and to wander in and out of those identical houses as though we lived in all of them, which in a way we did. When the newcomers invited us for dinner, it seemed wise to be friendly. To my horror, I discovered that the other journalists had not been invited, and that the guests were all diplomats. The conversation was therefore not about whether Harry Evans was really living with Tina Brown (my conviction that he was stemmed from a night on which I had gone to review her rather good first play, and found the small theatre almost entirely filled with *Sunday Times* executives) but one of, to me, toe-clenching boredom about the political state of the world. After what seemed like several hours, I could bear it no longer. I apologised profusely, said that I had to be at work unusually early next morning, and asked if perhaps we could be forgiven for leaving. As we got to the pavement, Margaret asked me if I had any idea of the time, then told me it was ten past nine. At least we were never asked there again.

Other *Punch* outings that stick in the memory include a day-trip to Calais, where we were given a several-course lunch in the mayor's parlour in return for a page or two of free advertising. The mayor rose to make an emotional speech about how thrilled he was to welcome his brave allies from the Second World War, whereupon it was left to Geoff Dickinson and Alan Coren to point out to the aghast Frenchman that not all of us had technically been his allies: Bill Davis had been born in Germany under Hitler, and only escaped with his mother and brother to England as a small boy. Like other quintessentially theatrical Brits, such as George Sanders and Leslie Howard, Bill was deeply foreign, which is paradoxically why he has always been so good at seeming English: unlike the rest of us, he had to learn it all, and remains almost certainly the only German to have ended up as head of the London Tourist Board.

Then there was the weekend given us by the Hennessy Cognac family at their splendid chateau, to which we were flown in their private plane, then invited to inspect the grapes and the resulting brandy, a bottle of which was thoughtfully left by each of our bedsides. Alan Brien returned a little late and shakily to the bus for the homeward journey. 'I was just going around the rooms,' he explained, 'finishing up the brandy bottles. I didn't want us to leave the wrong impression.'

These celebrations were maintained at the weekly *Punch* lunches: the system was that once you had written sufficiently for the magazine, you were invited to carve your initials in the historic *Punch* table alongside such legendary predecessors as Thackeray, Mark Twain and Charles Dickens. One week we decided to invite Prince Charles to lunch, and Buckingham Palace sent a detective a day or two ahead to do a security check, this being the time of the IRA bombers. I took him proudly into our dining-room and showed him where His Royal Highness would be lunching. The detective ran his hand across the carved initials. 'I see, sir,' he said. 'Have much trouble with vandalism here, do you?'

The theory also was that once you had carved your initials you were entitled to a free weekly lunch at the table until you died, but that, like so much that was wonderful about *Punch*, seems to have disappeared with the coming of United Newspapers. For about a century, up to and including my early days there, the old magazine had been owned by a family of antique dealers, Bradbury Agnew, into whose portfolio we fitted perfectly as a valuable, cherished but slightly foxed old treasure.

However, in one of the 1980s recessions, the antiques business had taken a dive and the family were forced to sell out to the *Daily Express* owners, United Newspapers. The splendid old chairman, Bill Barnetson, took Coren and various others of the resident staff out to lunch, where we asked him nervously about the position in which the takeover had left us. 'You are now in roughly the position of the mayor of a small French town early in 1941,' he said benignly. 'The Nazis have arrived. You can get shot, flee to the hills, form a resistance, but never forget that you are henceforth under occupation.'

And that was exactly how it felt: men in suits with clipboards began lurking around the corridors, advertising revenue became a regular problem, and gradually everything that *Punch* had been about disappeared into the hands of those who thought of us as just another title to be tracked on the computer. We were overrun by people who didn't have the faintest understanding of our history, our purpose or our future. We were an anachronism, like a thatched cottage in the middle of a motorway.

Bill Davis soon went off to form his own publishing company, wisely taking the hugely profitable *High Life* with him, and Alan Coren became editor. Eventually he also left, to edit the BBC's *Listener*, and David Taylor briefly succeeded him, before the magazine went into meltdown. I hung on for as long as I could, largely because even I could see that what was happening to *Punch* was happening to most other publishing houses, magazines and newspapers where I might have wanted to work. Thatcherism, technological breakthroughs, union disputes and the manic greed of the eighties devastated all the old establishments where the writers had been allowed to dominate the accountants and managers. But not any more.

Besides, I had another problem: I was going barking mad.

23
This Way Madness Lies

'It starts as something small,' as a character says in Nicholas Wright's brilliant Van Gogh play *Vincent in Brixton*, 'and then it becomes everything.' 'It' is depression, and I had better start this chapter with the ritual disclaimer that what follows is purely my own account of what happened twice to me. It might not chime exactly, or perhaps at all, with the memories of my wives, my mother or my children, or indeed Leslie Morrish, the psychiatrist who was eventually brilliant, kind and patient enough to get me out of it – yet another debt that I am well aware I can never repay.

All I have are my own memories, and those are agonising enough without asking others for theirs. In my family the way you deal with painful memories is to deny that they exist. This is the first time I have written about any of this: I was terrified for more than fifteen years that if I publicised my own mental breakdowns I would become even more unemployable than usual. Suddenly, at sixty, one ceases to care quite so much. It's one of the many great things about growing old, I guess. Besides, I now have this vague hope that the more those in public life talk about their depression, the less terrifying it may come to seem for others.

The first time I was made aware that something was seriously wrong with me was in the last stages of my marriage to Margaret. One morning I was about to drive as normal, or so I thought, up the M4 from Berkshire to the *Punch* office in London, when Margaret threw a cup of coffee over my clean shirt, in order to get me to go back upstairs to our bedroom and stay there until she could get me a doctor and some sedatives. I was, I suspect, making no sense.

Various unforeseen things had started to happen to me: *Punch* was in the aforementioned meltdown, and those of us who were still clinging to the wreckage had so much to worry about professionally that we were not bothering any longer with each other's private lives. Some years later I worked out that Miles Kington in the next-door office had been going through a very similar marital breakdown, though we never compared notes.

At this time, I'd just had a considerable success with the first biography of David Niven, *The Other Side of the Moon*, in which I attempted to tell the real story behind the man we all thought we knew but hardly knew at all – not least because his own two great bestsellers, *The Moon's a Balloon* and *Bring on the Empty Horses*, sold as memoirs, were largely fictional, hence the title of my book.

I had also discovered something curious about biography: you might imagine that if someone's memoirs have sold well, there would be little demand for another book about them by someone else. Not true. Or, at least, not in my experience: I did well with books about Niven, Coward and Gielgud, all of whom had published several bestsellers about themselves or (in John Gielgud's case) their work, while my first biography of James Mason sold as badly as his own memoirs had. The public wants to read about some people and not about others, no matter how much they admire them.

Anyway, I was on the road selling the book in America – in those pre-satellite days one travelled from town to town like some demented evangelist, turning up on all the local radio breakfast shows and, in my case, getting to identify with Arthur Miller's Willy Loman, out there on a smile and a shoeshine and not much else. As always, when I got to New York I rang Ruth Leon, the girl I had first known as a teenager at Oxford.

Through our long first marriages to American partners, she and I had always kept in touch: after starting her career as a researcher and producer at Granada while I was still at ITN,

Ruth had married Michael Mosettig, the (still) boyishly handsome foreign editor of what was *MacNeil-Lehrer* and is now *The Jim Lehrer News Hour* on American public television. But Michael has always been as obsessed by Washington as Ruth and I have been by the theatre. Gradually their marriage had started to go its separate ways when Ruth moved to New York, where she made a considerable reputation in her own right as the Emmy-award-winning producer and often director of documentaries about Aaron Copland, Isaac Stern and many other classical-music giants.

She also directed live television broadcasts of many operas, ballets and concerts from Wolf Trap, Carnegie Hall and the Lincoln Center in New York. When they were building the Kennedy Center in Washington in the early 1970s, it was to Ruth they decided to prove that they had thought of everything, including cable ducting in the concrete for her TV cables. 'Just one little problem,' she murmured to the architects. 'These trenches are for black-and-white television cables. We now broadcast in colour, and colour cables are twice as thick.' Several acres of concrete had to be dug up at considerable expense in mid-town Washington.

When we met again in New York while I was on that Niven tour, her marriage to Michael was by no means over, although they were only meeting at weekends – either Michael flew to New York or Ruth to Washington – and they were keeping two lives and two homes going quite happily.

But as I travelled on around America, I realised something tricky: for the first time in twenty years or more – in fact since Margaret and I had first met on that student campus in Hawaii – I was falling deeply in love. Ruth and I had known each other, albeit distantly, for even longer than Margaret and I had, and suddenly we seemed to have so much more in common: a passion for theatre, Broadway, television, the showbiz and big-city life, which Margaret had always (and now, of course, with good reason) distrusted.

What was I going to do about it? Both Ruth and I were still, at least in theory, happily married, we lived on opposite sides of the Atlantic, I had three children, the youngest of whom was only about ten. All in all the whole thing seemed ludicrously beyond the barriers of possibility.

The trouble was that I couldn't get her out of my mind: from our offices we wrote long love letters to each other, and it became clear that her life was undergoing a change not entirely to do with me, or even with us. The funding for her classical-arts work on television was drying up in New York, as it soon would in Britain, and although New York is really her spiritual home, her sister and parents in London wanted her home after a couple of American decades.

Accordingly she began to look for work in London, though often still for American television employers, and I began to look for excuses to spend more and more time with her in New York. I felt very guilty about Margaret, even though I knew, if only subconsciously, that she was growing as out of love with me as I with her. We had developed in our middle age into different people and we were no longer held together by young children.

After one particularly passionate weekend with Ruth in New York, the guilt got the better of me and, unable to tell Margaret the truth, I left some credit-card bills lying around in the knowledge that, once she had read them, she would have a pretty good idea of my infidelity. It was at about this time that I ceased making a lot of sense, and that she was kind enough – and I mean just that – to throw the coffee at me. I was not safe on the streets, let alone behind the wheel of a car, and if you are even as vaguely familiar a figure as I am, it is neither advisable nor career-enhancing to wander the streets talking to yourself with a mad-eyed stare.

The kindly local GP who came to have a look at me that coffee-stained morning saw that something was pretty wrong, and recommended bed-rest and a local psychiatrist. *Punch* kept paying my salary, the late Robin Ray kindly wrote my theatre columns, and I spent a good deal of time chatting to an avuncular therapist in a nearby village about my childhood, my life, Ruth, Margaret, the children, my parents, more or less anything that came into my head. Gradually it occurred to me that none of this, although mildly enjoyable, was resolving anything. What was worse, I seemed to be disturbing even my doctor: eventually he, too, went into a deep depression.

I finished up in the Cardinal Clinic in Windsor, run by Dr Morrish. The Cardinal is wonderful. I often think that if, by any ghastly chance, I were to outlive Ruth (unlikely: she is deeply into health and fitness while I, you will be amazed to learn, am not and never have been) I would like to end my days there, although it is not a retirement retreat. Otherwise I'll go to the old actors' home, Denville Hall, if they'll have me, to be surrounded by thespians so forgetful that I could, as usual, tell the same stories day after day but without the usual complaints.

The wonderful thing about Leslie Morrish was that, after I had begun on the usual soul-searching chat, he decided on a purely chemical rather than conversational solution: find the right pills, allow them time to kick in, and depression can sometimes be cured or, if not, held at a low enough level to allow a return to fairly normal life.

In my case, the pills presented a problem. I have not only been vastly overweight all my life, but of a curious medical constitution: in the occasional event of a headache, I need to take several times the usually prescribed number of aspirins before I notice any effect. This has certain advantages: I am such an appalling driver that police cars often pull me to the side of the road (on one occasion rather embarrassingly just as Ruth and I were driving out of Buckingham Palace after an intimate dinner with the Duchess of York). I am then routinely breathalysed, but even if I have been drinking all day, the machine never changes colour. The alcohol must sink to my feet or something. Anyway, when it came to the depression pills, Leslie had to prescribe for me several times the normal dosage. To this day, when I go to the chemist to get the prescription refilled, they ask for how many people the pills are required. When I tell them, proudly, just me, they telephone the Cardinal to verify the situation.

Once you are lucky enough to be at the Cardinal, it becomes an incredibly difficult place to leave: the nursing staff are magical and the conditions are – thank God for BUPA – as luxurious as your four-star country-house hotel. I sometimes thought I would be there for the rest of my life. Indeed, I began to believe that the doorknobs and the telephone in my bedroom would give me a severe electric shock if I touched them. I suppose I was giving myself permission, in a roundabout way, to cut myself off from the outside world full of people with whom I could no longer deal on any meaningful level.

Looking back, I feel guilty and ashamed that I allowed a nervous breakdown, however real and unavoidable at the time, to remove me from the chaos of *Punch* and my now failing marriage. My father took the view that there was nothing wrong with me that couldn't be fixed by a good long lunch at the Garrick, and my mother has never referred to any of this. I have a terrible feeling that I might inadvertently have brought back to her memories of the suicide of her own disturbed brother.

As for the children, having a temporarily deranged father must have impacted on them, but they, too, seem to have got on with their own lives relatively unaffected. If I ever start to probe them nervously for scars, I can honestly say that I have never found any. My brother and sister, long resident abroad, managed to avoid the whole bloody thing.

Although the depression recurred a few years later, and I was rapidly back in the Cardinal, albeit for a shorter stay than my initial twelve weeks, thanks to the pills it seems now under reasonable control. Again, I think ageing must help: everything somehow seems less awful at sixty than it did at forty-five. The mortgage is paid, the children have grown up, Ruth also works, and although I live still on the borderline of debt, the amounts seem somehow reduced. I can just about foresee myself getting into marginal profit before I die, which cannot be said of many in my family.

Has depression made me a better, more considerate or less selfish person? Almost certainly not. The only definable difference I can ascribe to the illness is that I can now instantly recognise it in others, often in total strangers. Something goes dead behind the eyes, and we depressives belong to a curiously semi-secret society, not unlike Masons or Mormons. We know at once who we are, not that it does any of us much good. And the depression itself is always there, waiting in the wings like Hamlet's dread ghost: all you ever learn is how to fend it off before it really kicks in. Have I been incredibly lucky, with the medical help of Dr Morrish and the love of first Margaret and then Ruth? Yes, of course I have. Would I wish the illness even on my worst enemy? Not for a moment. It really can be a killer, as my uncle John discovered.

So much for all of that. In the end I got it under control, moved out of the marital home to London, started to live with Ruth whenever she was over from New York, and gradually tried to rebuild a life after *Punch* – I resigned when they appointed an editor, David Thomas, who had no previous connection with the magazine. I suspected by then (and Thomas later confirmed) that had I not resigned he would have fired me anyway, not from any personal dislike but because his brief was a total makeover of the magazine to bring it into line with all the then new weekend giveaway supplements and 'lifestyle' titles.

Punch itself lurched through various appalling reincarnations before ending up as the house magazine of Mohamed al-Fayed at Harrods. I had always taken pride in being only the twelfth drama critic of the magazine in a hundred and forty years. When I resigned, David Thomas gave my column to an American woman, who had, so far as I could determine, no previous experience of the London theatre or of *Punch* and all it had stood for across a century and a half. I developed immediately such a passionate loathing of her that I have seldom been able to read a single word she has written anywhere. In the summer of 2002, when al-Fayed admitted financial defeat and closed *Punch* for good, I was torn between relief at seeing the old mag put out of the agonies of the last fifteen years, and rage that United Newspapers should have been allowed to destroy a national institution with such apparently careless and wilful disregard for the past. A nation that preserves, protects and takes pride in, for instance, Radio 3, the National Theatre and the V&A should, it seems to me, have been able to preserve *Punch*.

And there's another thing: what about those free lunches we were promised until the end of our days, once we had carved our initials on the *Punch* table? A few of us old hands, who also belong to the Garrick, once tried to kidnap the table and find it a safe home in the club, but we failed. For all I know, it still lies buried in the vaults at Harrods.

With the hostile takeover, I was now effectively homeless: I took to going home to Fairmans at the weekends, but I was not a barrel of laughs and, if anything, was beginning to depress my usually undepressable parents. In London, Ros Chatto was kind enough to give me office space high above the Prince of Wales Theatre, and for a while I rented various flats around Baker Street; Ruth came to live with me in them, when work or parents brought her to London. By now we had realised, almost by osmosis, that we were going to get our divorces and marry each other, but I was still worried about what effect this might have on the children. It wasn't until one Christmas when Alexis and I went to a chamber-music festival in Mexico, and Michael came to stay with Ruth in our London flat and noticed that all the Christmas cards were addressed to her and me as a couple, that things came to a head – as in an Ayckbourn bedroom farce of mismatched marriages.

Understandably, Michael said that Ruth would now have to choose between him and me. With reservations, given that I had recently come back to her from a nervous breakdown, had just lost my most regular and constant employer in *Punch*, and would now be faced with alimony and child-support payments, she settled for me. Margaret and Michael found other partners to marry, and have seemed admirably settled and sorted for a long time. So that's all right, then – although of course it wasn't at the time.

The last of at least a thousand columns I had written in my *Punch* office was a savage attack on our new chairman David Stevens, to whom I ascribed personal and direct responsibility for the brutal murder of a once great magazine. The piece did not appear in *Punch*, but across half a page of that week's *Sunday Telegraph*, and I made a mental note never again to apply to United Newspapers for a job, although in the event the vow was very short-lived.

My ego suffered a short, sharp shock some months later, when Ruth and I found ourselves at a small dinner party with Stevens and his then wife: 'We shall have to leave at once,' I whispered, 'after what I wrote about him,' but it was already too late. For the next couple of hours I sat directly across the table from Stevens, who showed no sign that he had ever read the piece or, indeed, heard of me. Some months later, when Eve Pollard offered me the film column on the *Sunday Express*, also then managed by Stevens and his clipboard-Mafia, I warned her of the problem: 'Don't worry, darling,' said Eve. 'Proprietors never notice articles like that if they are not on the City pages, where they can affect the shares,' and, of course, she was absolutely right.

One of my major concerns in these intermarriage years was that my two beloved daughters, who had by now moved on from Brigidine Convent in Windsor to Rye St Antony in Oxford, would awake to find the collapse of their parents' marriage all over the tabloids. I had known too many children of too many showbiz parents suffer this, and I also knew the potential cruelty of fellow pupils.

Eventually I decided to tackle the situation full on. I wrote to Nigel Dempster, whom I had got to know distantly when he occasionally wrote for us at *Punch*, and told him the whole story, most of which he already knew. I said that if he would keep it to himself until I was ready to go public, I would then give him all the quotes he needed. He was as good as his word, and I have always been grateful to him.

24
Starting Again: Ruth and a New Life

The financial chaos that would normally have resulted from our divorce was solved to some extent by the fact that, yet again, I come from that luckiest of generations: the one that left university to full employment, and got its feet on the property ladder at precisely the right time – albeit more by luck than judgement. The family house we had bought some fifteen years earlier in Berkshire for less than £20,000, where all the children had grown up, now turned out to be worth well over £300,000. When we had divided that in half, Margaret was able to buy the house in Binfield where she still lives, just across the road from Alexis and our two grandsons, while I was left with enough to buy a little flat in the then brand new Chelsea Harbour.

Although Ruth never cared for it, I loved it. Chelsea Harbour is now little more than a glitzy interior-design centre on the river just off the King's Road, but when it first opened fifteen or so years ago, it boasted a pub, several shops, four restaurants and amazing door-to-door service: you could get croissants, dry-cleaning, eggs, milk and newspapers delivered to the porter downstairs, and the place seemed to have been designed for recently divorced men, like Tom Stoppard, Ralph Halpern and me, unreconstructed as we were and therefore unable to deal with daily domestic details. Michael Caine also had a restaurant and a flat there, and among the other showbiz residents were Ian McShane, the film producer John Woolf, and the veteran agent Laurie Evans, who had represented Olivier, Gielgud and Richardson. The Harbour even had its own wine merchant. People used to come and photograph our pads for glossy design magazines, though in my case they usually sent someone over first to tidy up.

There were one or two shadier characters, or at least men living with women not likely to have been their wives. The lift outside my flat only served the two apartments on each floor. One morning I got into it, and it stopped, unusually, at the floor below. As the doors opened a man dressed for the City was being seen off by an entirely naked and breathtakingly glamorous woman. He and I travelled down to the lobby in a somewhat embarrassed but very English silence, and I never saw either of them again.

All of my three children came at various times to live or stay with me in the flat, and if Ruth was there too it got a little crowded. When we got married, I persuaded her that the Harbour was still the only place to live, and we bought one of the townhouses across the street for considerably more than either of us could afford. I was blissfully happy there too: the house ran up five floors, so the views from the vast study at the top were spectacular, and there was even a little garden, not to mention enough spare rooms to have all the children and various American guests staying at the same time. The only problem, of course, was the size of the mortgage, which I managed never to think about. However, it kept Ruth awake at night, so after about five years we sold up – again at a reassuring profit – and moved across the river to Plantation Wharf, on the river in Battersea, where we have lived ever since, vaguely within our means, and in a house about which the best thing is a vast ground-floor study. It contains my library of nearly three thousand theatre books, all now in alphabetical order, thanks to the brilliant assistance of the playwright Paul Webb, on bookcases that slide around the walls on railway tracks, thereby providing double-density. So much for our domestic arrangements: I knew you'd be interested.

On my death, I have vague plans to leave the library

and, indeed, Ruth to the nation, rather as Nelson left Lady Hamilton, or Scott of the Antarctic left his son Peter, or as Serge Gainsbourg left Jane Birkin to the French. Jane bought an ultra-luxurious Parisian flat after Serge's death, so modern that it had no keyhole in the door, but one of those number-pads you see in American hotels. The following Christmas, her veteran mother Judy Campbell – with whom Michael Law and I still do cabaret, some sixty years after she first sang about the nightingale in Berkeley Square – was arriving with her usual collection of trunks, presents, cousins and animals. 'Just punch in the year of my birth,' said Jane, who was filming that day, 'and the door will open.' Judy punched in the correct year, the door failed to budge, so she sat on the pavement for an hour or so in driving rain until Jane got back from work. 'Your bloody new-fangled French door—' began Judy.

'Oh, my God, Mother,' exclaimed Jane, 'I forgot to tell you— I lied to it about my age.' Even after you have worked closely on a play with nearly all of the Redgraves, as I have, lying to your doorknob about your age still counts as eccentric.

In the aftermath of *Punch*, I drifted around various other magazines and newspapers, grabbing what columns I could, but resenting the loss of the old mag and with it a way of life that I knew I was never going to enjoy anywhere else. I served about a year as a television critic of the *Evening Standard*, another year of TV for *The Times*, and then a year or so of radio criticism for the *Sunday Telegraph*, plus all the book reviewing I could get. I was also working as a writer or reporter on BBC radio and television arts documentaries, and doing whatever interviewing or hosting jobs that any commercial ITV, American, Australian or Canadian company offered.

But I soon realised that I could never write about television as wittily as either Clive James or Alan Coren, who were then leading that field, and the terrible truth was that I didn't care enough about it to get very exercised one way or the other. Television, as Noël Coward once said, is for appearing on, not for looking at, and I established semi-regular homes as a guest on such daytime panel games as *Countdown, Call My Bluff* and *Going for a Song*. Later I even managed to creep on to painting shows like *Awash with Colour* and *Watercolour Challenge*, thereby proving to myself my theory that on daytime television anything is possible.

Of all the regular radio shows I did during the 1970s and 1980s, few gave me greater pleasure than Radio 4's *Start the Week*. Long before the Bragg or Paxman eras, the programme was hosted by Richard Baker, a broadcaster of neatness and efficiency who ran a tight ship. I was employed below decks to come up with a little weekly comic relief.

Some genius of a producer had also installed the late Kenneth Robinson, a figure of incredible subversion. Although he dressed and spoke like an undertaker, Ken was a seething mass of barely suppressed rage and eccentricity; I sometimes persuaded him to write for me at *Punch*. He was at his best on live radio, and would often sit silent and fairly well behaved until, quite late in the proceedings, he would suddenly take against some unsuspecting guest. Then he would launch into a manic tirade against their clothes, their hair, their parentage and even their sexuality.

Richard Baker and I would try, usually without much success, to calm him down. But as often as not, in the worst of all BBC crimes, the sacred pips at ten a.m. cut in on him while he was still foaming about some perceived insult, or just his life in general. No Python, no Goon, ever achieved the heights of Ken's real-life surreality.

Also, for a short but magical time, I had my own early-evening BBC1 television series, flatteringly entitled *Sheridan Morley Meets*: for some arcane reason this came out of Norwich, and to qualify as a guest you had to have East Anglian connections. I recall walking along the beach in

Aldeburgh with Laurens Van der Post – I believed, as we all did in those days, every word of his largely self-manufactured autobiography.

I also had a lovely decade or so hosting the British Airways inflight videos. The airline has always been especially good to my family – for years Robert was their commercial spokesman, and could even be heard on their New York telephone number, apologising if the lines were engaged. The only problem he experienced with filming their commercials all over the world was that other passengers who lost their luggage or missed connections would associate him in some vague way with whatever airline they were flying, and duly accost him with their grievances as if he was some sort of ombudsman. Eventually he took to hiding in the gents' at airports the world over, until just before his flight's final call.

I hosted a 'What's on in the Arts in London' for BA's inflight television, and loved the idea that friends somewhere over the Atlantic or the Indian Ocean would wake from fitful sleep to find me looming at them out of the mid-air darkness.

Mine was now, for the first time, a freelance life, with neither *Punch* nor *The Times* nor *Line-Up* nor ITN to give me a regular place to hang my hat, except that I have never owned a hat. In at least one way, though, I was better equipped for this abrupt change than many of my older friends and colleagues, who had worked most of their lives for one newspaper and suddenly, in the Wapping diaspora, found themselves forced into a home-working life. I had, however, come from a family of actors. My father, even in his eighties, would sit happily by the phone placing his bets on the TV racing then wait for it to ring with the next job, whereupon he would tootle off and do a day or two's acting on a film or TV, before happily settling back into his armchair in time for the next race meeting. His, my grandmother Gladys's and my uncle Robert Hardy's lives had always been freelance, and once the collapse of *Punch* made mine that too, I fell back into the old family ways with a resigned and even optimistic familiarity. We are all much like mini-cab drivers, waiting for the next fare, wondering where it will take us and if we will like it once we get there.

True, I was still having my fair share of disappointments: a series of *Theatre Annuals*, which I had started editing in the 1970s, came to a grinding halt after about five years, and as I advanced into my early fifties it was dawning on me that perhaps I would never get the first-string posting as drama critic of *The Times* or the *Daily Telegraph* that I had always taken to be my natural destiny. The truly terrible thing, though, was that I now no longer cared so very much. Not that my interest in the theatre had diminished – precisely the opposite: I had begun to want to take a more active part in it than is traditionally permitted of a reviewer. In Kenneth Tynan's famous definition, I was fed up with being the man who knew the way but couldn't drive the car, or the diner in the restaurant who never got to write the menu. However, Ken's own diminished end as a National Theatre bureaucrat and the creator of *Oh! Calcutta!* offered a potent warning as to how wrong that crossover ambition could go. I suspected also that I was never going to be Bernard Shaw either: he was the only drama critic I could remember who had given up reviewing for something better.

I began to grab every book contract that came along, publishing in rapid succession critical celebrations of the careers of Katharine Hepburn, Audrey Hepburn, Ingrid Bergman, Elizabeth Taylor and Ginger Rogers, several of which, to my secret chagrin, sold considerably better than some of the full-length biographies to which I had devoted many more years of my life.

Ginger Rogers made me laugh twice. Once she told me proudly that 'Everything Fred Astaire ever did, I did backwards in high heels.' On the second occasion, I was interviewing her about her interminable memoirs on a live Radio 2 show. I noted that she had described at least four of her five husbands as alcoholics. 'But were they,' I queried, 'when you married them?'

There was a long pause while she thought about this. 'Jesus, God, you're right,' she said. 'They weren't.'

As for my home life, in the years between leaving Margaret and marrying Ruth, I was dimly aware that my family and friends were having trouble adjusting: I have never understood the rule whereby on divorce others are supposed to separate, rather as they did in church at the time of the wedding, into 'friends of the bride' and 'friends of the groom'. To my amazement I lost, albeit temporarily, a few old mates, although there again I was in for a surprise or two. My beloved cousin Catherine had been married for many years to David Barham, a one-time High Sheriff of Kent and a landowning farmer of considerable local prestige. They were, I figured, the conservatives most likely to have a problem with a divorce in the family, and yet they were the ones who, with my beloved aunt Sally, proved most welcoming to Ruth when we started living together. Others especially kind to us in those early, tricky days were Cameron Mackintosh and his partner, the photographer Michael LePoer Trench, who let us use their French home as a refuge – and no, since you ask, that has not made me any more generous in print to his shows, although when they have been wonderful, as they often are, I have had no trouble in saying so.

It was also indirectly thanks to Cameron that my working life turned round in this last decade or two: one weekend I was in Vienna reviewing a brilliant Gillian Lynne production of the everlasting *Cats* when I met the agent Barry Burnett, an old friend of Cameron and, indeed, the first to give him office space when they were starting out in showbusiness. Who, asked Barry, one morning over breakfast, was my agent?

I told him Michael Shaw at Curtis Brown. No, said Barry, who was my stage agent? I explained that, as a journalist, I had never thought I needed one. Nonsense, said Barry, and set about finding me a vast range of work on daytime television, voiceovers, *Judge John Deed*, whatever comes down the line. More importantly, he, his mother Celia and his partner Richard Wellington have all become to both Ruth and me loving and loyal friends, always there in a crisis and usually good for dinner at Joe Allen's. As with Mike Shaw, I have this guilty feeling that I now owe Barry vastly more in hospitality than he has ever had back from me in percentages. Or is ever, despite all his efforts, likely to get.

Early in the 1980s, I had a phone call out of the blue from a man called Martin Tickner. Like me he was a Coward addict, but he made his living editing theatre programmes and presenting the occasional small-scale show on the road or in the West End. He had been asked to supply the Hong Kong Arts Festival with yet another Coward singalong. *Cowardy Custard* already existed, as did an American variant called *Oh Coward*, but Hong Kong had already seen both of those revues, and Martin wondered now whether there might be a third line on which to string some of Noël's songs and sketches.

At once I knew that there was. Soon after Noël died, I had published, at his suggestion, a biography of his love and partner Gertrude Lawrence, which I called *A Bright Particular Star*, handing over that title some years later to Michael Coveney when he wanted it for his life of Maggie Smith. There is no copyright in titles so I can hardly claim especial generosity there, though I usually do anyway.

I soon put together an early draft of *Noël & Gertie*, a kind of double stage biography that, through Noël's songs, sketches and memoirs, Gertie's rather sketchy autobiography and a lot of linking material I invented in what I hoped were their voices, would tell the story of their remarkable lives both together and apart. Edward Fox was to be my first Noël, and Maria Aitken my first Gertie, but as they didn't sing, I would have

Mark Wynter and Liz Robertson to do that, plus me as the narrator. I had recently toured in the UK as a replacement for Ned Sherrin – he and I did so much similar work on stage and radio that he was once introduced by a slightly confused ladies' lunch-club hostess as 'Mr Ned Sherrindan Morley' – in *Side by Side by Sondheim* while he went with the original cast to triumph in the show on Broadway. I was hooked on the 'book-and-stool' format, as Caryl Brahms had memorably christened it, while having six people on stage in a show that named only two in the title did not seem at first a problem.

Early in rehearsal we lost Edward Fox to a television job, briefly acquired Ian Ogilvy, then lost him too, so that by the time we reached Hong Kong it was Gary Bond as the non-singing Noël and Cheryl Kennedy as the singing Gertie, with the rest of the company still intact. We were in the best of offstage hands: Alan Strachan, the most intelligent and faithful of all contemporary Coward directors, was in charge of the acting, David Toguri did the choreography, and the gowns were by some incredibly fashionable couturier called Yuki. For our one-night gala Winchester tryout, we also had the unbelievable good fortune of being joined by Alan Jay Lerner, then about to take Liz Robertson as his eighth wife, and from him I learnt more about the musical theatre – over some long rehearsal lunches and after-show dinners – than I ever have before or since.

My own sharpest memory is that we hit Hong Kong on the weekend that the British government announced to the understandably irate and terrified local Chinese that when the mandate ran out in 1997, a decade or so hence, we would not be contesting the handover back to China. Rioting broke out in the streets, and even carried over into the stalls and dress circle of our little theatre. We decided for the sake of safety (at least, that of the rest of us) to send Mark Wynter on stage with the veteran and venerable Bill Blezard, who had served as accompanist to both Marlene Dietrich and

Joyce Grenfell, so that he could calm the advancing hordes with a song or two.

The rest of our stay was comparatively uneventful: we were treated royally by the local expats, many of whom asked after Noël and Gertie, and were more than a little distressed to hear they were both dead – expat time is not the same as real time. During the Hong Kong run, I received an anguished cable from Arthur Birsh, the *Playbill* publisher in New York for whom I had been writing a London column for several years. He and his wife Joan Alleman were organising a gala Broadway benefit for some theatre festival or other. They had already sold several tickets at about a thousand dollars each, including dinner, and had suddenly lost whatever was to be the show that night. Would we, asked Arthur, like to fly home via New York and fill in?

None of us needed asking twice, and on the Monday after we had closed in Hong Kong on the Saturday we found ourselves playing a one-night stand on Broadway with *Noël & Gertie*. To suggest that we were not a success would be like suggesting that the Japanese had just possibly made a mistake in bombing Pearl Harbor. We were all jetlagged, the audience had been expecting something a little more glitzy, and I knew we were in trouble when the backstage scene from *Red Peppers*, which had them rolling in the Hong Kong and Winchester aisles, passed without a titter. As I sweated my way into the wings, I asked the stage manager what had gone so wrong. 'Mr Morley,' he explained patiently, 'that whole scene is about two showbiz failures. We on Broadway have never considered failure to be a laughing matter.'

Arthur, surveying a disenchanted audience, was heard to murmur: 'Maybe we should do this in a double-bill with the Zoë Caldwell *Medea*, and send it out on the road. Boy, would that be a fun evening and a half . . .'

I am happy, indeed relieved, to report that in the intervening years *Noël & Gertie* has had two long, successful New York runs, one uptown at the York Theatre and one downtown at the Lortel with Twiggy – but, then, we weren't charging a thousand bucks a seat.

Undeterred by our spectacular failure, Maria Aitken announced on the plane home that it would be ridiculous just to fold our tents after short stays in Hong Kong and New York and we should show London audiences what they had been missing. I was deputed to find us a theatre, and before long fell into the arms of Dan Crawford at the King's Head, for whom I have happily worked ever since, not only on *Noël & Gertie* but also on a celebration of another great songwriter of Noël's period, Vivian Ellis, *Spread a Little Happiness*, and then Noël's last full-length play, *A Song at Twilight*, all of which transferred to the West End in slightly different forms.

But the wonderful thing about Dan, Penny Horner at Jermyn Street and Bill Kenwright just about everywhere else is that they will allow people like me, often from a non-directing background, to devise and/or direct shows on their stage, putting the same faith in us that they accord to more experienced writers and directors. All we have to do is not let them down, and so far, over about seven fringe shows and one in the West End for Kenwright, I never have. By the time you read this, of course, things may have changed for the worse: no run of luck in the theatre ever lasts for ever – one of the first lessons I learnt at my family's knees.

Dan agreed at once that we could play *Noël & Gertie* for a month at the King's Head, and with Alan Strachan still in charge. All went well until about ten days before we were due to open, when Maria rang with the glad tidings that she had just landed a lucrative television series, and would not therefore be joining us in Islington. I managed through clenched teeth not to remind her that the whole thing had been her idea in the first place, and somewhat frantically rang Joanna Lumley, whom I had remembered in the nick of time was a distant cousin on my father's side of the family.

Now, I told her, was the time for our family to stick together. Could she please, therefore, play Gertrude Lawrence very quickly at the King's Head?

'By that,' said Jo, in her best head-prefect voice, 'do you mean I have to say it all very fast, or that there's not much time to rehearse?'

'Both,' I told her. The next day she was, enchantingly, in rehearsal and already almost word-perfect. By now we had also lost most of the others on the original team to more lucrative TV work, so we were joined by three splendid newcomers: Simon Cadell, Gillian Bevan and David McAlister. Jo herself has already published in her memoirs a wonderfully funny account of our initial stay at the King's Head so I won't take you through all that again, except to add just one story. Even though Jo was thrown off a horse while filming a commercial on the day of the dress-rehearsal, and therefore had to play in considerable agony, we opened triumphantly with – as is traditional at the King's Head – almost no advance publicity. On the morning after our first night, to my amazement, there was a box-office queue stretching down Upper Street almost as far as the cinema. 'You see?' said Dan proudly to me. 'It's what I've always said. No need of posters or any expensive publicity: word of mouth does it every time.'

I thought about that for a little while. There had been about sixty people in the house the previous night, most of them critics in non-paying seats. 'Dan,' I said, 'if every member of our audience last night had gone home, rung three friends each and told them not just that they had to buy tickets to see our show, but that they had to turn up this very morning at the box office, you still would not end up with a queue as long as that.'

'But there the queue is,' said Dan, 'so how would you explain it?' I went to the newsagent next door and bought him that week's *Radio Times*. 'It's called television,' I told him. 'You don't watch it, I don't watch it, especially if we are in rehearsal, but millions of others do. Last night, had we but noticed, ITV began to rerun the Jo Lumley series of *The Avengers*, while over on BBC1 Simon Cadell was starring in a hit new sitcom about a holiday camp, *Hi-de-Hi*. We just happen to have the two hottest television stars in the country this week. Hence the queue.' Dan still seemed unconvinced, but we sold out instantly for the rest of the month, and could have stayed at the King's Head for years, had Simon and Jo not had to return to television.

And there was something else: it had dawned on me that there was something ludicrous about having six people (two actors, two singers, the pianist and me) on stage for a show in which only two were named in the title. What was needed, I decided, was to combine the acting and singing, delete the narrator, even if it was me, and get the cast down to a more logical and manageable three, counting the pianist.

Although we had several offers from leading managements to transfer my show to the West End – which was flattering, given that I had never devised anything on stage until now – I decided to take the whole script back to the typewriter for reworking. Over the next year, rewriting intermittently when not on other (paying) projects, I got *Noël & Gertie* into its present shape, using much of Noël's still then unpublished diaries for the narration, but inventing all of Gertie's private lines, as she had left nothing behind but one rather dodgy, ghosted memoir.

I am proud that about thirty per cent of the show is purely my own writing, although in the 'voices' of Noël and Gertie – people naturally assume that I have simply stitched together their own words. I completed the new version, popped it into a drawer and promptly forgot all about it: by now interest had waned and all the original team were off on other projects.

About a year later, my old friend Chris Matthew rang: 'I am instructed,' he announced solemnly, 'to invite you to dinner to meet Patricia Hodge. Have you any idea why Miss Hodge would want to meet you?' Oddly enough, I had: London theatre is a small world, and I suspected that she had somehow got to hear that I had a new 'improved' *Noël & Gertie* in my bottom drawer, one for which, as I should have realised, she would be perfect since she could sing, dance and act, unlike either of my previous Gerties.

Over dinner at the Matthews', Patricia made it clear that this was indeed her interest in me. I sent her the revised script, with a weary note to the effect that we had already played the King's Head, declined several transfer offers, and that I couldn't face the sheer sweat of raising the money, let alone organising a tour or a West End theatre. Luckily, my darling Patricia is made of sterner stuff: within a few weeks, she had enlisted the Australian actor-dancer Lewis Fiander, a new director and organised a season in rep at Salisbury and then at the old Donmar Warehouse in Covent Garden. After that success, she re-enlisted Alan Strachan, Simon Cadell and the choreographer David Toguri, found yet another new management, made up of the photographer Zoë Dominic and the impresarios Howard Panter and Bill Freedman, and arranged a major tour starting at the Yvonne Arnaud in Guildford, and finishing up for nine months at the Comedy Theatre in the West End.

None of that, and therefore none of the *Noël & Gertie* 'afterlife' around the world, where we are now approaching sixty different productions, would have happened without Patricia's energy and single-minded devotion to the project, and I owe her everlasting gratitude. I am only sorry that the ludicrous ongoing battles between British and American Actors' Equity denied her the ultimate dream she had with my show, the chance to play it on Broadway.

Yet even that first long run at the Comedy was not without its headaches: Patricia became pregnant and had to leave the cast for a while, then Simon Cadell began to suffer the first agonies of the cancer that was all too soon to kill him. He was a wondrously funny man and a subtle actor. Although Patricia and I went on doing Coward in cabaret at the Pizza on the Park in Knightsbridge with the nostalgic American pianist Steve Ross, neither of us ever felt quite the same about *Noël & Gertie* after we lost Simon. I have seen countless others play Noël and Gertie, some brilliantly, but inevitably none lingers in the memory with quite the magic of my first great West End team, and to this day I can never see or hear the show without thinking nostalgically of the way Patricia and Simon first brought it so heartbreakingly to life. If I had done nothing else in the theatre as either writer or director or even (lately and very occasionally) as an actor, that first *Noël & Gertie* would have been more than enough to take to my grave. Ruth and I used to stand at the back of the theatre most nights, on our way home from reviewing other shows, and apart from those moments when my children and grandchildren were born, I cannot ever remember feeling more proud that something I had invented and for which I was loosely responsible actually came to life – apparently for hundreds, perhaps thousands of others as well as me.

One last thing about Simon: like his old schoolfriend Gyles Brandreth, and Ned Sherrin and me, he was a compulsive collector of backstage anecdotes. His best concerned his early theatrical life with Ralph Richardson. They had been doing a William Douglas Home comedy together. Simon was fresh out of drama school and, as always, immaculately mannered. One night he came offstage to find Ralph on his hands and knees in the wings.

'Sir Ralph, Sir Ralph, let me do that. What is it you have lost?'

'A little thing, old boy. A little, tiny thing.'

'A coin? A pill? A cufflink?'

'No, no, much smaller than that. It is my talent, but if you should find it, I would so love to have it back.'

Another night, Ralph suddenly stopped the play with a cry from the heart: 'Is there a doctor in the house?'

'Yes, Sir Ralph, here I am in the stalls. What can I do for you?'

'Oh, Doctor,' replied Ralph, 'isn't this a terrible little play?'

Although the royalties from *Noël & Gertie* were more than welcome, I still had to maintain my day job as a critic and interviewer. Luckily Radio 4's *Kaleidoscope* ran on through the 1980s, and when that came to a close David Hatch, then head of BBC Radio, asked if I would like to start Radio 2's first-ever regular *Arts Programme*. His initial idea was that I should run this three nights a week, Friday through Sunday, from ten in the evening until midnight: six hours of me and the arts. Although I was thrilled and flattered by the offer, it soon occurred to me that this might prove too much of a good thing, if not for me then certainly for my listeners.

The West End success of *Noël & Gertie* had led me to believe, perhaps optimistically, that I might be able to do other theatre work, and years of experience had taught me not to put all my eggs into the basket of a single radio or TV programme. I also remembered how furious BBC regional listeners always were about the way that radio arts programmes were so London-centric. I persuaded David and the then Radio 2 Controller, Frances Line, that the three arts nights should be treated separately. Fridays we would give to the regions, allowing each in turn to make its own programme, Saturdays would be my magazine-format arts round-up (which now goes out on a Friday), and Sundays we would give over to 'specials', arts documentaries, many of which I would make, the rest to be offered to specialists in whatever field we had decided to cover.

Frances gave me the best of all possible producers, a cheery soul called Stella Hanson, who – because she was the daughter of John of *The Desert Song* – had spent a vast part of her childhood, like me, backstage on regional British tours with her dad. We soon developed a kind of shorthand about the programmes and our own lives. We travelled together making shows abroad, to Hollywood for the Oscars or New York for the Tonys, and once even to Japan, which was memorable because neither of us is small or agile, and we were forever stumbling over the Japanese, falling into jetlagged sleep at their beloved *kabuki*, or in my case once falling out of a taxi door, which I had inadvertently demolished to the fury of the driver.

Stella also came up with the idea of Proms in the Park, an open-air celebration for Radio 2 linked to the Last Night of the Proms at the Albert Hall but with its own *al fresco* audience, who were encouraged to bring picnics and sit under the stars in Hyde Park. It has been up and running for nearly a decade, has slipped firmly into the London summertime agenda, and also now happens at other parks around the country. That first summer, we had no idea who, if anyone, would turn up on the night, and as the original host I have never forgotten the thrill of watching twenty thousand people settling down on the grass as the result of an invitation we had broadcast on Radio 2. In those days we also used to broadcast entire West End and Broadway musicals from the Golders Green Hippodrome, another idea of Stella's for which, as so often happens in the history of broadcasting, she was never really credited.

Over the next ten years, the arts programmes were whittled down to the one ninety-minute show a week that I cherish and guard jealously. Stella eventually took early retirement, but I now share a strong production team, led by Anthony Cherry and Judy Elliott, with Michael Parkinson's Sunday show. Over the last five or six years Jim Moir has been a commendably generous and non-interventionist Controller, sharing my passion for large, long Garrick lunches, and actually listening, from time to time, to the programmes. I couldn't ask more of any BBC employer, especially one who is reassuringly of roughly the same shape and size as me. Somehow I have always distrusted very thin radio or TV controllers.

25
The Apple Doesn't Fall
Very Far from the Tree

Although I tried for some time to disguise this from myself, let alone my wife and family, since I couldn't see how to make it into a paying second career, the time I was spending backstage at rehearsals of *Noël & Gertie* all over the place was teaching me that the theatre was where I wanted to end up – not just at night with a notebook, but as a day job too.

Accordingly, I began to work on another musical for the King's Head, this one devoted to Vivian Ellis, then still a sprightly late-octogenarian who would come to rehearsal most days with still more of his 'trunk songs'. He remained wonderfully unperturbed and cheery, even if we threw them out after one play-through.

Ellis was a contemporary of Noël Coward and Ivor Novello, and the last survivor of that great musical generation. As he was neither an actor nor a singer, he had never achieved their personal recognition, and because his songs were written in many different styles, few recognised them all as his. He had, however, composed such classic English musicals as *Mr Cinders* (which the King's Head had recently and triumphantly brought back to life after half a century), *Bless the Bride* (which had outlasted even *Oklahoma* in the West End just after the war) and *The Water Gypsies*, as well as countless single hits for stars as diverse as Sophie Tucker, Jack Buchanan, Sonnie Hale, Bobby Howes and Flanagan and Allen.

Aided and abetted by Vivian, I cobbled together a song-by-song anthology that Dan Crawford directed with considerable success. We assembled a starry cast, headed by

Frank Thornton, Thelma Ruby and two gorgeous newcomers, Rachel Robertson and Fiona Sinnott.

Helped by some rave reviews (my Critics' Circle colleagues – with one or two exceptions who shall be nameless but I know where you live – are nearly always more than generous to me), we sold out for a month in Islington and then faced the usual King's Head transfer problem. It is best summarised by something I learnt some years later, when Bill Kenwright took over a production I had directed at the King's Head of *A Song at Twilight* and moved us on to Shaftesbury Avenue. The day before we began rerehearsing for the West End, Bill took one quarter-page box ad in the *Sunday Times* Culture section, listing those of us involved and the Gielgud box-office phone number. Then he rang me, I think meaning to be reassuring: 'Out of interest,' he said amiably, 'I have just spent more on one quarter-page ad than you spent in seven weeks at the King's Head, counting rent, salaries, rehearsals, the set, costumes, the lot.' Never again in a review did I express astonishment that a fringe hit had not made it to Shaftesbury Avenue: the costs of moving a few miles up West are now almost totally prohibitive.

But we found some backers willing to take the risk, and moved to the Whitehall Theatre. Frank Thornton had to return to his triumphant *Last of the Summer Wine* television series, but we replaced him with Ron Moody. It was a slow summer, and previews were sparsely attended: whatever else American tourists had heard of, they sure as hell hadn't heard of the songs of Vivian Ellis. I was functioning as narrator, because I had failed to find any string of plot on which to hang the show together, and in one of the last previews, I was surprised to find Ron hurling assorted props across the footlights.

'They were a bloody lousy audience,' said Ron backstage, by way of explanation, 'and, besides, there weren't nearly enough of them'; within about twenty-four hours of the first night, we came to an abrupt parting of the ways. Another old revue trouper, Jimmy Thompson, kindly stepped into the breach but understandably had to read all the songs and sketches off a script on stage, which made for a somewhat hesitant press night. Even so, most critics took pity on us but audiences did not. All in all, that summer of 1992 was about as bad as it has ever got in my otherwise charmed life on stage and off.

In the gap between the King's Head and the Whitehall, I had gone as usual to New York with Stella to cover the Broadway Tony awards for our Radio 2 *Arts Programme*. When we got back to Heathrow early on the Tuesday morning, both Ruth and Alexis were there to meet me. Although I had got no warning, and certainly no premonition, I knew at once why they had come. The previous Sunday my father had woken up feeling a little under the weather, and decided he would not join Joan in going over to Margaret and his grandchildren for lunch, but would instead spend a happy day in bed with the weekend papers.

After lunch, Hugo decided that his grandfather might like to have the television in his bedroom to watch the racing or the old movies, and drove home with Ma to carry it upstairs. They found Pa slumped across the bed, having suffered a massive stroke. He died three days later, peacefully in hospital, having never regained consciousness. He was just eighty-four, and it was Derby Day, 3 June 1992, one of the few he ever missed in a long, generally happy life.

Luckily, he and I didn't have much of what American psychiatrists call 'unfinished business', although our last few years together had not been easy. He never really forgave me for leaving Margaret, not because he cared very much about our marriage but because he was devoted to Margaret who had become invaluable to him, helping him with his *Book of Worries* and *Book of Bricks*, which they triumphantly anthologised for charity, driving him once or twice a week to the Ascot and Windsor race meetings, which Ma (like me) never terribly enjoyed, and generally taking the place of his three absent children: I was always working in London, my sister was settled with her family in Sydney, and my brother was in Tampa, Florida. I think Pa was terrified that, once we were divorced, Margaret might return to her native Boston, thereby depriving him of his last 'best friend'. Peter Bull, Sewell Stokes and Tom Chatto, who had always been cast in that role, were all recently dead, and Pa even saw less of his beloved agent Ros Chatto, now that he never did plays and therefore had less reason to visit London. His life when he was not filming now consisted of Ma, Margaret, and his faithful driver John, and the thought of losing even one of them was more than he could bear to contemplate.

I have always been every bit as selfish and egocentric as my father and understood his position but vaguely resented it, feeling that he might have been a bit more focused on me and my new-found happiness with Ruth. He was also very fond of her, and once, whispering like a naughty schoolboy, even told me that he understood why I had left Margaret for her, but it was Margaret who came first with him in these last few years. That I was still financing her leisure, despite the fact that she could in at least my view have gone back to work now that our children were off her hands, did not do much to improve my general feeling of having somehow come out of that whole divorce deal very badly indeed. But then I guess everyone probably feels the same way about divorce, and she had certainly given up much of her early life to our family.

One of the last things Margaret and I did together as a reasonably happily married couple was a three-week tour of China: we went by train from Hong Kong, fairly soon after the time of the Red Guards, and across the border were bundled into a minibus that also contained a couple of homegoing Chinese, and a fabulously wealthy couple who had travelled from Panama to be among China's first tourists.

Disappointment was the order of the day: our guide told

us first that we would not be going to either Shanghai or Beijing because, she explained sweetly, both cities had limited tourist accommodation and were unfortunately full. Instead, we would spend several of our precious days in Wushi, a kind of local Lake District of breathtaking dullness, where there was little to do but watch the rain. Hotels being virtually non-existent, we were boarded in weird youth hostels where they left a comb, a single sheet of loo paper and some improving tracts by each bedside. The Panamanians didn't care for this, but Margaret was stoic and I think she realised she could get a novel out of the experience, as indeed she did. As for me, once you have been to an English boys' preparatory school, you can sleep anywhere on anything.

Eventually we got to Shanghai, where to my great delight there was a hotel with black-and-white television on which I managed to find Arthur Miller's own production of *Death of a Salesman*, albeit in Chinese. After that we reached Beijing, which was full of people building twelfth-century tombs by the roadside. 'Regrettably,' explained our guide, 'the real ones were destroyed by the Red Guards, but now that we are trying to attract tourists, we find they need something to look at, so we are building lots of brand new historic ruins. They will all be ready by October latest.'

Also in Beijing, they had just built the first western-style hotel, a partnership between Hilton International and a local hotelier. We arrived in perfect time for the gala opening. An equally brand-new western-style coffee shop was advertised in the lobby. We fell into it. The menu promised spaghetti, then apple pie with ice cream and we ordered it. All we had eaten for the last couple of weeks had been a very old owl in water, which mysteriously followed us from town to town – apparently all the really good Chinese-food chefs had left the country years earlier. A few hours later, a beaming waitress returned with steaming bowls of spaghetti, in the middle of which, as per local custom, she had carefully placed the apple pie and ice cream. The Panamanians nearly killed her.

Our marriage had been over for almost a decade by the time Robert died but, as always in my family, we had managed to bury any feelings of bitterness or guilt under the usual façade of cheery sociability. In the summer we'd all have Sunday lunch on the Fairmans lawn, Pa at the end of the table as the *patron*, determined to re-create in the Thames Valley the high *alfresco* life that he had once glimpsed on a French Cognac commercial. Then, he and I used to swim – or, rather, float – in his pool, a couple of water-buffalo terrified of looking too far beneath the surface in case we should come face to face with some ghastly truth about who we really were.

Of course Robert conditioned me: he conditioned me to flee in terror from any really emotional situation; to believe that loving people was the same as looking after them; to know that my only real talent was for living precariously on my wits, and that I had better make sure to keep them about me, never allowing them to be interfered with by others trying to get too close. Robert never frightened me, or bored me, or tried to advise or instruct me, and I have tried to be equally hands-off with my own children and grandchildren; he never tried to make me into anything I hadn't already become by heredity or accident, education or desire; if I ever disappointed him, he had the grace not to tell me, and in our own curious way, I think we loved each other as much as it is perhaps possible for fathers and sons to love each other across half a century.

I took his death badly, God knows why, as it was about as good a death as you could hope for. 'Clifton,' as Noël Coward had said, when Mr Webb was proving inconsolable over the death of his mother, 'you really must stop all this weeping and grieving. In my experience, it is not entirely unusual to be orphaned at seventy-four.' But this sudden bereavement, added to the stage disaster at the Whitehall, sent me into my second nervous breakdown. It lasted less time than the first, and I was nursed through it by Ruth and, once again, Leslie Morrish.

What also got me out of this one was the terror that BUPA might stop funding my long stays in the Cardinal, and, oddly enough, the offer of a job. The then editor of the *Spectator*, Dominic Lawson – encouraged I have always thought by the splendid Michael Heath, who was our last cartoon editor on the old *Punch* and has fulfilled the same function ever since on the *Spectator* – rang with the offer of the theatre column. I grabbed it with delight: although my job at the *Herald Tribune* was safe, I had long missed having a local British readership.

I lasted on the *Spectator* for precisely ten years, rather longer, I think, than any other drama critic in its two-hundred-year history, and was fired, somewhat peremptorily, by Boris Johnson on my sixtieth birthday in December 2001. I took this rather hard (why do I never get used to being fired from press columns? It has happened so often without any lasting damage to my career, finances or journalistic well-being. Pride, I suppose), feeling doubly aggrieved as Johnson had just become my mother's local Tory MP in Henley-on-Thames. This was not, I somehow felt, the constituency behaviour of a gentleman, and my mother at ninety-two has kindly promised never to vote for him again. Should I find myself at a loose end come the next general election, I may doorstep some of her neighbours if I am still feeling indignant – which I doubt I shall be. At least I hope not: it isn't as though I have all that much time left in which to pursue daft grievances. Suppose I live to my father's age – that gives me just over twenty years. I hope to God I find something more useful to do with them than settle old Fleet Street scores, addictive though that can sometimes become.

I am, anyway, well aware that I have been more than lucky as a drama critic: fifteen years at *Punch*, almost thirty at the *Herald Tribune* and ten at the *Spectator*. And I have just been asked, in the autumn of 2002, to take over the theatre column on the *New Statesman*. Quite apart from the political spectrum covered – or, rather, not covered – I can't think of any other drama critic of my lifetime who has had the spread of those four titles in four decades.

My private life was now reasonably settled with Ruth, or as settled as it was ever going to be. Her apartment by the Lincoln Center in New York, and a timeshare I had bought from her first husband in Aspen – she is addicted to the annual August music festival – exerted a powerful influence on her travel plans. In June 1995, by which time our respective divorces had finally come through, we decided to have two weddings, as befitted Ruth's transatlantic life. In New York, we took the boat to Staten Island for our licence (the queues tend to be shorter there), accompanied on the ferry by a gorgeous New York producer, Dasha Epstein, who gave us a magical wedding party at her equally gorgeous apartment on Park Avenue. We had a couple of weeks' honeymoon in our beloved Hawaii, where Sheila Donnelly (now married to the novelist Paul Theroux) and her ex-husband Dave spoiled us rotten, then returned to London for another wedding. This time our marriage was blessed by Rabbi Julia Neuberger and was followed by a party at the hotel in Chelsea Harbour.

Apart from that, and the ongoing theatre reviews, an increasing amount of cabaret hosting and, of course, the weekend Radio 2 *Arts Programmes*, I spent most of the 1990s writing my biography of Sir John Gielgud. It was a lengthy task, involving hundreds of interviews both in the UK and abroad, as he had lived to be ninety-six, had seldom been out of work, and I was therefore writing, through his life, the history of the twentieth-century British theatre.

Towards the end of that marathon project (which I would never have completed without the help of a brilliant young biographer, playwright and researcher called Paul Webb, who luckily shares my passion for theatrical nostalgia), I got my first chance to direct a West End play. It happened, as so much else in my life, by sheer luck.

26
Curtain Calls

At the time of the Coward centenary in 1999, I felt strongly that we should try to remind people of, or at least introduce to younger audiences, the extraordinary range of Noël's work – he had written over four hundred songs, of which only about a dozen are still familiar: we persuaded the Pet Shop Boys to release an album of some of the others. With Michael Law and Alison Williams of the Piccadilly Dance Orchestra, Ruth and I took a Coward cabaret, *Out in the Midday Sun*, around the Far East, playing in such great hotels as Raffles in Singapore and the Oriental in Bangkok – both have a Noël Coward Suite in recognition of the many times and even months he stayed there in the 1930s and wrote many of his best songs, short stories and plays.

Back home, Patricia Hodge, Steve Ross and I also had the considerable joy of reviving a Coward cabaret we had done fairly often at Pizza on the Park, but this time in a private performance for the Queen Mother, in recognition of the fifty years she had served as a patron of the Red Cross. She sang virtually all of the songs with us, word-perfect, and explained to me afterwards that she was now, after all, Noël's longest-living fan: she had been singing his songs, often with him at the piano, since 1924.

I also worked on gala centenary concerts at Drury Lane, Carnegie Hall – with the great New York cabaret impresario Don Smith – and even in Hollywood with Kirk Douglas, but it was the plays that Graham Payn and I really wanted to re-establish. Noël had written more than sixty of which barely half a dozen ever seemed to get regular revival.

Over long, nostalgic weekends at Noël's house in Switzerland, where Graham and his partner, the award-winning painter Dany Dasto, keep the Coward flag flying, he and I began to wonder what more we could do to underscore the versatility of Noël's writing. They have always been the most generous of hosts and friends to Ruth and me, not only there but also in the South of France, where they have a summer apartment and where the surviving Coward clans gather, usually with Hilary and Roy King's brilliant little English-speaking Red Pear company at the Theatre Antibea, to celebrate Graham's birthdays.

Noël has been dead now for almost thirty years, so that many of his original team, those who looked after him and his work throughout the first two-thirds of the last century, have also vanished. Graham and I, however, have been blessed not only with Dany in Switzerland and Alan Brodie, who now runs the estate in London, but such relative newcomers as Robert Gardiner, Jo Karaviotis and the Coward Society, godfathered by Michael Imison. All of them, in partnership with the University of Birmingham's drama department under Joel Kaplan, keep a watchful eye over various aspects of the Coward legacy. In America we have been equally blessed with Geoffrey Johnson, Barry Lee Cohen, Don Smith and Barry Day, who recently edited a superb collection of Noël's lyrics.

But estates are curiously vulnerable: in America, Ted Chapin presides over a breathtakingly efficient and effective Rodgers & Hammerstein office, so that their work (and also the scores of many other composers) is protected by an army of caretakers, who ensure that every single production of their scores, no matter where in the world it is staged, lives up to the highest original standards. The R&H estate is worth millions of dollars a year in royalties and Noël's brings in rather less, yet we still have the obligation to watch over it, policing it as well as we can on limited resources. We don't demand a series of museum-piece revivals but that, wherever and however he is staged, there should be at least some understanding of the man and his intentions.

My centennial patience finally gave way when I discovered that Trevor Nunn at the National Theatre, instead of reviving the two-hundred-cast *Cavalcade* or the nine plays that make up *Tonight at 8.30*, or some other Coward project that only a heavily subsidised permanent company like his could now contemplate, was planning nothing more ambitious than yet another revival of *Private Lives*, a two-set, five-cast comedy that any local amateur society, or any surviving regional rep, can and does stage at a moment's notice.

If nobody else was going to bother about 'the unknown Coward', I figured I would have to do it myself. Just as the centenary started, the British press in general and the *Daily Mail* in particular suddenly became obsessed with gay 'outings'. There was the business of Jeremy Paxman on *Newsnight* inadvertently raising the private life of Peter Mandelson, then the Welsh minister caught on Clapham Common in a compromising situation. At this point I remembered Noël's last full-length play, the one he had been working on while I was writing his and my first biography back in 1966.

A Song at Twilight had been the last play in which Noël had appeared, somewhat shakily, on the London stage a year or so later, in a sequence called *Suite in Three Keys* at the Queen's, which marked his farewell to the West End, as he was already far from strong; the play had seldom been revived since, and was certainly nowhere near the top ten of his more popular scripts. Yet it happens to be, though the term itself had not yet been coined and is therefore nowhere used in the script, a drama almost entirely about homosexual outing.

I knew at once that this was the play of his I most wanted to direct and took it to Dan Crawford, who was good enough to let me try my luck with a third show at the King's Head, albeit the first straight play I had ever directed. Although lately I've been working more often at Jermyn Street – largely because the casts I assemble on fringe salaries seem happier there than in Islington – I still retain a deep affection for the King's Head and gratitude for Dan's willingness to let me have my head there.

Song at Twilight – I eventually dropped the *A* – tells the story of an old, Nobel-prizewinning novelist staying in a Lausanne lakeside hotel with his German wife. Noël himself said the character of Sir Hugo Latymer was loosely based on that of Somerset Maugham, and indeed made himself up to look remarkably like that 'old party' for the first production. But you can also find traces of Max Beerbohm in Sir Hugo, and of Noël himself, and even maybe of Vladimir Nabokov, who lived for many years in the same Swiss hotel where the play is set. I have only just realised, incidentally, that it was while Noël was writing this play that my Hugo was born and named after Pa's stage character, and of course my old Oxford tutor Hugo Dyson. Did Noël borrow his last godson's name for the play, or did we both arrive at it simultaneously by coincidence?

Early in the play, a woman arrives from the old writer's past: she is an actress with whom he once had an affair and now, some forty years later, after a rackety career in Hollywood, she is about to write her memoirs and intends to use his love letters to help sell the book. Resentfully, he points out that he still owns his copyright, even though she holds the letters, and that he will not allow his elegant writing to dignify her trashy autobiography.

Furious with his arrogant unhelpfulness, she tells him that in that case she won't use those letters but will paraphrase some others in her possession: love letters he once wrote to 'the only person you have ever loved in your whole rotten existence', a man called Perry Sheldon. So much for act one; the whole of act two is a debate about the morality of homosexual outing in which the film star, the author and eventually his wife discuss all the issues of secrecy and privacy, of British middle-class intolerance towards gays, even of the way in which a novelist can be warped and defeated by his own refusal to face the truth about himself.

I knew at once that, if I could just get it together, I had here a play that would astonish even the Coward addicts, and maybe surprise those of my critical colleagues who had long since written him off as a Shaftesbury Avenue boulevardier. In the best sense, *Song at Twilight* is a return to the 'problem' plays of Galsworthy and Granville Barker with which Noël had grown up almost a century earlier.

My problem, once Dan had given me the go-ahead for the King's Head, was to get it cast – not only on the usual King's Head pittance, but also over Christmas, since we were due to open early in January 1999. After countless refusals from actors for the other two leading roles, I began to think about the German wife and remembered Kika Markham, who has made something of a speciality of women from middle Europe. Her immediate enthusiasm for the play, given her radically different background from mine, confirmed my belief that we were on to something special. By another kind of miracle I was doing a charity fund-raiser when across a crowded room Ruth saw exactly who I wanted for the ex-movie star. Carlotta, as she is called in the play, says that she has been out of public vision for several years, and I had some daft ideas of trying to find Samantha Eggar or one of those other sixties stars, who seemed to have dropped off the local radar. Nyree Dawn Porter was not looking forward to Christmas, as her daughter was away in Canada and she would be alone. She agreed to join us, but that still left me without Sir Hugo. Just as I was getting desperate enough to think of postponing, Kika had an idea. 'Have you,' she wondered, 'considered my husband?'

As it happened, I hadn't. My memories of Corin Redgrave were still of his barricade days with Vanessa and the Workers' Revolutionary Party, and I had not always written him the most enthusiastic reviews. I could hardly have imagined a less Cowardly leading man.

'Would you mind,' persevered Kika, 'if he came over this afternoon and read it to you?' I took a deep breath, and tried to explain to her that she was asking if I, having only ever directed my own *Noël & Gertie* in cabaret and concert, would mind being read to by an actor who had not only directed many plays but to whom I had often been less than polite in print. No, I heard myself answer, I would scarcely mind at all.

That reading was a revelation. Corin, like all great actors, has the chameleon ability to inhabit whoever he plays, and for me he turned himself into a crotchety, old, gay, Nobel-prizewinning novelist. I also realised, though was careful not to say so, that he had seen in Sir Hugo a great deal of his own father, Michael Redgrave, who had left his wife to spend his last night of shore leave before the Second World War with his then lover, who just happened to be Noël Coward.

We were suddenly into a lot of family closets: my father and Michael had made four films together; I had always been devoted to Lynn; and although Vanessa and I had had occasional public battles, I suddenly saw that in various odd ways our two families had been interconnected almost all our lives.

But we were still not out of the wood: Corin had a film to finish, which meant that our precious rehearsal time would be whittled down to barely fourteen days before – such was the King's Head schedule – we had to open to the critics, many of whom were just waiting, or so I became convinced, to watch me come a serious cropper. Corin and I reached an immediate agreement: the only way I could do the play that fast would be to treat it almost like radio. We would learn it, block it and do it, keeping all discussion to a minimum. If I lacked any real directing experience, I figured I could make up for it by knowing the play better than anyone – I had, after all, been with Noël while he was writing it.

Once we'd opened, I told Corin, he was welcome to redirect the show any way he liked, but for the twelve days or so at our disposal, he would just have to trust me to get it right. Generously, he went along with that, and we had an almost trouble-free rehearsal period, one which also gave me a new friendship with both Kika and Corin that I cherish to this day. We turned back into a working partnership recently, when I directed them, Jo Lumley and Thelma Ruby, in an audiotape of *Blithe Spirit*.

We only had one real rehearsal crisis: one morning, rather like Macavity the Mystery Cat, Nyree Dawn Porter was simply not there. Her answerphone was taking messages, but she wasn't, and by the end of that day I had started wondering frantically about a replacement, given that we were now only a week away from opening. That night, briefly to take my mind off the whole crisis, Ruth and I went to a dinner party we'd accepted weeks earlier, and I found myself sitting next to an old friend, the actress Maureen Lipman. She asked what I was doing, I told her, and then she asked about the casting. When I mentioned Nyree, without telling her of the day's crisis, Maureen said simply, 'Has she done her bolt yet?'

'What?'

'Her bolt. Nyree is famous for disappearing from shows without a word of explanation.'

'Well, yes. As a matter fact she did that today.'

'Then you're extremely lucky. She usually does it just before the first night, and that really causes chaos. In this case she's gone early. She'll be back tomorrow morning in rehearsal. Just don't mention it, and you'll find she'll be utterly reliable for the rest of the run. She only does it once.'

And, sure enough, Maureen was right. The next morning Nyree was answering her phone, and I was reminded of how, almost fifty years earlier, Pa had dealt with an equally recalcitrant Peggy Ashcroft when she locked herself in a dressing room just before the first night of *Edward My Son*. 'If you don't come back to us now,' I told Nyree, probably quite untruthfully, 'you will never have the courage to go out on any stage again,' and by lunchtime she was back in rehearsal as though nothing had happened. None of us mentioned her disappearance, and she never missed a performance.

A week later, we opened at the King's Head to the kind of reviews you dream about in the shower: far from attacking me for crossing the line, almost without exception my critical colleagues discovered to their amazement an altogether different Coward from the one they thought they knew, and within about a day we were sold out for the whole six-week run in Islington.

Flatteringly, we were also visited by several West End managements, all of whom agreed that we deserved a transfer; but then something happened that is often now the fate of off-West End shows. As the run progressed, playing to full houses – which, at the King's Head, means about 150 people a night, say around a thousand a week – West End enthusiasm for us faded, as managers did the arithmetic. If we were to have reached, by the end of the Islington run, around six thousand people, that would have carve a sizeable hole in the prospective Shaftesbury Avenue audience. Moreover, in the ludicrous new tourist and Hollywood film-star economy of the West End, neither Corin, Kika nor Nyree was considered hugely bankable. It looked as if we were going nowhere, after all.

Until, in fact, our closing Sunday matinée, when a standing-room-only audience was notable for two visitors: Corin's sister Vanessa, and the impresario Bill Kenwright. As we chatted in the pub after the show, a new idea began to form: supposing, just supposing, Vanessa could be persuaded to join us? We would then have two Redgraves (or three, counting Kika, by marriage) together for the first time in the West End and that, Bill reckoned, would be a package he *could* sell at thirty pounds or so a ticket.

The problem then, of course, was Nyree. Now that she has died an all too early death, I look back at our brief alliance with considerable affection. The curious thing about her, as an actress and a woman, was that she was easily thrown off balance by what most of us would consider normal life, but when there was a real crisis to be faced, or a sacrifice to be made, she invariably came good. Carefully, I explained to her that only with Vanessa did we have a hope in hell of getting into the West End, then stood well back expecting just about everything to hit the fan. Nothing did. Nyree said she entirely understood the situation, and would stand down in order that the show could move on. I always hoped and meant to work with her again, because at her best on stage she could break your heart, but that hope became yet another example of Noël Coward's old belief that if you want to make God laugh, you tell him your plans.

We now had to wait almost nine months for Vanessa to be free of a couple of movie projects, but in the meantime I had the joy of seeing my *Noël & Gertie*, now getting on for fifteen years old, given a whole new lease of life across the Atlantic by Leigh Lawson and Twiggy. They opened an American version of the show, retitled *If Love Were All* because even in America we reckoned that there were now far too many people who had not the faintest idea who Gertie was, and some who weren't even all that sure about Noël, at an enchanting little summer theatre out at Sag Harbor in the Hamptons, run by Richard Burton's first wife Sybil, and Emma, the daughter of Julie Andrews and Tony Walton.

Leigh had worked at Sag Harbor before, and even married Twigs there, I think, so they were totally at home. Although I had one or two reservations about the changes they had made in my script, once I saw Twigs on her dancing feet winning nightly five-minute standing ovations, I had to admit that I was lucky she had chosen to return to the American stage, after an absence of nearly twenty years, in a show of mine.

A few months later, joined now by the American actor and tap-dancer Harry Groener, we moved into the Lortel, the first off-Broadway theatre, founded in the 1950s, then still run by the redoubtable, legendary Lucille Lortel. We were her last production: having, to my great delight, approved the show, she died at a ripe old age just before we opened, casting the only shadow of sadness over a long, happy New York run, during which Twigs, despite acting, singing and dancing eight performances a week in which she was seldom if ever offstage, spent almost all of her spare time going out and selling the show. We seldom played to less than full houses. My admiration for her dedication, energy and sheer professionalism is boundless, and all I hope is that I get to work with her once more before I die. She clearly never has to worry about dying: she's the nearest thing there's ever been to an ageless, tireless Peter Pan.

Back in London, it was now time to put *Song at Twilight* back together for Bill Kenwright at the Gielgud, a theatre where, under its old name the Globe, my father had enjoyed several long runs in the 1950s, and which I therefore knew intimately. I had spent many months of my childhood lurking backstage but I had never expected to get back there fifty years later as a director, and it wasn't an entirely easy experience. On hearing that I was going to make my West End début as a director at fifty-eight with a play starring Vanessa, friends, and even a few enemies, took to laying bets as to how long I'd last. Nica Burns, of the Really Useful management, our landlords, even offered to bet me a hundred pounds that I would be fired by Vanessa in the first week. Sorely tempted as I was to take her money, I couldn't because I knew, as she did not, that as the literary executor of the Coward estate I had the play to myself. Vanessa couldn't do it without me. Had I not known that, I doubt that even with my rampant ego I would have risked taking her on.

And there was another problem: over nearly three months at the King's Head, counting the rehearsals and the run, the original cast had bonded well. Somehow, I had to get that back with Vanessa now parachuted into our midst. I decided the time had come to beg some advice. Nearly all of the directors I knew well, some of them from as far back as Oxford, told me I had not a hope of survival and would be wise to bring in a 'real' director, if not one of them then at least someone with a little more experience of the job. Only Trevor Nunn was truly encouraging, and he gave me the note I most needed: 'Don't even try directing her,' he said. 'Clear a flight path where she can land on stage, look after the others, and just don't expect her ever to do the same thing two nights running because she won't, and you can save your breath about giving her notes – whatever she does tonight, she's not going to do tomorrow night. That's all you have to remember.'

I tried to stick to his advice, but rehearsals were not easy: my chief concern was to preserve on a much broader stage in a much larger theatre what I knew were two wondrously intimate performances from Kika and Corin, and try to make sure that whatever Vanessa took it into her head to do that night, their work would not be damaged. I don't for a moment believe that Vanessa, who had only agreed to join us so that her brother and sister-in-law's work could be seen in the West End, had any intention of getting in their way, but she can be, to put it mildly, a loose cannon.

In the event, after some shaky previews, Vanessa gave on press night one of those mesmeric performances that has always had even the toughest critics eating out of her hand. We ran for about seven months at the Gielgud, until her new film commitments meant that we had to close: hers, as usual, was an impossible act to follow.

During the run, I began to realise that since leaving Robert's theatres I had never discovered what happens to a play once it has opened: both critics and directors tend to disappear after first nights. I used to go back to *Song at Twilight* most Saturday evenings, when I wasn't reviewing or working elsewhere. It was a truly fascinating experience: both Corin and Kika kept their performances pristine and rock-solid across another six months, while Vanessa remained unpredictable. Some Saturday nights I would watch her and think, Yes, however occasionally maddening she may be to work with, I do see why she alone, not Maggie Smith, not even Judi Dench, has won the *Evening Standard* Best Actress award in four consecutive decades. But other nights I would sit there thinking, How this woman has stayed in work for forty years, doing what she is now doing, I simply do not understand. And then, if you went backstage and said, 'Darling, that was one of the greatest nights of my life,' or 'Darling, that was near total and utter rubbish,' she would look at you with precisely the same faintly myopic surprise.

It finally dawned on me that Vanessa doesn't know what she does on stage; it is, as they keep saying in *Shakespeare in Love*, 'all a mystery', and it was as usual Corin, himself an expert theatre historian, who gave me the final clue. One night, when I was especially livid with her about something I've now forgotten, probably her performance, he said of his sister, 'Never forget, she's another Eleanora Duse.' I went home and read the only book on my shelf about the legendary nineteenth-century tragedienne. Sure enough, what nearly everyone said about her, as they do about Vanessa, is that it all depended on which night you went to see her. But then again, if that isn't in and of itself a definition of the essence of live theatre, and what keeps it separate from film or television, what is?

I am sometimes asked, after the event, if I would ever work with Vanessa again: the answer is yes, in a split second, especially as, since the show closed, we have carved out a wary friendship, built around our devotion to her long-lived mother Rachel Kempson. But will I ever be asked to work with her again? That I rather doubt: as Louis B. Mayer used to tell recalcitrant Hollywood movie stars, 'You're fired . . . unless and until I really need you again.'

Looking back, I gained so much from *Song*: the friendship of, eventually, all the Redgraves, the joy of working for Bill

Kenwright, who commendably left me alone to survive, asking only that on the press night I would make myself scarce – he had decided that seeing me in the stalls might so annoy my critical colleagues that they would give us lousy reviews. I therefore found myself tramping Shaftesbury Avenue in the rain, wondering how the hell they were all getting on without me. That, too, was a lesson I learnt for the first time: up to the press night, the director is, for better or worse, the leader of the pack, and in near-constant demand to sort out each day's problems. But once the notices are in, the cast grows up and leaves home: when you go back, they look at you in mild surprise, as if they thought you were dead.

My other cherished memory of that production is a cable that came a week later from the great director Michael Blakemore, who had been good enough to teach me to read and write backstage in Australia on *Edward My Son* almost fifty years earlier: 'I don't mind a critic becoming a director; what I mind is him having a hit.'

By now I had discovered something new about myself: although I knew I'd be unlikely to make a full-time living at it, I enjoyed directing more than writing, broadcasting, cabaret-hosting, or lying on a beach in Hawaii. If you are, as I am, temperamentally bossy and in love with the sound of your own voice, only preaching or teaching offer the same opportunities, and at my time of life I am unlikely to make it as a vicar or a professor.

So directing it is, and I got really lucky again: not only Dan Crawford and Bill Kenwright seemed prepared to trust me with the occasional production, but so did the redoubtable Penny Horner at Jermyn Street. Over the last four years, thanks to the faith and generosity of yet another remarkable woman, the choreographer Gillian Lynne, I have been able to direct four very different shows there.

Under Gillian's management I opened safely enough with yet another *Noël & Gertie*, which we took into Jermyn Street from Sally Hughes' enchanting riverside Mill at Sonning; then, getting a little more ambitious, the next year I put together a *Jermyn Street Revue* with an amazing cast led by the veteran Judy Campbell, Frank Thornton, Thelma Ruby, Jonathan Cecil, Stefan Bednarczyk, Peter Land, Sophie-Louise Dann and Issy van Randwyck – perhaps the most fun I have ever had in rehearsal, especially as it was choreographed, like so many of my shows, by the ageless, magical Irving ('the feet') Davies.

The year after that I did yet another 'lost' Noël Coward play, *Shadows of the Evening*, as a double-bill with his much more familiar backstage *Red Peppers*, and again, despite minimal Jermyn Street salaries, I attracted another wonderfully starry cast: Jeremy Clyde, Jane How, Jeremy Nicholas, Peter Land and my darling old Oxford friend Annabel Leventon.

The fourth year I decided it was time to abandon, if only temporarily, the nostalgia market and try directing something new: Paul Webb, who had been working with me on the Gielgud biography, had written a remarkable one-man play about an actor who, in the 1950s, runs foul of the anti-gay laws that had seen Gielgud arrested and many others imprisoned for homosexual soliciting. But Paul's mythical actor has a still worse problem: once he comes home from prison – we meet him only on the night before his trial – he is likely to be unemployable: not only has he a police record but, still worse, he is also a chorus boy and the West End world has changed, almost overnight. His beloved Ivor Novello is dead, and Noël Coward has gone to live abroad.

It struck me at once that, having already written the best Novello biography, Paul had a unique understanding of that abrupt changeover time in Shaftesbury Avenue, and of what it meant to be gay around the summer of the Coronation. The only problem with *The Lodger*, so far as I could see, was that we needed to find an actor who could sing, dance and play the piano, while holding the stage alone for ninety minutes.

We found him in Garth Bardsley, who was not only a joy to work with – one-man shows make for curiously intimate rehearsal periods – but also delivered us a batch of smashing reviews. Then, of course, we faced the old problem: how to achieve the afterlife with a Jermyn Street hit, given that to transfer to any even slightly larger theatre multiplies your budget by a factor of at least ten.

Because I am always so blissfully happy in rehearsal, whether for a stage play or a cabaret or whatever, and the *Spectator* had come to an abrupt halt on my sixtieth birthday, I decided that maybe I should look around for some alternative form of employment to get me through the rest of my life. For more than ten years, between other assignments, I had been engaged on writing, at his request, the life of Sir John Gielgud. When that was finished soon after his death, I realised that I was never again going to find a stage or screen figure so totally absorbing. As Noël Coward had once been able to remark, 'I am England, and England is me,' so John could have said, were he not so modest, 'I am Theatre, and Theatre is me.'

But during the long writing period of the biography, an obvious problem arose: John and I had always agreed that, because of the trauma of his 1953 arrest for homosexual soliciting, my book could never be published in his lifetime. He understood that it would have to cover the only real-life drama of his stagestruck life, but understandably did not want every tabloid reporter in the country phoning to ask how it felt to be outed in his late nineties.

Our agreement, with my original editor at Hodder, Ion Trewin, who had offered me the job on the death of John's original biographer Richard Findlater, was that the book would be published a year after his death. As John showed every sign of living for ever, that gave us a flexible deadline. John was also eager to see what his authorised biography was going to look like, and took to phoning regularly to ask how old he was now. After a while, I think he forgot I was still on the case, so when another writer, Jonathan Croall, approached him with the request to write a book about his career, John agreed to that, too.

Some months later, I noticed that when I went to interview one of the two or three hundred witnesses to John's longevity and classical stardom, they would often tell me about 'another author' who had been around asking similar questions, not only about John's career but also about his life.

This, I soon discovered, was Croall, who had decided that he, too, would go for a fully fledged biography. When I pointed out to John that even he could hardly have two of us as his authorised biographers, Gielgud at once wrote to Croall withdrawing, in a letter of which I still hold a copy, any permission he might have given him. Yet Croall went ahead with his own biography, leaving in its preface a note to the effect that it had been written 'with John's blessing'.

Our books appeared more or less simultaneously in the spring of 2001. Although the clash had a happy outcome for me in that, thanks to Roland Philipps at Hodder and Michael Korda at Simon & Schuster in New York, we outsold Croall's effort substantially, the whole unhappy affair somehow put me off the idea of another massive biographical project.

I had grown up, I realised, in an altogether less cut-throat biographical climate. If Croall and the barbarians were at the gates, maybe I'd be better off spending my sixties and, hopefully, seventies elsewhere. But where?

Well, in a theatre, obviously: I was still getting regular reviewing work from various British and American magazines including *Playbill*, the *Lady*, and also a brilliant new invention called Teletext whereby you go to the theatre, write your first-night review, slip it on to a fax machine at midnight then see it in print on your own television set about an hour later. It never ceases to thrill me in all its technological complexity.

Sure, there were other biographies I ached to write, but either these were already assigned elsewhere or the subjects, understandably enough, wanted to do it themselves. One that I regretted losing to the admirable John Coldstream was Dirk Bogarde: I had already written, much against his will, a critical picture-book about the man who I believe was one of the greatest home-grown movie stars we ever had, but something about his buttoned-up, closet-gay character continued to fascinate me. Like David Niven and Noël Coward, with both of whom I had been lucky to publish my biographies ahead of all the others, Dirk was his own greatest invention and was conditioned as much by his exile as his roots. His best performance, all his life, was the one he gave as Dirk Bogarde.

As I started out on my sixties, I realised that I was, yet again, in a certain amount of career trouble: the old system, whereby you could find an actor or actress you cared about and settle down to write a biography of them, had long gone. Just as press profiles are now in the hands of publicists and minders rather than the interviewers or even the interviewees, so actors, in the wake of Anthony Sher and Simon Callow, have discovered that they can write as well as most biographers. Why put their lives in others' hands?

Moreover, in the current climate of publishing, both in Britain and in America, the books that publishers really want, or at least those that will justify a large enough advance to allow the author to stay on the case for the requisite two or three years and travel the world in search of evidence, are not likely to be about great stage actors with only a limited market outside the National Theatre bookshop. What they want are books about Madonna, and apart from the undeniable fact that I am of the wrong generation and background for her, it remains to be seen whether the fans of a young movie star, or even a middle-aged one, ever find themselves in a bookshop, given the worldwide collapse of attention spans.

Equally, I was becoming dimly aware that the role of the drama critic was being subtly downgraded: when I started writing, the first-night review was the first thing you heard about a show. But a combination of escalating costs and professional marketing has made us critics now almost the last stop on the track. What you get first today is the profile, the background piece by the author or director, and then often, if a star like Madonna is involved, a full-length review by a news reporter (or sometimes just someone who happened to be there) of the first preview, which can often be days or weeks ahead of the official press night. This, combined with the technological revolution that has actually made it slower to get a paper to bed than the old hot metal, has destroyed the overnight reviewing system in all but a couple of papers, and with it goes the sheer sexiness of getting an instant verdict into print that could be read a few hours after the opening night. In New York they now have a whole series of press nights before a première, which is reserved for friends and relations of the cast. As a result of all these changes, the first-night review sinks further and further down the page, weighed down by a vast bulk of pre-publicity, which is, of course, much more welcome to the management concerned since it tends to be promotional, and therefore good for advance bookings, rather than critical. The days when a critic like Kenneth Tynan could make or break a show overnight are long gone.

So, looking back over almost forty years as a London drama critic, what if anything have I achieved? What difference, if any, have I made? I am lucky enough to be able to check it all out in some detail because, thanks to four very different but incredibly generous publishers – Jeremy Robson, Naim Atallah, John Curtis and James Hogan – I have been able to collect virtually all my reviews into four hardcover volumes.

One of the first reviews I ever wrote was of a truly appalling (I thought) Anna Neagle musical called *Charlie Girl*: 'This,' I announced firmly, 'deserves to last a night, and might just survive a week.' In the event it ran seven years at the Adelphi, and for all of that time they left my review outside the theatre, presumably meant as a terrible warning to others of critical fallibility. Oddly enough, it didn't seem that way to me at all: I simply realised that in Britain, unlike America, a critic could say what he or she thought, and have little effect on the final outcome because the public would decide for itself whether or not to go. Never again did I worry about what effect a hostile review from me might have on people's incomes or careers, and that, for someone brought up as I was in the theatre with actors and directors for friends, was liberating.

Have I ever campaigned or feuded successfully for anything? Well, yes and no. One of the first sustained battles I ever fought in print was when, towards the close of Olivier's years at the National Theatre, it seemed to me that some of those around him were exercising behind-the-throne powers that were not entirely in the theatre's best interests, and that the battle for the succession was disfiguring what the National was meant to be doing. It all felt to me too much like a real-life *King Lear*, with an old and ill man being deposed and too many claimants clustering around his throne.

Although I was told later how hurt Larry had been by some of my writing about his last few months at the National, he and his wife Joan Plowright remained generous to a fault, never allowing anything I wrote to colour a friendship that, in Larry's case, went all the way back to Noël and my grandmother Gladys, both of whom had given him early career breaks, and in Joannie's, to the time we all spent around a play called *Hook, Line and Sinker*, in which she starred with my father at a moment when she was about to embark on her new life with Larry. My family has never been good at keeping secrets, and I remember to this day Pa and I biting our sizeable tongues whenever the subject of Joannie and Larry came up, which it did a good deal as both were still married to other partners and being pursued by every gossip-columnist in town.

Years later still, when I was writing the biography of David Niven, I found I needed some evidence from Larry: at the time of *Wuthering Heights*, I was reasonably sure that David had been sleeping with Merle Oberon, and that she had got him his role in the movie. David always refused to acknowledge this in his own memoirs, suggesting that he had just happened to be in the right studio at the right time. Larry was the only star survivor of the film, and I needed his recollections.

It was the last summer of his life, and he was sitting in the white hat he had taken to wearing in his garden, fragile now but at last, thanks to Joannie and his new family, having achieved a kind of peace. His memory for current events was a little shaky, but he still had perfect recall of *Wuthering Heights*, and confirmed for me that it had indeed been Merle who had got David into the picture.

I turned off my tape-recorder, rose to leave him, then suddenly felt sure I was never going to see him again. I started to thank him not just for a cup of tea, but for years of interviews about himself and all kinds of other people. 'No, no,' said Larry. 'Before you go, one thing you absolutely have to understand, very important for your book – both Niven and I were deeply in love with Merle Oberon, but I was the one who married her.'

'Er, no, sir,' I had to say, 'not Merle Oberon. Vivien Leigh.'

'Oh, my dearest boy, you are so right,' and they were the last words I ever heard him utter. Sometimes I wonder if it might have been better to let him go to the grave convinced he had married Merle Oberon: she might have been a little less trouble to him than Viv.

Twenty or so years later still, when it seemed to me that Adrian Noble had totally lost the plot of the RSC, and was anyway occupied elsewhere with *Chitty Chitty Bang Bang*, I was the first critic to call in print and on television for his resignation, which duly came a few weeks later. But I had become so used (as a theatre writer) to demanding changes that never took place, or if they did they were not in the form

I had suggested, that I remained amazed when, for once, I had called a situation correctly – not that I would imagine Adrian sees it in quite the same light.

I have, for instance, campaigned for years without result for a more intelligent use of London theatres: here are these vast, mainly late-Victorian palaces, many on prime sites, hugely expensive to maintain, staff and run, yet open to the public for only about three hours out of every twenty-four. Wouldn't it make better sense to use them all day every day as art galleries, cinemas, bookshops, wine bars rather than let them gather dust until every evening? If that were done, their landlords would be able to charge less for the shows that play nightly, and would spend less time hoping secretly that their listed buildings would fall down, so that they could use the space more profitably as a twenty-four-hour car park.

Some things do come good, however. Twenty or more years ago, I began working for a still-unsung theatrical genius called Graham Jenkins, who had noticed one blindingly obvious problem: who are the heartland theatregoers for old musicals and starry revivals of a certain familiarity? Ladies, often widows, of a certain age. And what do they have in common? A terror of driving at night, car parks in city centres, and public transport at its perennial worst.

So, what is the answer? To bus them in and out of town. Hence the launching of Arts & Heritage, a club Graham and his wife Jill have run for many years – matinées a speciality, cream teas and stately homes also on offer. And, if they are not careful, a chat from me thrown in. Americans do it all the time: there are regular coachloads of Broadway matinée matrons, Elaine Stritch's 'ladies who lunch'. Over here, we just have Graham and several thousand grateful senior theatregoers. The man should have been knighted years ago.

Just when I was wondering if the game was still worth the candle, or if maybe I had done enough shouting in the dark to no avail and should try to make my late-life career lecturing on cruise liners, the phone rang. Yet again my life was turned around in about thirty seconds. The caller was a writer called G.F. Newman, with whom I had once shared a book tour in the 1970s. Did I, he wondered, ever act?

Not since leaving Oxford in 1963, I told him, and even then not very well. Undaunted, Gordon said he was starting to write a BBC television crime series called *Judge John Deed*, and he had a small, faintly sinister role to offer me as Judge Robert Home. That job led to two series, and I've come to the conclusion that if I go on writing, acting, directing, lecturing and broadcasting wherever and whenever anyone asks, I might just make it through to the grave. I've also learnt to be deeply grateful whenever the phone rings with an offer of whatever, and there are still the cruise liners if things go hopelessly adrift. All in all, life could be a lot worse. My Judge Robert Home even made it into the second BBC series of *Judge John Deed*. In the summer of 2002, I had the considerable delight of taking my robe off after a long day in court and looking at the label: 'Outsize Judge,' it read, 'Robert Morley 1968'.

Time for a last family round-up: Ruth and I still live on the river in Plantation Wharf, when she is not pursuing her Manhattan life and career from her apartment at Lincoln Center. She was the founder-editor of *Theatregoer*, which for two years she ran for Madeleine Lloyd Webber. Now, while still writing from Broadway for the magazine, she is also working on a major cabaret series for American television. It all began when she and her business partner Howard Weinberg made a starry special, *New York in Song*, to raise money for the firemen involved in the Twin Towers catastrophe. In New York Ruth has a whole separate life of her own, which in my more cynical moments I think may well be the best way to conduct a marriage between two highly strung neurotics like us. In London we are wonderfully supported by two assistants, Peter Coller and Sally-Anne Pinnington, whose daily love and cheerfulness in the face of the chaos we cause, them is something that I know I can never adequately repay, but at least I can publicly acknowledge it here.

My mother still lives, alone but in remarkable health, at Fairmans in Wargrave, the house she and my father bought more than sixty years ago, and where she is looked after by John and Jean Jonas, who seem to have been in our family for almost as long as we have. My son Hugo still owns and operates with my brother Wilton the best restaurant and bar in downtown Tampa, Florida; my sister Annabel still teaches and lives with her Australian family in Sydney, but happily gets home to see us all a little more often, now that her children are leading lives of their own; her husband Charlie spends a lot of his time directing plays and lecturing on theatre, the difference between him and me being that he can also build and decorate houses, is an expert antiques dealer and, after all those years under the Australian skies, looks one hell of a lot better than I do. As for my daughters, they have both found careers and talented, long-suffering husbands in Reg Smith and Stefan Drury. Alexis and Reg now have two little boys, Barnaby and Tom, whom Ruth and I are occasionally allowed to kidnap for London weekends.

My actual sixtieth birthday in December 2001 was a suitably nostalgic gathering: Peter Young and I had celebrated our joint eighteenth in a Henley pub; by twenty-one we had graduated, in thick snow, to the Phyllis Court Club there. For our third venture we gathered a hundred or so from our Thames Valley childhood and our Oxford youth at the Garrick, not to mention several more recent acquaintances, wives and children. Also there was Robin, Peter's half-brother, who had awoken that very morning to find his son Will the most famous singer in the land.

A day or two later, interviewing the American actor Robin Williams on radio, I was still talking about the party. 'Sixty?' he said. 'That's wonderful, just wonderful. Like some great Cheddar or Gorgonzola, you are now starting to mature, to come truly into your finest age. And, of course, like some great Cheddar or Gorgonzola, you will soon be starting to smell a little.'

It occurs to me, rather late in life, and after hearing all the marital and parental troubles of most of my friends, how blessed I have been, not only twice as a father-in-law, but also twice as a son-in-law. When I first married Margaret all those years ago in Boston, her Irish Catholic family took me to their hearts, and I am only sorry to have lost all of them as friends in the aftermath of our divorce.

But I now have another whole extended family, this one as distinctly Jewish as the first was Catholic, thanks to Ruth's many relatives: her sister Adrienne, her husband David Landau and her cousin Mildred Metter were all wonderfully welcoming when I began rather tentatively to join their family when their girl was still married to another man. Ruth's parents, now well into their nineties, live near us in a superb retirement home called the Nightingale, where they both lead lives of high soap-opera drama and trauma: whatever else those two may be doing, they are not going quietly into any good night.*

As for me, unlike my wife, children and now grandchildren, I still lack the technological or even logical skills to make any sense of mobile phones, euros, computers or the Internet. I can, however, just about manage electric kettles and the twenty-four-hour clock, and if you should ever need me urgently, I am in the phone book where I have been for the last forty years or so. Somehow I'd like better billing in there, but Directory Enquiries are quite good at finding me in a crisis, as are the AA and BUPA. Also, on a good day, the Garrick Club and Critics Circle, and our neighbourhood Battersea Police, who are brilliant at burglaries.

Last time we got done, they caught the burglar on a very

---

* Alas, I was wrong: Sam died aged ninety-six in August 2002.

good and exciting video: you see him shin up the drainpipe, go inside our open window, and then, if you wait a bit, you see him in close-up, exiting the back door with the video-recorder. We've never actually seen the man in person, of course, and neither have the police. But if he'd like to see himself on home video, he only has to pop round. Except that now we have nothing to play it on.

And, as we approach the final curtain (I debated going on for two volumes, but decided I wouldn't be able to cope with the ultimate humiliation of there being, perhaps, no takers for the second), I start again with my new column on the *New Statesman*, and the vague hope that it might see me out.

It occurs to me, and only in the nick of time, that someone who has spent most of his life writing biographies, and the last few years directing plays, might have been expected to deliver some general and conclusive thoughts on these two occupations.

Reader, you are to be spared all of that. I have no particular theory of biography, except that, as with marriage, you had better be bloody certain at the outset that you really wish to spend several years with your chosen subject. A divorce in mid-typescript is hard to achieve, and could prove expensive. As to how to do it, arm yourself with a reliable tape recorder, a back-up notebook and ideally a large enough advance to allow for giving lunch to several hundred prospective witnesses. It is the least they expect, and you will then find yourself picking up the tabs for large numbers of people who turn out to know a great deal less about your subject than you have already discovered. Begin at the beginning, and end if possible with a really good memorial service: living subjects are usually more trouble than they are worth at the bookshop.

As for directing, I have taken my only real note from the aforementioned Michael Blakemore, in my lifetime simply the greatest. 'Directing,' he said to me once, 'is all about telling stories.' Because most, though not all, of the actors I now direct know a great deal more about their business than I do about mine, I believe my job is host-like: keep them happy, buy them meals and drinks whenever possible, stop them bumping into the furniture, and try to clear some flight paths so they don't all crash into each other on stage. If you wish to teach them the play, as I usually do, try to make sure at the outset that you know it better than they do. Beyond that, you are really only a traffic controller, and once the cast reach a first night, they are never again even going to notice you standing in the middle of the street, still desperately trying to give them directions. As with my children, and I fear soon my grandchildren, there suddenly comes a day when they can all manage very nicely without you, and the trick then is simply to move on in search of some new children, no matter their real age.

And Robert? He stays with me most nights in some theatrical form or other, whether I am reviewing or acting, directing or just hosting. Sometimes others find him too. Almost the last time I saw Nigel Hawthorne on stage, it was in Alan Bennett's *Madness of George III*. In an opening scene, Julian Wadham comes to him as the younger William Pitt. 'Married yet?' asks the King. 'No,' says Pitt gloomily, whereupon the King sets off maliciously on a lengthy hymn of praise to the married state.

On this one night, when the King asked the usual question, Wadham said, 'Yes.' Hawthorne could hardly believe his luck.

'Who to?' he asked, as Wadham realised his mistake.

'Er, um, a sister of the Duchess of Marlborough.'

Hawthorne paused for another gleeful moment. 'Tell me,' he said, 'all about her,' whereupon Wadham gave up the uneven contest and returned to the text.

A few nights later, I ran into Hawthorne at Orso's, and told him how glad I was to have caught this historic exchange. 'Yes,' said Hawthorne thoughtfully. 'I rather suspect your late father was with me that night, too.'

So that, as they used to say at the end of network bulletins on American television, is the way it is tonight: Sheridan Morley, sixty, overweight, flat feet, non-injecting diabetic, ex-depressive, wildly out of condition, reasonably sober when working, available for anything enjoyable, only too well aware that the world has moved on beyond him into a new, alien century, and that he is bloody lucky still to be considered employable in it, let alone alive. Father of three, twice married, grandfather of two, hoping to get through to the end of his life without causing too much more trouble, or annoying anyone any more than he undoubtedly already has.

Not a lot to ask, really, and that's roughly that, at least for the time being. In the curtain-call words of John Osborne's Archie Rice, the old Entertainer himself and arguably the greatest stage character invented in all of my theatregoing lifetime, you've been a good audience, very good. A very good audience. Let me know where you're working tomorrow night, and I'll come and see you.

27
For Ruth

'Typical,' she said, 'absolutely bloody typical.' She had been reading this typescript on a flight home from New York, and although she didn't exactly throw it at me, I got the feeling that only its weight was preventing her.

When you have been married as long as I have, twice, you learn to anticipate most marital trouble. Sometimes I think I must have been born married. You learn the key words, the key situations to avoid if you want to get through the day in reasonable harmony without the terrible silences that are also a part of married life, or at least have always been a part of mine.

Chris Matthew even has a friend who comes down to breakfast every morning blinking regretfully at his large, assembled family. 'Good morning,' he says, 'and I am most terribly sorry. Whatever happens today to any of you, I just want to apologise now, in advance, since it will almost certainly turn out yet again to have been all my fault.'

Memoirs, however, are an altogether new marital hazard. 'They are fine,' Ruth said, handing them back rather too firmly. 'As far as they go.' One of the joys of being sixty is that you have usually been there before, or somewhere very near by, but I had the sudden feeling that I might now have wandered into a new and unexploded minefield.

'As far as they go?'

'Well, yes. As far as you go.'

'But they're my memoirs.'

'And what about me? What about all the others in the book who will never get to tell their side of the story? What about all those years we've lived together, travelled together, the books we've written together, the shows we've staged together, the team I always thought we were supposed to be? Nobody reading this book would have the faintest idea why you married me. I come over as just another problem in your life, a sort of alternative to your first wife. She's tall and dark, I'm short and fair. Apart from that, we're just two names in the vast bloody cast list of your life, with not very good billing.

'Nothing about love, nothing about respect, nothing about why you wanted to change one whole marriage for another. Nothing, even, about why you really love me, or what we mean to each other.'

I read the book again, as one would. Like most critics, I have always reacted badly to criticism of any kind, and I especially dislike it from close relatives, of whom all I really ask is that they stand around cheering, especially on the frequent occasions when nobody else seems to be doing so. Ruth has never understood this: she regards criticism as a central component of love, and believes that relatives should be the first to raise it; I have always preferred to receive their knives last, if at all.

But, as usual, she is right: like a lot of Englishmen and women of my 1940s generation, I write badly and minimally about love, perhaps because I am terrified of being thought sentimental and also, of course, because I don't really understand how it works. I think it's a prep-school, Garrick Club kind of problem. I know I love Ruth – am, indeed, in love with her. I also know now, as I never did before, that I lack some kind of marital gene. This is not to suggest that I am unfaithful to her, or that I do not, in some vague way, thank God every day for allowing me life with her.

My problem, Doctor, is that, although I desperately want to be and stay married, I have not much aptitude for it. It's like I desperately want to be a good father and grandfather, yet have never quite learnt how to play the roles. I hate being alone, and yet I am, I think, emotionally a loner. I can write, have written, happily enough with Ruth, and yet I think I write better alone. I *think* better alone. I react better alone. I don't really understand sharing, or partnerships, although all my life I have tried, without much success, to be part of a double-act.

So why, then, did I marry – let alone twice? Why didn't I settle for being a bachelor, or go off into some kind of working life (a university for instance), where eccentric isolation is still just about acceptable, and sometimes even cherished and admired?

Because the very idea of all that still terrifies me. I want and need to be with someone, and preferably the same someone. Parents die – although two of our four have luckily refused to do so – and children leave home. Marriage is supposed to last and this, here, now, is me trying to say that I hope ours always will, even if sometimes against all the odds.

Selfish as ever, I don't want to die alone any more than I have ever wanted to live alone – and I do love Ruth more than anyone else in the world, except, in a different way, my mother and children and grandchildren. Beyond that, I really don't know very much: what keeps us together is, I think, as unfathomable as what keeps any partnership together. I look at the marriages of my friends in all the bewilderment with which I arrive at a foreign airport. God knows what keeps those two together, I think – but if they split, I'm usually equally amazed.

I don't know why I can't write about Ruth as she would wish; maybe it is because we are in the present, and this book has really been about the past. I am also suddenly, and shamefully, aware that I have never managed to write about my mother, any more than my father did. She too has always just been there, central to my lifelong well-being, but somehow always impossible to paint – as though, surrounded by so many egos, she has managed to make her own vanish.

We are now in real time, and real time has never made much sense to me. But, Ruth, if you are still reading, yes, I do love you very much, yes, I am glad we have managed to stay together these last fifteen years, and yes, I am well aware that I am not really quite what you had in mind.

I am not really sure what you did have in mind, even now; I begin to think that maybe no one is ever quite what anyone else ever has in mind. Perhaps there ought to be somewhere sensible, like Peter Jones or the General Trading Company, a counter where you can go and turn in, for credit, those people who have somehow never quite lived up to the expectations aroused by their labels. The only trouble would be having to queue for so long.

Sheridan Morley
Summer 2002

Index

SM = Sheridan Morley
Titles given in italics refer to stage productions unless indicated otherwise.

Index

Index

Index